Provocations

omplicated

A Book Series of Curriculum Studies

William F. Pinar
General Editor

VOLUME 13

PETER LANG
New York • Washington, D.C./Baltimore • Bern
Frankfurt am Main • Berlin • Brussels • Vienna • Oxford

Provocations

Sylvia Ashton-Warner
and Excitability in Education

Judith P. Robertson & Cathryn McConaghy

EDITORS

PETER LANG
New York • Washington, D.C./Baltimore • Bern
Frankfurt am Main • Berlin • Brussels • Vienna • Oxford

Library of Congress Cataloging-in-Publication Data

Provocations: Sylvia Ashton-Warner and excitability in education /
edited by Judith P. Robertson, Cathryn McConaghy.
p. cm. — (Complicated conversation: a book series of curriculum studies; v. 13)
Includes bibliographical references and index.
1. Ashton-Warner, Sylvia—Influence. 2. Education—New Zealand—
Experimental methods. 3. Feminism and education—New Zealand.
4. Feminism and literature—New Zealand. I. Robertson,
Judith P. II. McConaghy, Cathryn. III. Series.
LB880.A67P76   370'.1—dc22   2005013861
ISBN 0-8204-7877-6

Bibliographic information published by **Die Deutsche Bibliothek**.
Die Deutsche Bibliothek lists this publication in the "Deutsche
Nationalbibliografie"; detailed bibliographic data is available
on the Internet at http://dnb.ddb.de/.

Cover design by Lisa Barfield

Cover image of Sylvia Ashton-Warner is reproduced with the permission
of the Alexander Turnbull Library, Wellington, New Zealand.
It is held in catalogue no: PAColl-2522-7-01-01

© 2006 Peter Lang Publishing, Inc., New York
29 Broadway, New York, NY 10006
www.peterlang.com

For Allan Kathnelson

and Di Bloomfield

with love

Table of Contents

Preface

Dearest, Something Good Will Come of This...

Selma Wassermann

There were days, I must confess, when things went rather badly at the university—the sort of stuff that occurs in any workplace—cruel, frustrating, disheartening. There are such times in the life of most members of the academy, I fear, and the results take their toll in the form of brewing anger, rage against the powers that be, and retreat to a safer place. Any of us who have lived an academic life know about such events, and know too the pain these experiences can bring.

It was my habit to stop off at Sylvia's house after a teaching day, to share the news and maybe a lager or two. We had made a pact about these visits. If the patio door was open just a crack, she was "at home." If the patio door was closed, she was likely to be writing and not to be disturbed. No one used the front door—all visitors entered through the patio so that she could check us out through the glass.

She could tell immediately, from my face, what kind of day I had had. Was she that sensitive? Or did my face so easily betray all the feelings? Nonetheless, she would always ask: "So tell me dearest, what kind of a day did you have?"

She was so genuinely interested in knowing that it was easy for me to let the words and feelings pour out—my troubles spilled like yesterday's sour milk. Practiced in "taking your Key Vocabulary," she always listened attentively—her gaze somewhere far away, as if she were envisioning the scenes as I described them, nodding her head, signaling understanding. After I had poured out my heart, she would be quiet for a few moments and then look me in the eye.

"Dearest," she'd say, "something good will come of this."

When I first heard this response, it fueled my anger as if she had dismissed my feelings, rendering them not worthy of further consideration. I had wanted some comforting words, some solace, some indication that I had an ally to stand with me against the "enemy." Instead, I got this inane platitude, which I felt was worse than useless. I was disappointed, hurt. How could anything good come of such a mess? What on earth was she talking about?

There were at least three more times, over a period of two years, when I took my "troubles" to my friend and she responded in this way. But by then I had accumulated some wisdom of my own and could see the deeper meaning this response had for me. For as rain is surely followed by little girls with umbrellas, what good did come was what I was able to build from the disaster that had initially overcome me. One makes "good" from teaching oneself how to climb out of disaster. It is not the easy road, of course. One can choose to remain in the ruins, sucking one's thumb and endlessly whining about one's troubles. Or one can build anew with greater vigor, greater creativity.

Wasn't it Nietzsche who said, "What does not destroy me makes me stronger?" Somehow, I don't think this was quite what Sylvia had in mind. In fact, she loved sending cryptic messages and playing the mysterious woman role. I'm not even sure *what* she had in mind. But I took her message as a mantra ever after that, having learned from it that I did not have to sit in the corner, sucking away, but could come out stronger, using my creative forces to build anew.

Sylvia was my teacher—from very early days before I met her, when I bought a copy of her first book, *Spinster.* She continued to be my teacher during our time together at Simon Fraser University. She is my teacher still—and I am eternally grateful.

Now, a new book is being created that will spur others to experience some of the provocative ideas of this fascinating writer and teacher. To all of you readers, I would suggest: Dear ones, something good will come of this.

Simon Fraser University
November 2002

Acknowledgments

In *Playing and Reality* (1972), Donald Winnicott reminds us of how we come to establish our independence from the authority figures we so admire, and how, in the process, our beloved provocateurs can only become real for us when we are able to release them from the omnipotent fantasy that we can control them. Such a process, Winnicott cautions, is beleaguered with experiences of love and hate, which the beloved must be able to survive; the beloved's survival, in fact, ensures something called independence for us as thinkers. It seems our ability to imagine ourselves as separate entities in the world is in fact predicated on the capacity of our icons to be absolutely dominated and destroyed by us, and—even more so—that subjectivity itself depends on our capacities to find sources outside of our own wishes and frustrations to sustain us.

This book is a distillation of over two decades of individual work and four years of spirited collective dialogue about the uses and possibilities of playing with the reality of provocation and excitability in education through the life and ideas of Sylvia Ashton-Warner. During this time we have grappled with the project of controlling, surviving, and sustaining ourselves with, through, against, and beside this difficult figure, who has moved us through her flawed words and stubborn sounds—someone who has affected us deeply as women and teachers whenever we have tried to talk about what is important to us about education in our time. In the course of collaboration on this co-edited book and several conference papers, our interests have been held, energized, and elaborated by the pleasurable voices of others, those colleagues who have joined us in shaping snippets of a life-narrative and practices of interpretation around what has moved and continues to move us about Sylvia. We want to acknowledge several debts.

We thank William Pinar of the University of British Columbia for inviting us to contribute to a series of complicated conversations around the problems of provocation and desire in education. His concept of curriculum as *currere*—as running the course of movement in the life of the mind—has encouraged us to think through our entanglements with Sylvia in time and to frame a wide-ranging investigation into elements of her life-narrative in moving from subject to theory. We appreciate Bill's direct involvement during some difficult moments in bringing our book to creation. Chris Myers and Bernadette Shade guided us through various stages of the project and helped us not to lose what inspired us.

We are grateful to Deborah Britzman for not taking for granted our interest in Sylvia Ashton-Warner and for prodding us to keep good faith with Sylvia's clues and cues about education as disturbance. For a book that addresses the excitement of enacting alternative, often puzzling interests in education, acknowledgments seem particularly crucial for those who have tolerated our idiosyncratic drifts of attention and desire, as well as the complexities of pan-Pacific collaborations, throughout this book's time of creation. We are grateful first and foremost to all of our contributing authors who have kept good faith throughout the project. Thanks also to Alice Pitt, Allan Kathnelson, Zachary Kathnelson, Naomi Kathnelson, and Pat Palulis, whose interest and ingenuities helped Judith to feel lucky, awake, and alive throughout the pages of the book; to Debby O'Brien, who can find the humorous side to any research task, and to Keith Woodley, for spirited conversations about his lifetime of teaching in Maori schools; to Di Bloomfield, Alex Taylor, Charlotte McConaghy, Liam McConaghy, Wendy Cannon, Robyn Lewis, and Kevin Jordan for their loving and generous support; to Avril Aitken, Kathleen Connor, Nectaria Karagiozis, Linda Radford, Lorraine Graham, and Cynthia A'Beckett, in whose company at different times the ideas in this book developed. We are grateful to others who helped us keep our promise: Ken Arvidson, editor of the *Journal of New Zealand Literature*; Susan Bartel at the National Library of New Zealand; Jeannine Bordeleau of Interlibrary Loans at the University of Ottawa; Chris Bourke, producer of *Saturday Morning* from Radio New Zealand; Stephen Burridge of the New Zealand High Commission in Ottawa; Diane Campbell of the *Otago Daily Times*; Yves Herry for financial support from the University of Ottawa; Jack Ingram, distribution manager at the New Zealand Film Commission; Sue Jamieson, curator of the Katherine Mansfield House in Wellington; Rachel Lord, chief sound archivist of the sound archives at Alexander Turnbull Library; Paula Maihi, librarian and listener at Alexander Turnbull Library; Valerie Morse, research services librarian at Alexander Turnbull Library; Jane Smallfield, assistant archivist at the Hocken Archives; Ronald Soulliard, senior systems administrator at Mugar Memorial Library; Irene Strong of the New Zealand Film Sound Archives; and Sally Williamson of the New Zealand Television Archive. Janet Horncy, recently retired Reader Education Librarian at the Alexander Turnbull Library, kindly assisted with permission to reproduce the book cover image. Our thanks are also due to Charlotte McConaghy for compiling the index for the volume. Selma Wassermann, Herbert Kohl, C. K. Stead, and Carole Durix are long-time advocates of Sylvia's distinctive brand of literary and pedagogical genius, and we are grateful to have their insights enrich this text. To the anonymous contributors to an online discussion we conducted about the painful post-colonial politics of Maori/English translations, thank you.

We are grateful to have had the opportunity of presenting earlier versions of chapters to various university departments and educational researchers in Australia, Canada, New Zealand, and America, including the School of Education at the University of New England, the Australian Association for

Educational Research, the New Zealand Association for Educational Research, the American Educational Research Association, the Canadian Society for the Study of Education, and the Language and Literacy Association of Researchers, Canada. These audiences, we hope, will notice their contribution to the final version of *Provocations: Sylvia Ashton-Warner and Excitability in Education.*

The authors wish to thank the department of English and the office of sponsored research at the University of South Carolina for travel grants that supported research for this project. We are also grateful to the heirs of Sylvia Ashton-Warner for permission to quote from unpublished manuscripts. We are indebted to those who granted us permission to quote portions of manuscripts in their care in the Mugar Memorial Library and the Sylvia Ashton-Warner Collection at the Howard Gotlieb Archival Research Center at Boston University, as well as the Alexander Turnbull Library in Wellington, New Zealand. Sylvia Ashton-Warner's intelligent beauty also lives on through the generosity of the Alexander Turnbull Library's permission to use her image on our book's cover. We are especially indebted to Joy Alley and to Sylvia's children—Jasmine Beveridge, Elliot Henderson, and Ashton Henderson, for their willingness to be interviewed in 1998 and for their generous insights.

This book would not have been possible without the spirited attentiveness of Dr. Emma Stodel, who worked as our editorial assistant on the project, and who was assiduous in her persistence, patience, and good humor. We are grateful for her meticulous and caring attention, which saw the book through to final completion.

CHAPTER ONE

Sylvia Ashton-Warner:
Reading Provocatively from Subject to Theory

Cathryn McConaghy and Judith P. Robertson

There are things that nobody would know about teaching unless Sylvia Ashton-Warner had written them. Pedagogy has an impoverished language for the senses. We know this because Sylvia attempted to create a new one. Her favorite thing was to go where no other teacher had been before. She understood very well that wherever the relevance of language is at stake, as in her work in the Maori infant rooms, matters become political by definition, for language is what makes us political beings. She has been described as a tough and noisy woman, a prize fighter, a demon, a maniac: you name it. Some called her Mother Courage. For Ashton-Warner, a chief moral deficiency would have been not indiscretion, but reticence. In order to go on living, she had to escape the death involved in perfectionism. She postponed stasis by suffering, by error, by risking, by berating, by loving, by creating—these moments of provocation punctuating her life-poem.

This book draws together feminist scholars in education and literary and cultural studies to reconsider the life and legacy of Sylvia Ashton-Warner (1908–1984). In particular, we focus on what her work provoked and continues to provoke, the creative and transformative elements at the heart of her thinking and practice. Ashton-Warner "lived at the edges of perception where reality is just beyond the finger-tips of the conscious mind" (Shallcrass 1984, 342). What was it about her mind and work that provoked shunning, silencing, exclusion, book burning, exile, adoration, seduction, emulation, idealization, inspiration—and what resources did Ashton-Warner draw upon to embrace the embattled universe she inhabited? How did she find the ability to absorb the hardships of her life—

poverty, war, isolation, the Depression, patriarchy, abuse, and transgression of gender roles for women—in order to perform a balancing act that associated education with world peace-making, and creation with loving relationships with women? And how do we read the story of her work and its reception in terms of what it reveals of antipodean sensitivities and sensibilities, now and then? Importantly, in what ways do the creative and generative aspects of Ashton-Warner's life/work travel across oceans and continents and decades?

In thinking about women educators and educational researchers as provocateurs, our attention is drawn to issues of composure and excitability in education and its manifest formations. We are interested in what it means to resist or submit to the excitability of ideas—of the new, the unorthodox, and the discomfiting—particularly if excitement is occasioned by the ideas and actions of a woman. Part of the story we want to tell examines the vicissitudes of "transcolonial narrative"—what complicates and inspires its emergence, and how various readers "each recuperate a history and a meaning in their own way, from their own point on a specific periphery" (Boire 1989, 199). Hannah Arendt once said that under conditions of tyranny it is far easier to act than to think. Sylvia Ashton-Warner sometimes considered her life as one of living under conditions of tyranny and under those conditions thinking, writing, and being fully alive were one. In fifty years she never had a day when she did not have to think about someone else's needs. And this meant the writing had to be fitted around those needs. At the same time, to assess the damage of education in writing was for her a dangerous act.

In the chapters that follow, we read between the acts of Ashton-Warner to examine the forces in teaching and learning that seek to subvert excitability, to cultivate self-surrender, to instill borders, and to restore composure as stasis. In thinking through the links between the life and work of Sylvia Ashton-Warner and contemporary theory, we have chosen to think of this process as a provocation, rather than as the work of interpretation or translation. Elizabeth Young-Bruehl's (1998) insights into the process of moving from subject to biography and Shoshana Felman's (1993) notion of feminist bonds of reading have been central to our collective endeavor to read provocatively into Ashton-Warner's life and work.

Why write about Sylvia Ashton-Warner at this time? What is the central motivation for people to write about what has provoked them? According to Young-Bruehl (1998), a great deal of happiness occurs when two people, whose fantasies of contentment conjoin, find each other. All human beings, she says, desire to be two people in relatedness. The biographer can enact this fantasy complex in writing a biography. The subject belongs to the biographer, who may even dream that the subject has been waiting for her to come along. We find these relations alive in the landwash of the chapters that follow, as Sylvia

Ashton-Warner appears alternatively to our contributors as a ghost, a phantasm, a haunting, a storm, a namesake, a lost child, a shrill wind piping. "Missed meanings haunt us," writes Mary Jacobus (1999, 30), noting, "There is something about meaning that is distressing to the reader, but there must also be something about this distress that excites or incites the reader" (4). Sylvia's missed meanings haunt us because they matter to us, but, like an apparition, she "remains elusive, felt but not quite perceived" (Jacobus 1999, 4). What is the story, this volume wants to know, that can be made of the missed meanings of Sylvia Ashton-Warner?

Those of us whose writings appear here are connected, somewhat disparately, through the bonds and missed meanings of enduring, intense, sometimes ambivalent, and always lively attachments to the life and writings of Sylvia Ashton-Warner. If Young-Bruehl (1998) is right when she says, "The biographer relates in the medium of fantasy to the subject's fantasy, insofar as it can be found" (3), then perhaps it can be said that we have all struggled in our chapters with the fantasy (also a dilemma) of Ashton-Warner's personal excesses and her measure as an educator. Young-Bruehl signals toward two sides of this complex relationship when we choose to write about someone. The biographer's subjectivity is implicated in her subject: "The biography subjects the subject to study and writing. But the biography and its subject also subject the biographer to the claims of the biographer-subject relationship and the biographer-biography relation" (Young-Bruehl 1998, 4). This is a web of conditions in which subjectivity is furiously implicated. After Young-Bruehl, we might call our method here "psychotheoretical criticism." We are interested in where women's ideas come from when Sylvia resides as provocateur. Thinking is conversational. Writing about Sylvia Ashton-Warner is a "field for the playing out of fantasies" (Young-Bruehl 1998, 8).

The drift of this playing field has something interesting to say to women and education, about the shifts from subject to biography and subject to theory. In the movement from subject to biography, Young-Bruehl suggests that the major task is not to problematize the subject, but rather to call into question the subjectivity of the biographer. Our biographies so often are infused with our own idealizations of our subjects that what is revealed is not so much the subject's but the biographer's own "family romance" (Freud 1908). We begin our biographies with a search for connection. When our idealized subjects fail to materialize— that is, when Sylvia turns out not to be as she seemed—disillusionment and antipathy may foreclose what began as a love affair. Readers of this volume will detect in some of the chapters snarled threshes of a story of biographical loss and mourning in relation to Sylvia as a lost love-object. Such signs, we suggest, are illustrative of the journeys that many of us have had with this glorious, impossible creature. However, Young-Bruehl (1998) suggests that the task for biography is to disrupt "the complex mirroring role the subject comes to play in the biographer's psyche" (46) and instead to seek out the differences between the self (as biographer) and the subject. Further, she cautions biographers not to fall into the trap of finding a simple relation between the strengths and weaknesses of the subject's personality and those of her work: Young-Bruehl argues that admiration and envy in relation to the subject's work are positive responses. Our collective readings emerge as a complex dance of both connecting and disconnecting ourselves with Ashton-Warner. In the face of Sylvia's obvious talents and successes we catch ourselves in an ambivalent embrace, on the one hand wishing to celebrate and understand her work as significant cultural production, while on the other hand seeking to delve into the more intimate, disarming spaces of the life that occasioned such work. We have found it difficult to separate out Ashton-Warner's work from her life.

According to Shoshana Felman (1977), in reading the work of any author we encounter the text as "a subject presumed to know" (7), where meaning and knowledge of meaning reside. For Felman, language effects carry meaning, but they also implicate unthought material—provocations that are both its conditions of possibility and its self-subversive blind spots. For a character who has lost the way of desire (as did the early Sylvia, who suffered mental breaks), the text is a pivot that helps the character progress toward a rendezvous with the self.

Part of our problem, then—if it is a problem—has to do with this precarious spin of selves and imbrications that comprise Ashton-Warner's written corpus. The voice of the author addresses us "not as the story of the individual in relation to the events of his own past, but as the story of the way in which one's own trauma is tied up with the trauma of another, the way in which trauma may lead, therefore, to the encounter with another, through the very possibility and surprise of listening to another's wound" (Caruth 1996, 8). Sylvia Ashton-Warner addresses us as a voice we cannot fully know, but to which we must bear witness, commanding us to awaken to something that "burns" at our edges (Caruth 1996, 9).

Shoshana Felman (1993) further displaces the picture for us when she describes literature, autobiography, and theory as "resisting one another" (133). The notion of resistance creates a significant dilemma to women searching for theory to use in writing autobiography and biography, particularly in relation to the texts of another woman. Indeed, if "women must turn to one another for stories" even now (Heilbrun 1988, 44), then part of what has motivated us to write this book is our desire to make certain stories thinkable: stories of women's subversive hopes, of their unacceptable desires, and of their provocative demand for something incompatible with the status quo, the writing into pedagogy of a fiction of desire.

And yet Ashton-Warner's literary, autobiographical, and theoretical texts defy, in complex and compelling ways, our capacity to talk about desire with anything resembling ease. This reminds us of that "counterfeit integration of the subject" in biography warned about by Roland Barthes (as discussed in Heilbrun 1988, 50). How can it be otherwise, when Sylvia's desires so confound? Her fiction is infused with her pedagogy and her losses and longings; her autobiographies are, in part, curiously and endearingly fictional; and her pedagogical treatises read as good novels. Perhaps more than any other educational theorist, her theory is lavishly bejeweled with both literary and narcissistic devices. Thus in our search for Ashton-Warner's educational or literary theory, in our desire to move from subject to theory, our meanings get deferred by her cross-writing. In light of these flirtatious exchanges, what we have attempted in this volume, if not in individual chapters, is a shift from subject to theory occasioned by our collective reading practices.

But here again Sylvia's ghost confounds. Perhaps this is what Alice Pitt (2003) gestures toward in her history of learning called *The Play of the Personal*. Pitt implicates James Strachey's notion of *Nachträglichkeit* (deferred action) to consider how learning inevitably springs out of something belated, like the wake that follows furious action. Pitt signals the importance of being able to distinguish, as readers and as learners, between an encounter with knowledge and an encounter with she who presents knowledge.

For Felman (1993) also, women's texts can only become stories through the bonds of engendered reading, bonds that women make between themselves as readers and with the author through their search for the "forms of resistance present in the text" (6). In describing feminist writing, Adrienne Rich (1979) observes that the point of writing is "not to pass on a tradition but to break its hold over us" (35). In breaking the hold of a text's belated address, the reader is challenged to find the points of resistance and to discover that against which the writer (and its reader) are resisting. Far from falling before the shrine of "objectivity," this volume acknowledges its own spaces of subjectivity and the importance of Sylvia as a subject in our lives, despite her damnable difficulties. Sylvia offers us alternative ways of knowing—and for that eludes us; occasionally we disparage her for it. Even so, we use her provocations to remind ourselves that there are ways of building a life around a core of want so deep that everything that follows—loving, teaching, writing, mothering—can be drenched in the waters of longing. We do not always like Sylvia for making this life-story familiar to us, but we need her.

This is all to say that the authors of this volume both agree and disagree about what Sylvia provokes in us as readers and writers. We disagree, for example, over the degree to which Ashton-Warner was writing "as a feminist": indeed, in these times when the word "feminism" may carry with it a foul odor, not all of the contributors to this volume even self-identify as feminists. And yet not to read Ashton-Warner as breaking—and breaking with—tradition is to miss something vital of her provocations. Reading as feminists requires the insertion of our own autobiographies into the texts. Thus, while wary of Young-Bruehl's (1998) warnings about the dangers of narcissism in biography, we acknowledge in our entanglements with Ashton-Warner that everyone reads from somewhere. To read autobiographically is to do more than get personal: it requires reading into texts "our differences and our own biographies as missing" (Felman 1993, 13). None of us as women has as yet an autobiography; we each have a story "that is not a story but must become a story" (Felman 1993, 17). Sylvia helps us to "engender, or to access our story only indirectly—by conjuring literature, theory, and autobiography together through the act of reading and by reading, thus, into the texts of culture, at once our sexual difference and our autobiography as missing" (Felman 1993, 17). But if Felman is correct in saying, "I cannot write my story (I am not in possession of my own autobiography) but I can read it in the Other" (Felman 1993, 17), what, then, can we read in Sylvia's story or stories?

Sylvia Ashton-Warner's stories constitute testimonies to teaching in difficult contexts, both the contexts within and external to the teaching self. As testimonies they present a number of ethical issues to us as readers. For our purposes, Cathy Caruth's (1996) contributions to an understanding of testimony and trauma are central. Sylvia's traumas (her mental breakdown, isolation, alienation, rejection, loss) might appear, in light of stories that have been told, to be natural (although as Žižek [1998] reminds us, never neutral). But her testimonies call forth an ethical response that generates an excess greater than the experience. Caruth examines how in writing, trauma "repeats itself, exactly and unremittingly, through the unknowing acts of the survivor and against his very will" (1996, 2). Such repetitions beat at the heart of catastrophe. There is a wound released in prosody that is a form of address, whose crying out asks us to witness a truth that the survivor herself cannot know. The reading/writing bond is part of a parable about how the unassimilable aspects of violence present a truth that is again belated in its call. Knowing and unknowing are thus inevitably entangled in the language of trauma, and these shadows compete for attention in the listener, asking us to consider not only how to transmit but how to theorize around "a crisis that is marked, not by a simple knowledge, but by the ways it simultaneously defies and demands our witness" (Caruth 1996, 5). For Caruth, particular repetitions ("insistently recurring words or figures") function as literary dimensions of communication that cannot be reduced to thematic content or meaning (1996, 8). These repetitions are figures of "departure," "falling," "burning," or "awakening" in their insistence. What impacts us as Sylvia's witnesses is not only her wounds but their polyvocality—not only what we know about the reality of the violence that beset her, but what is not yet fully known and therefore continues to haunt us.

The story of reading and writing Sylvia, then, is also a story, as Pitt (2003) has said, of the trauma of belated learning. The ongoing experience of having survived something (in reading Ashton-Warner, we survive what wounded her) constitutes a double telling, a telling that includes the unbearable nature of surviving education in our time. As women we possess a common experience of feeling trapped in an educational script we did not write. Slowly we are beginning to analyze and dig a way out, seeking a "bid for freedom from the assigned [roles]" (Heilbrun 1988, 42). But few models exist, few stories that are larger than plays of refusal or suicide. As Heilbrun notes, there is still no organized sense of what a woman (teacher's) life should look like in writing. Accordingly, Ashton-Warner's testimonies, the enigmas of her survival, draw the reader into her dramas through an empathetic connection with our own: for women disavowed within educational institutions, women teaching in indigenous or remote contexts, women inhabiting the shifting uplands of biracial, bicultural, hybrid public spaces, women juggling heteronormativities in their professional and personal lives, and women seeking a place within national schooling imaginaries, Ashton-Warner's testimonies constitute an enduring call for justice, as powerful now as in her own time.

But as with all testimonies, there are limits to the power of her relevance and points at which readers variously move from empathy to antipathy (Young-Bruehl 1998). Such is the provocation of her narratives that readers, although endlessly curious, find themselves loving or hating the meanings Ashton-Warner calls forth. Her biographer, Lynley Hood (1988, 249), writes, "The potency of her ideas and her astonishing power to polarise her audience, lives [sic] on beyond death." Hood continues:

> What is the secret of her impact? What life force enables her to move people so? Perhaps the power of Sylvia Ashton-Warner to attract and repel lies not in her, but in ourselves. Perhaps it is the shock of recognising ourselves in the flashing mirrors of her soul that drives us to frenzied celebration or fevered denial. It may be in Sylvia Ashton-Warner that we see our own suppressed irrationality, and the embodiment of our own dreams. (1988, 249)

And yet it is precisely Hood's appropriation of Ashton-Warner's life and dreams that Anne-Louise Brookes critiques in this volume: there is a fine line between appropriating the subject narcissistically (thus erasing her) and reading the subject autobiographically (reading as a form of resistance). The difference may be political. Unlike many of the reviews of Ashton-Warner's work over the years, a number of the chapters in this volume are political in the sense that they seek the forms of resistance in Ashton-Warner's own texts: the move from subject to theory requires a political investment in the subject. It may be, in these chapters, that the reader is relating "less to the specific content of the subject's fantasy than to the feeling that the subject had a fantasy of contentment, the feeling of kindredness" (Young-Bruehl 1998, 3). "Tangles of implication," Britzman (1997, 31) calls them. Such a move to theory is transformative in a number of senses: in the search for Sylvia's excesses; in the search for theory within Ashton-Warner's psychic and social conflicts; and in the "worlding" (Heidegger 1977 as cited in Khanna 2003, 3) of Ashton-Warner in the critical examination of both the sayables and unsayables of her presencing in the contemporary world.

Selma Wassermann's poetic and affectionate prelude to the volume remembers foremost Sylvia's continuing role as teacher and comforter. Sylvia Ashton-Warner was both an irritant and a form of consolation for Selma, but if it had not been for Selma spiriting Sylvia to Vancouver in the 1960s, a generation of teachers would not have had such intimate access to Ashton-Warner's teachings. Wassermann incites us to think better because of Sylvia; we think through her relationally and against her in conversation. Sylvia becomes the object that makes thought bump against itself and thus take on a name and a shape. Thinking as life-story telling is for Selma Wassermann a way of relating to Sylvia in friendship and hospitality, "a way of finding or refinding the world as a home" (Young-Bruehl 1998, 10). Thinking through the biography of a subject can, as Young-Bruehl writes, "make actual the being of the thinker" (1998, 10).

Alison Jones is also interested in the notion of thinking and relatedness, and like Wassermann, Jones also had a personal connection with Sylvia Ashton-Warner. Jones's chapter reads Ashton-Warner's contributions and resistances within a genealogy of dangerous and passionate pedagogies and postcolonial sensitivities around remembering and forgetting a difficult Maori schooling history. Jones explores the tensions between classroom erotics and proper teaching, then and now, and identifies Ashton-Warner's provocations as a form of resistance against pedagogy as ordered, logical, and rational. She asks: what does it mean to be a proper teacher, what forms of censorship and taboo are at work in today's classrooms, and in what ways is pedagogy never innocent, but rather an aspect of everyday social relations of power? Jones sets her analysis of Ashton-Warner within an analysis of the regulation of classroom excesses and important historical questions about the dangers of both classroom intimacy as a form of surveillance and the material effects of passionate pedagogues. Read within contemporary contexts of social anxieties about the dangers to children, Ashton-Warner provokes us to consider what the limits to teachers' interferences should be. In grasping Sylvia Ashton-Warner as subject, Jones helps us to exercise a subversive and yet caring recognition of ourselves.

We said earlier that biographical subjects also perform like figures in a family romance, providing us entry to "a new and better, more elevated and self-flattering heritage" (Young-Bruehl 1998, 20). Reading Sylvia allows us to break with our pasts and to finish creating a place of exile. Several contributors to this volume rendezvous with Sylvia in ways that construct, deconstruct, and recover their way back over a landscape of contested New Zealand educational history and into a space of reconciliation, at least with the self, if not fully with the subject. For example, beginning with an appreciation of the significance of voice and creativity for women's sanity, Sue Middleton considers the embodied nature and historical and spatial situation of Ashton-Warner's educational theories within New Zealand educational and social history. Middleton finds irritation with Ashton-Warner's claims of persecution and disavowal as an educational theorist and seeks to correct the myth that her theories were in contradiction to those prevalent at the time. Presenting what she refers to as a postmenopausal reading of Ashton-Warner, Middleton finds Ashton-Warner's romanticisms, paranoias, and ambivalences less seductive than she once had as a younger educator and academic. Reading through the lenses of experience and archival research, Middleton considers the significance of Ashton-Warner's attachment to the notions of "kiss" and "ghost" and locates these in her transferences as an educator. Middleton presents a more nuanced analysis of the complex relationship between Ashton-Warner and various educational figures and institutions, establishing that Ashton-Warner, rather than having been shunned by New Zealand, was a product of her location in a contested yet progressive educational context.

In theorizing the empathy required in writing a woman's life, Young-Bruehl (1998) points us toward the need to possess a feeling for the subject's cultural formation. There is a need to give way to the core, formative desires that follow another's lifeline, to move "along the shape of a life ... particularly sensitive to turning points, junctures, moments of high density—particularly as the subject herself constructs these, sometimes in the form of those complex condensations of experience that Freud called screen memories" (Young-Bruehl 1998, 24). This involves hearing the notes by which individuals present the melody of their lives to themselves, usually through counterpoint. These are the fault/lines—want, breakdown, woman-love, art, flight, marriage, writing—that are the distilled images of Sylvia's lifetime, the condensed notes that resound if we truly attend to her (and to ourselves) as desiring subjects. Accordingly, through the surges of Ashton-Warner's work, Cathryn McConaghy considers the fantasy that the objects of our teaching are other than our teaching selves. McConaghy explores the possibility of reading Ashton-Warner's texts as testimonies to teaching in difficult contexts. Reading Ashton-Warner as a witness to her students' and her own traumas makes possible a revisioning of Ashton-Warner's pedagogies as pedagogies of witnessing. Ashton-Warner emerges as an ambivalent witness to education at empire's end, developing her pedagogies as forms of self-consolation for losses linked to her own postheterosexual longings and to her difficult relationship with teaching in the stony headlands of remote colonial contexts.

McConaghy makes clear that there is no natural empathy with the subject of biography; rather, she argues, we need to see what role the subject plays in our wish structures and as our ego-ideal. It is easy to appropriate and use Sylvia's dream of love in teaching as a fantasy structure through which to serve others and to conserve the self in privilege. The conditions of this illusion, however, need to be made explicit in any reconstruction of her life and effects. But the challenge here lies in the difficulty of loving Sylvia as a subject. Maybe she consoles our recognition of ourselves as difficult and wounded in our capacities to love. Or maybe we can accept Sylvia's difficulties without having to digest her or dissolve her. She was a woman who had a history and a life. She is not us. We need to distinguish between what she wanted for herself and what we want for ourselves. "The life-story should not be directly used for purposes external to it, or forced to answer questions over which the subject herself did not ponder," writes Young-Bruehl (1988, 45).

Judith James and Nancy Thompson describe their decade-long immersions in Sylvia Ashton-Warner's life and texts and explore the creative and destructive impulses in her life and work through her fictions. Taking Sylvia's dream life as their starting point, James and Thompson explore the repetitions of Sylvia's passionate attachments to Joy Alley, expressed as a key character interwoven in many of her novels—frequently in masculine guise. Sylvia's longings and painful separations from Joy find focus in her literary texts. James and Thompson closely examine unpublished archival material to construct a genealogy of Sylvia's homoerotic longings. Their psychotheoretical reading of Sylvia's primal hunger for both love and control needs to be read against the heteronormative sensibilities of the times and Sylvia's own repressions and homophobias: Sylvia's passionate and enduring love for Joy could be said to act as an insistent point of resistance fashioned on the edge of human grief.

What did Sylvia Ashton-Warner really want? What did she most deeply want, for her entire life, so strongly that her obsessions grew up around this pearl of desire, even if as a denial of it? For Sylvia, her deepest desire was love; she said it over and over. It is evidenced in her quest for companionship in her marriage, her devotion to her children, her loving friendships with women, and the enormous tenderness lavished upon her creativity and writing. We need to be able to understand the subject in biography as other to ourselves. As Young-Bruehl (1998) says, "This must be mine in a way that I do not yet understand" (23). Thus James and Thompson cross-write to Anne-Louise Brookes, who cross-writes to Lynley Hood's biography of Sylvia by challenging Hood's claim to writing "the truth" about Ashton-Warner. Describing Hood's texts as damaging, alienating, and a form of "textual violence," Brookes talks back to Hood's need to rescue Ashton-Warner from her same-sex desires and to disavow the passionate attachment between Ashton-Warner and Joy Alley. Brookes writes of the offensiveness of Hood's depictions of Sylvia as vulnerable and Joy as parasitic, of her portrayal of lesbian love as possessive and desperate, and of Sylvia's affections for Joy as a ploy to forestall depression. Hood's attention to what she describes as "the lesbian question" in Sylvia's life, argues Brookes, works as a heteronormative mode of address, a challenge to the women in the story to identify. Brookes raises important questions about the writing of biographies and the normativities that produce forms of heterosexual censure in biographies of women passionately attached to other women.

Roland Barthes once said that biography is a "novel that dare not speak its name" (as cited in Heilbrun 1988, 28). Tess Moeke-Maxwell explores the dynamic between bi/multiracial identity, colonialism, and national identity formations in Sylvia's novel *Greenstone*. *Greenstone* was a relative latecomer to the Sylvia Ashton-Warner oeuvre and has received scant critical attention. Its bi/multiracialized protagonist, Huia, provides the prescient body upon which old nationalist, colonialist, and corporate battles play out, led by those who want the old bifurcations, the devastating categories of self/other, to remain intact. Reading her own autobiography into the text, Moeke-Maxwell reconsiders the strategic potential of hybrid identifications and their power to disrupt the designated spaces reserved for colonial subjects. In her analysis of what she describes as a tale of bicultural tensions and river/border crossings, Moeke-Maxwell interprets the River as a colonial space, a border to be crossed from This Side to That Side in diasporic negotiations. For readers of Moeke-Maxwell's narrative interpretation, the possibility arises that the River as colonial space could have also been a code for heteronormative space, a space of vulnerability symbolized and disrupted in Sylvia's expression of her homoerotic yearnings. Although Moeke-Maxwell suggests the River presents the hybrid bi/multiracial woman with possibilities for emancipation and survival, it is also possible that Sylvia's River functioned as a force for seclusion and self-marginalization, a liminal and transitional third space for mourning her own losses.

"Woman's selfhood, the right to her own story, depends upon her 'ability to act in the public domain'" writes Carolyn Heilbrun (1988, 17, citing Jehlen). Heilbrun reminds us that in writing a woman's life, it is difficult (even today) to admit achievement, ambition, or recognition in their narratives—an observation that Jill Ker Conway also once made in a study of accomplished women. Kathleen Connor and Linda Radford, with Judith Robertson, interviewed several notable international educational and literary theorists, including C. K. Stead, Carole Durix, and Herbert Kohl, about the influence of Ashton-Warner's ideas and writings on their own. Curiously, as with our own interpretive community of readers in this volume, those interviewed by Connor and Radford with Robertson were at times hard pressed to put into simple words the meanings that they have made from Ashton-Warner's work. Even so, the respondents' poetic testimonies provide evidence of rich genealogies tracing back to the radical interpretive communities of Ashton-Warner's own lifetime. Their structures of feeling challenge the cultural politics of the contemporary veil of amnesia shrouding Ashton-Warner's memory. In so doing they open the way for new grounds of understanding of humane educational praxis, Sylvia's "humane image of the calling" that invites us to assume our place at the table of an expansive and extraordinary educational imaginary.

The volume concludes with Judith Robertson's psychoanalytic reflections on the nature of Ashton-Warner's provocations and of the tendency in education and life to censure excitation and find comfort not in our ability to create excesses, but in our abilities to return to composure as stasis. Robertson's theorizing of provocation as education's "twin sister" returns to us the insight with which we began this introduction, from Elizabeth Young-Bruehl (1998), that a great deal of happiness occurs when two people, whose fantasies of contentment conjoin, find each other. Recovering education as provocation invites us to view it as something dynamic and unfrozen, or as Phillips (1994) would say, "as a resource to be thought about rather than endlessly re-enacted" (69). In tracing the sparkling havoc of Sylvia's provocations, Robertson finds us desiring Sylvia's epic performances of subjectivity: as herald of the new woman teacher, as cartographer of education's unconscious, as official mourner to the living obituary of education as loss, as a woman's woman, as anthem of her generation, and even (because it excites our curiosities) as a perpetual plague to biographers. "Missed meanings haunt us," we remember from Mary Jacobus (1999, 30). Such issues raise important and difficult questions for both literary criticism and education.

Indeed, our bonds of reading and our collective search for theory in our subject have raised a number of significant issues for education and literary and cultural studies that we could not have predicted. Sylvia Ashton-Warner's texts call forth important and challenging questions about teaching that remain as provocative and productive now as they were twenty-five to fifty years ago. The readings we present pry open and complicate the ongoing conversation around educational theorizing, remembering, and forgetting. While there is perhaps little new in our recognition that pedagogy comes populated with censures and taboos, the different kind of story we tell takes us into the heart that beats within everyday relations of social power, even as it registers through historically situated contestations around proper teaching. What gets revealed, then, are the fascinating dilemmas of classroom erotics, the dangers of intimacy in teaching and learning, and the powerful fantasy that the objects of teaching lives are other than our own teaching selves. Quite specifically, our volume takes up the measure of transference in meaning-making, in teaching, and in writing, and examines what it is that pedagogy consoles throughout its life of myriad declensions. Sylvia's life and work call us to witness the difficult and ambiguous nature of postheterosexual attachments in women's biographies, the violence of regulating excesses in women's lives, and the ghostly skirts that envelop women's lives as semiotic provocation. Ashton-Warner's haunting texts—and they did haunt us, in dreams and phantasmatic presences—trouble easy assumptions about what it means to live and create as a woman/teacher. This volume turns on the significance of reading and interpretive communities in understanding the complexities of woman/teacher identification. We have tried to capture the psychosocial dynamics that give shape to shadows in reading teaching and literary histories. In desiring Sylvia, we have endeavored to listen into the historical and spatial situatedness of educational and cultural theorizing and to ask how reading effects might radically disrupt composure and stasis in the tides of pedagogy. The insights and troubling questions that emerge from our collective embrace with Sylvia speak not only to her enigmatic survivals, but also to our own submission to excitability in education. Our volume puts into public memory a story that is immediately graspable as one that is contemporary and feminist, thereby connecting us with Sylvia across seasons and decades of womanhood, continents, and disciplinary divides. Ultimately, we offer here our response to Sylvia Ashton-Warner's enduring calls for justice. The process of reading provocatively enables us as women to make new meanings of both her life/work and our own, despite or perhaps even because of our disparate autobiographies and our varying tolerances for composure and excitability.

References

Ashton-Warner, S. 1966. *Greenstone*. New York: Simon and Schuster.

Britzman, D. 1997. The tangles of implication. *QSE: International Journal of Qualitative Studies in Education* 10, no. 1: 31–37.

Boire, G. 1989. Thieves of language. Review of "Dreams of speech and violence: The art of the short story in Canada and New Zealand." *Landfall* 43, no. 1: 199–224.

Caruth, C. 1996. *Unclaimed experience: Trauma, narrative and history*. Baltimore, MD: Johns Hopkins University Press.

Felman, S., ed. 1977. *Literature and psychoanalysis: The question of reading: Otherwise*. Repr. Baltimore, MD: Johns Hopkins University Press, 1980.

———. 1993. *What does a woman want? Reading and sexual difference*. Baltimore, MD: Johns Hopkins University Press.

Freud, S. 1908. Family romances. In *Standard edition of the complete psychological works of Sigmund Freud*, 17th ed., ed. and trans. by J. Strachey, 217–52. London: Hogarth Press, 1953.

Heilbrun, C. 1988. *Writing a woman's life*. New York: Ballantine Books.

Hood, L. 1988. *Sylvia! The biography of Sylvia Ashton-Warner*. Auckland, New Zealand: Viking.

Jacobus, M. 1999. *Psychoanalysis and the scene of reading*. Oxford: Oxford University Press.

Khanna, R. 2003. *Dark continents: Psychoanalysis and colonialism*. Durham, NC: Duke University Press.

Milford, N., ed. 2002. *Selected poetry of Edna St. Vincent Millay*. New York: Modern Library.

Phillips, A. 1994. *On flirtation*. Cambridge, MA: Harvard University Press.

Pitt, A. 2003. *The play of the personal: Psychoanalytic narratives of feminist education*. New York: Peter Lang.

Rich, A. 1979. *On lies, secrets and silence*. New York: Norton.

Shallcrass, J. 1984. In memoriam: Sylvia Ashton-Warner. *Landfall* 38, no. 3: 342–44.

Young-Bruehl, E. 1998. *Subject to biography. Psychoanalysis, feminism, and writing women's lives*. Cambridge, MA: Harvard University Press.

Žižek, S. 1998. Love thy neighbor? No thanks. In *The psychoanalysis of race*, ed. C. Lane, 176–92. New York: Columbia University Press.

CHAPTER TWO

Sex, Fear, and Pedagogy: Sylvia Ashton-Warner's Infant Room

Alison Jones

Let us begin by putting the slight sense of indignation on the table. Here are two academics, an Australian and a Canadian, presuming to edit a book about *our* Sylvia. Once our ruffled feathers flatten down, the question remains: Why did this book not come out of New Zealand's education community? That unsettling query must lurk behind any New Zealand educationist's contribution to this book. Although she is apparently recognized among educators elsewhere, not much is known about Sylvia Ashton-Warner among educators in New Zealand. Certainly, in my recent conversations with dozens of teacher-trainees, teachers, and teacher-educators in Auckland, most had only a vague idea of who she was. Some knew that she "once taught around the East Coast [of New Zealand]" and wrote books. New Zealand's largest teachers' college library is named after her and (since 2001) contains a small exhibition of some beautiful watercolor illustrations from one of her reading books, yet few students at the college seem to know anything much about her.

There are many possible explanations for Sylvia Ashton-Warner's disappearance in New Zealand, most of which I suspect would be based in responses to her difficult personality, in particular the local cultural distaste for anyone (especially a woman) who "blows her own trumpet." Reading between the lines of her novels and autobiography, Sylvia was far *too much* for us—she was self-opinionated, arrogant, deluded, badly behaved, self-pitying, a drama queen, obsessed with sex (or at least with falling in love), and intent on being a misunderstood victim. And she had a drinking problem. These characteristics are unpopular in any woman, at any historical moment. She was an embarrassment best ignored.

Other explanations include the fact that few New Zealanders know much, if anything, about the fascinating history of Maori schooling. Such social amnesia (Simon and Tuhiwai Smith 2001, 1)—whereby a dominant section of a society systematically forgets its problematic past[1]—may have influenced our memory of Sylvia Ashton-Warner, the teacher of rural Maori pupils in Native Schools. But I suspect that this is not the whole story.

The explanation for her ultimate obscurity that seems most likely to me, and which is borne out in Lynley Hood's (1988) excellent biography of Ashton-Warner, is that far from being neglected, Sylvia actively and consistently undermined her own reputation, both with publishers and with the New Zealand education establishment.[2] As some of them attempted to praise and encourage her outstanding writing talent, her intense ambivalence about public admiration and acceptance caused her to seriously alienate the very people who supported her work. In short, she was a brilliant, charismatic, but quixotic individual who was literally impossible to work with and who ultimately and actively ensured her own "rejection."

Despite this preamble, my chapter is not an attempt to explain or justify Sylvia Ashton-Warner's obscurity in her own country and its links to her complex character. Nor do I wish to contribute some hagiographic recuperation of Ashton-Warner. Rather, I want to consider what was—and remains—at stake in the approach she took to her teaching. In particular, I am most interested in the philosophy and practice of her pedagogy, which, considered in the light of today's social anxieties about children, make her work both compelling and dangerous for contemporary educators.

Ghost Story

Before I begin, I need to get another seemingly trivial and personal thing out of the way. I am guilty of being a New Zealand educationist who, despite my public interest in gender and the body and Maori education, has never given Sylvia's work much thought beyond a mild curiosity about her pedagogy. I have read some of her books and met her on one or two occasions—she was a friend of my mother's in her later years and lived nearby. But I might not have given her much more attention if she had not haunted me one night.

I had been invited to speak at my old secondary school in Tauranga about my recently published book—a somewhat bitter ethnographic study of the impact of social class on Pacific Islands girls' schooling in New Zealand (Jones 1991). The host teacher's family had, as it happened, purchased Sylvia's house after her death and I was invited to stay overnight in the semidetached guest room. After a lively seminar, I retired there for the night. This room was Sylvia's last Selah.[3]

I fell asleep quickly and was "woken" by some beautiful clear piano-playing that seemed to come from somewhere in the room. Then I experienced a tremendous rushing sound in my ears, a rolling sensation, and felt myself to be rising up and standing inside someone else's body. I was looking out through the eyes of an enraged person, and I knew I was about to angrily sweep some ornaments off a nearby table. I thought immediately how embarrassing it would be to have to explain this vandalism to my hosts the next day. For some reason I said loudly, "Sylvia! Stop it!" Clearly, I assumed it was Sylvia's body and her rage. The sensation ceased immediately, as though the ghost were ashamed, and I sat up in my bed. I turned on the light and, warning Sylvia not to return, slept fitfully until morning.

At breakfast, my host was unruffled by my strange tale. She merely said, "Yes, Sylvia is still around," as though it were nothing out of the ordinary. It was certainly out of the ordinary for me—I am an atheist, and a scientist by training, with enormous skepticism about the supernatural. My host's apparent indifference made me think that even as a ghost, Sylvia could not gain educators' attention.

Later, a psychologist friend suggested that the anger I experienced that night was my own. Maybe she was right; it was true that I did not feel I could satisfactorily express my distress about the talented but turned-off young women in the research study I had come to Tauranga to speak about. The excitement, energy, and talent the working-class Pacific girls in my study displayed in their church singing or in their various cultural groups was completely at odds with their flatness, boredom, and lack of engagement in class. How to unlock passion—and success—in the classroom? This was Sylvia's domain and her desire as a teacher. Maybe the unconscious rage I felt about the schooling of working-class Pacific Islands girls was expressed through Sylvia, the educator who had worked passionately with Maori children. Perhaps.

It occurred to me that if Sylvia the teacher was considered problematic as an educator, the problem lay in this desire—a desire for passion when good teaching is about rationality, a desire for abandonment when good teaching is about order and control, a desire for erotic passion when proper teaching is precisely *not* about the body, emotion, or sexuality. In short, Sylvia's threat to teaching in this country (and universally, in fact) was her symbolic threat to what counted—and counts—as *proper teaching*.

Fear, Sex, and Reading

In his preface to a 1966[4] reprint of *Teacher*, Sir Herbert Read, the great English war poet, philosopher, and promoter of the arts (from whom Ashton-Warner got her ideas about organic expression), wrote without blushing that Sylvia Ashton-Warner made "the child's inherited drives: self-preservation and sexual gratification" the foundation of her teaching (9). By welcoming the presence of these drives in the infant room, he suggested, Ashton-Warner provides an example of pedagogy that "should have a beneficial effect on teaching everywhere" (*Teacher*, 11).

Sylvia put it more bluntly: the organic instincts of sex and fear drove children's passions and interests, she said, and allowing these elements free expression in the classroom would incite learning. Her reading scheme for new readers, an exemplar of her educational philosophy and her claim to pedagogical innovation, revolved around this idea. The key vocabulary, a system of encouraging children to name their own words to learn to read, "centres around two main instincts: fear and sex" (*Teacher*, 34).

Read through today's sensitivities, it is evident that Ashton-Warner (let alone Sir Herbert) is on uncomfortable and dubious ground bringing "fear and sex" into the infant classroom (five- to seven-year-olds). As members of the risk society of a late modernity characterized by obsessive anxiety about children's (sexual) safety, we are uneasy if children are exposed to any experience of sexuality or threat; any possibility that their environments are not completely sanitized in the interests of innocent happiness is literally a criminal or at least a "social welfare" matter (Scott, Jackson, and Backett-Milburn 2001).

Fear and sex were far from the worlds and words of the reading books originally on offer in Sylvia's infant room. The *Janet and John* books, replete with blond happy children in socks and shoes playing in a bright, ordered English landscape, were standard issue in New Zealand primary education. The lives of Janet and John could scarcely be further from those of rural Maori children of the time, for whom bare feet, mud, wild pigs and lively, often violent, family relationships were the stuff of daily existence. Rejecting the standard texts as without native charm and with "no instinctive meaning" (*Teacher*, 36), Sylvia encouraged the children in her classrooms to suggest their own word lists and captions for their pictures. She sought words from the children's lives, the words they had "inside":

> Out flow these captions. It's lovely flowing. I see the creative channel swelling and undulating like an artery with blood pumping through. And as it settles, just like any other organic arrangement of nature it spread out into a harmonious pattern; the fear words dominating the design, a few sex words, the person interest, and the temper of the century. Daddy, Mummy, ghost, bomb, kiss, brothers, butcher knife, gaol, love, dance, cry, fight, hat, bulldog, touch, wild piggy … if you were a child, which

vocabulary would you prefer? Your own or the one at present in the New Zealand infant rooms? Come John come. Look John look. Come and look. See the boats? The vocabulary of the English upper middle class, two-dimensional and respectable? (*Teacher*, 32–33)

Sylvia was not the only New Zealand infant teacher using homemade vocabulary lists and stories for readers. Teachers' production of purpose-written books based on the pupils' worlds had been encouraged, especially by Native School officials who recognized that the stories and images in imported reading books bore little or no relation to the cultural lives of local children, Maori or Pakeha.[5] In other words, Sylvia's development of readers and vocabulary lists from the children's words (as well as her encouragement of dance and free play) was entirely consistent with the child-centered philosophy of the Education Department of the time (Middleton and May 1997). Recollections by teachers and education officials in Judith Simon and Linda Tuhiwai Smith's (2001) superb book on New Zealand Native Schools (schools for rural Maori, in which Sylvia taught; see McConaghy, this volume; see Middleton, this volume) indicate that many Pakeha and Maori Native School teachers experimented with innovative, "relevant" pedagogy and curriculum for Maori children, especially from the 1930s to 1969, when the Native School system was abandoned. In many of these teachers' reading programs, squirrels and forests became sheep and bush, and Janet and John became, say, Hine and Rangi, to better suit the interests and knowledge of the local children—although, of course, in the English language.[6]

What made Sylvia *improper* as a teacher and different from other inventive local teachers was (as well as her ability and desire to write about her teaching) her primary interest in creativity based in emotion, particularly the dark feelings of fear and the disallowed excitement of sex. As Lynley Hood put it, "while most teachers felt that keeping the lid on their pupils' more explosive emotions was essential to effective teaching, Sylvia was determined to rip the lid right off" (Hood 1988, 135). The expression of such explosive creativity necessarily involved what would today be called inappropriate words. "Pleasant words won't do," insisted Sylvia, "Respectable words won't do. They must be organically tied up, organically born from the dynamic life itself" (*Teacher*, 27). One teacher who worked with Sylvia to develop books for Native Schools reported:

First of all there were Sylvia's books and they were full of murderous things like "My uncle said he'd do this to my brother" and they were all four-letter words—not quite the four letter words they use today but near enough. Another girl [teacher], hers were … good stories that ended up with good morals. Mine were somewhere in between. I think mine were the best. (Simon and Tuhiwai Smith 2001, 109)

Sylvia would not have been happy with the in-between solution. The child's raw language about his or her most basic emotions, she maintained, tapped into the child's inner being and unlocked the relationship with written words. She analyzed the words spontaneously chosen by the children and identified fear as the strongest emotion, with ideas related to sex following second. Sylvia's identification of the fear words, curiously, included "Mummy" and "Daddy," as well as the more obvious: "cry," "fight," "thunder," "knife," "yell," "crack." The popular sex words she identified as "kiss," "love," "touch," "haka," "darling," "together," "you-and-me," "sing," "dance."

The sex words identified by Sylvia are not the sex words we might imagine children knowing at the time—words like "bugger," "cock," "root," "cunt," "tits," or other more colloquial English words (after all, Sylvia was in the business of teaching English text to Maori children, despite the fact that she was unlocking "native" imagery). The children's sex words, according to Sylvia, were more related to love, feeling, romance, and relationships—to an erotic life above the crudities of physical sex itself. In other words, the children's own stirring sex games and sex talk did not make an appearance in the key vocabulary; it was Sylvia's views of children's sex words, not their own, that populated reading time. It was an adult, romantic (rather than crude, childish) notion of sex that interested Sylvia, given the focus on love in her personal diaries and novels, and it was her view that shaped the key vocabulary.

Whatever its link to Sylvia's own preoccupations, her approach to teaching small children to read was based in a pedagogical erotics within which passion, fear, sexuality, violence, and excitement were all to be harnessed in the interests of creative expression and learning ("unlocking the mind") (*Teacher*, 33). Sylvia and others report great success from her approach. She told of so-called slow children rapidly learning to read by articulating and collecting the words that excited and connected to them; her children learned sophisticated musical scores through emotional engagement with the passion of musical expression and dance. The "lovely flowing" of that which is within the child onto paper or into voice is a positive and enduring image—one that has excited generations of teachers who believe, like Rousseau, that good teaching allows and encourages the unfolding of the myriad talents of the natural child. While there is probably much to recommend in this noncoercive philosophy, it avoids altogether the difficult question of what the "natural, organic" child is, or is allowed to be.

Valerie Walkerdine (1981) some years ago pointed to the problem of the four-year-old boy who called his teacher "knickers" and another child a "cunt." She discussed the teacher's mild rebuke and her shrugging patience with such "silly talk" of the natural child—a tolerance and an undermining of teacher authority that arose out of a child-centered educational approach. It appears that organic expression, at least in the form demanded by the key vocabulary, also rules out the authority of the censoring or disciplining teacher: it is not for the teacher to decide what legitimately excites the expressive child. This is a fairly uncontroversial claim when children's sex words are "kiss" and "darling"; these words can only be seen as rather quaint and charming. But what about the child who wants to write, as part of his or her key vocabulary, such socially unacceptable words as "fuck," "dick," "shit"—what would Sylvia or any contemporary teacher make of those words in the infant reading list? They are undeniably "organic words, tied up with dynamic life itself" (*Teacher*, 27); such rude and naughty words are loaded with excitement for children and access to them would no doubt catapult some slow learners into word identification and reading.

The problem of the excessive, and truly independently expressive, child did not arise, it appears, in Sylvia's experience. (It might be suggested that children, sensibly, hide their true, instinctive "native imagery" from adults). She did encounter what she saw as the opposite of natural childish expression, though. When she came to teach later in Colorado, she found the children there tragically "civilized" compared with the simple, open Maori; they failed to produce the generative sex and fear words at the heart of the key vocabulary. At this, Sylvia was nonplussed. Instinct and native imagery in North American children, she presumed, had been overwhelmed by "man's concoctions," including politeness, selfishness, and emotional repression (*Spearpoint*, 86).

It is unclear how Sylvia would have handled children's words or sentences brimming over with crude sex, even though she lived at a time when there was far more positive educational and theoretical interest in children's sexuality than today (Tobin 2001). One assumes—though I am far from confident about this— she would have rejoiced as children got to the heart of the matter and "naughty" reading and writing took off. Whatever Sylvia's reaction, we know that in the late twentieth and early twenty-first century, denial and even criminalization of childhood sexuality means that any young child uttering such words is likely to be seen as a candidate for serious counseling and investigation or at least guidance (Levine 2002; Tobin 1997, 2001).

Surveillance

Here is the impromptu reading card on which one of my backward Maori five year olds at last learnt to read:

Daddy
Mummy
Ihaka
Hit
Cried
Kiss

Daddy hit Ihaka.
Ihaka cried.
Mummy kissed Ihaka. Daddy hit Ihaka. Ihaka cried.
Kiss Ihaka Mummy. (*Teacher*, 144)

Sex was dynamite enough—but Sylvia's children more often used what she called fear words. For overseas readers of *Teacher* in the 1960s, Sylvia's key vocabulary—as illustrated here in Ihaka's story—probably had a romantic, poignant ring to it, providing a glimpse into the exotic, if not harsh, lives of small native children in a far-off land. But what if the key vocabulary's tenets of "expressing the personal" and "connecting with that great instinct—fear" are relocated to the present? As mentioned above, while the vulgarities of fear and sex were no doubt considered best avoided as the proper basis for reading and writing in the infant classroom in the 1940s and 1950s, they are far more actively a source of anxiety and danger today. Any child developing his or her key vocabulary to write "My Dad gave my Mum a black eye" or "My uncle gave me a hiding" or "Rangi had a knife" or even "The piggie bite Ihaka" (as did the children in Sylvia's classrooms), would not be a "creative, expressive child." He or she would be a child at risk, an abused child, a child to be rescued by the authorities. In other words, such phrases and sentences would be dangerous to families. The child learning to read and write, generating his or her native imagery, could literally become a threat to his or her parents and family, and the hapless teacher would be expected to read the child's work as a sign of need for official intervention.

It is impossible to guess the attitudes of the parents to their children's writing about what Daddy did to Mummy or vice versa (or the fact that children may have invented exciting home stories to satisfy their teacher). Maybe some parents had no idea what their children told Mrs. Henderson, as Sylvia was known to her students. However, some did and were no doubt privately annoyed or even alarmed. Pere Hanara, a pupil of Sylvia's, recalled that when parents were invited to view their children's work on the walls of the classroom, "their complexions would go from brown through various shades of white and purple as they read it all" (Hood 1990, 229). Certainly there is no clear evidence that the exposure of personal lives and the reference to violence in the children's homes was problematic for the education authorities who assessed Sylvia's teaching. They had long advocated the use of children's experiences in the teaching of reading, and although they considered Sylvia's innovative espousal of emotional expression unusual—and at least one thought her pupils' words "vulgar" (Hood 1990, 51)—they did not appear to be officially concerned about the substance of the children's writing. If it worked as an instrument of learning, it worked. And it seemed to. As one of Sylvia's pupils told Lynley Hood (1988): "Our personal lives were exposed all round the walls. She encouraged it. She said it really makes you feel good. When she got a few with their stories revealed[,] there was peer pressure on the others to do the same. We really caught the reading bug from wanting to read those stories" (137).

Sylvia sometimes seemed to find the writings of her students "too jolly well hard to bear" (*Spinster*, 175), but the fact that they were writing and reading was the most important thing. From today's vantage point, however, ambivalence about privacy, voyeurism, and surveillance must lead us to take a critical position toward the idea that children's expressive prose in classrooms is merely an innocent means to literacy. The child's organic vocabulary—in a context where "dysfunctional" Maori or working-class families are seen as requiring official state intervention—can be a key player in a scene of social control and surveillance in which parents, children, and teachers become involuntary participants.

From this negative perspective, the distanced neutrality of imported vocabulary takes on a rather more attractive appearance. The sanitized texts of Janet and John, or even Hine and Rangi among the bush and sheep, may provide an important aspect of the peace of the classroom, a guard against voyeurism: protecting the teacher from knowing "too much" about the child and protecting the child, ethically, from being an agent of official family inspection. Another critical—though less powerful—point is that the self-generated vocabulary assumes that all children *want* to write about what is familiar. It may well be that imported vocabulary and imagery offer an alternative set of ideas and a temporary respite at school for a pupil who seeks, however unconsciously, to escape the limitations and tensions of her home. Amusingly, Pere Hanara—who had noted the color of the parents' shocked faces above—confessed to liking *Janet and John* better than Sylvia's readers (Hood 1990).

Such cautions about the child-generated transgressive vocabulary are not to suggest that children harmed at home should not tell their teachers about it, nor be encouraged to write about it at school. Indeed, teachers can and do provide needed sanctuary and rescue for some abused children. The point is that organic vocabulary is not merely an innocent mechanism for literacy. As Paulo Freire (1972, 1976) has already made clear, words are powerful, political things; they make worlds but they also destroy them. Our invitation to children to become literate is far from innocent; it is a compulsory invitation to be actors in the fraught and complex relations of power that surround them.

The family is not the only party in line for official scrutiny following the unimpeded flow of children's passionate expression. The contemporary teacher might also become an object of suspicion if the child's fear words or sex words turn toward her—or, more dangerously, toward him. With some relish, safe in the tolerance (or avoidance) of the times, Sylvia tells of the violence the children report from their dreams: "The violence of [the dreams] has to be heard to be believed. A lot of it is violence against me—which they tell me cheerfully enough. I come out very badly. My house has been burnt down, bombs fall on me, I'm shot with all makes of guns and handed over to the gorilla. Presumably it's the authority and discipline which I represent" (*Teacher*, 56). Such negative passion towards a teacher could cause serious concern among some contemporary educational authorities: what abuse must have been meted out by Mrs. Henderson to generate such violence against her in the writing and talk of the children?

Surveillance and voyeurism were the last things on the minds of Sylvia's adult pupils at Simon Fraser University in Vancouver, Canada, where she was a visiting professor in education. Thrilled by the idea that emotion might be productively unleashed in classrooms where previously order and rationality reigned, some said of her methods and approach, "It's about letting children be themselves," and "Here was someone working with kids who was willing to wade right into the emotional content of their lives … to open the wellsprings of their own souls" (Hood 1988, 222). No matter that the wellsprings may have been private or criminal or even fictitious.

For Sylvia and her more enthusiastic followers in teacher education, anxieties about surveillance would be an example of the academic, over-rationalized manhandling that kills good and creative educational ideas. I would argue that it is precisely *not* rationality that threatens the sort of culture or the emotional landscape of the classroom prized by champions of organic teaching. Rather, social anxiety and the current *irrational* obsession with risk and safety are arguably the main forces impacting on the possibilities for creative expression, passion, pleasure, and even common sense, as primary classrooms become increasingly sanitized, and "safe" relationships and behaviors become compulsory (Furedi 2002a, 2002b). The tension between children "naming raw life" in classrooms and the social impetus to regulate the negative excesses of that life was not something Sylvia had to be concerned with, but it is a tension that contemporary teachers cannot avoid.

Touch and Teaching

[M]y arms have become itchy on the inside to hold children. From the wrists on the inner side along the skin right up to the shoulders and across the breast I know a physical discomfort. If ever flesh spoke mine does; for the communion of hands, the arms stretching round my waist and black heads bumping my breasts…. The truth is I am enslaved. I'm enslaved in one vast love affair with seventy children. (*Spinster*, 188)

As her teaching career developed, Sylvia talked about her desire to touch and cuddle her pupils. Maori cultural practices enchanted and inspired her and she learned with enthusiasm, as she put it in *Teacher*, that meaning for Maori is in "expression, gesture, intonation, cadence and, above all, touch ... verbal conversation gives way to sensual and physical conversation" (114). The children would trace patterns on her smock with their fingers, untie her shoelaces, and sit on her knee, held close to her body. In *Teacher*, her account of such intimate teacherly scenes was imbued with romantic, sweet, innocent motherly affection:

> Tears break from the big brown eyes and set off down his face. "That's why, somebodies they broked my castle for notheen. Somebodies".
> I sit on my low chair in the raftered prefab, take him on my knee and tuck the black Maori head beneath my chin....
> "There ... there ... look at my pretty boy ..." (*Teacher*, 177)

But in *Spinster*, Sylvia's accounts of touching children, spoken through her alter-ego Anna Vorontosov, were more often expressed in erotic, even explicitly sexual, terms:

> He is heavy to lift but I can't resist the physical impact of him on me, on a person that has never been touched by a man since I left Eugene ... although I feel his paint brush wet through my smock I also feel that big something ... like a great instinct, unidentifiable and uncontrollable, take over. (*Spinster*, 43)

Some teachers reading these passages no doubt feel identification with Anna's/Sylvia's charged feelings towards her small pupils. The physical and emotional demands of little children, their small-animal need for love and nurturing, the giving and taking, the rubbing and pushing and physical closeness, the intense pleasures and pains that their care elicits from the engaged teacher all call forth a sensation that is sometimes akin to sexual engagement. And, as Sylvia's books so powerfully illustrated, teachers' own emotional lives—just as for any worker—impact on the trajectory of their workday.

Again, today's social anxieties and preoccupations ensure that we feel uncomfortable even reading such admissions. Modern teachers are not to feel (or should suppress) the pleasures of "physical impact" or the "big something" in their interactions with children. More than that, they are not to touch children, except when absolutely necessary. In fact, courses are these days offered for primary teachers in New Zealand to assist them in identifying and eliminating all nonessential touching (Jones 2003, 2004). The physical passions expressed in Sylvia's classrooms would be highly suspect today, and Sylvia would be told in no uncertain terms that positive intimacy with her children was not allowed. Any suggestion that good teaching of small children might elicit fleshly desires to hold and be held would be considered unethical, immoral, and even illegal. Indeed, many teachers have learned actively not to enjoy the "impact" of children's bodies. If a child attempts to climb onto a teacher's knee today, she is gently removed: the "great instinct" to hold and to love has been replaced by the need to remain at a safe nonabusive distance (Jones 2001).

Anxieties about abuse of children were also in play in the 1960s, and many would have found Anna's desire to cuddle her pupils creepy and immoral—because it met the teacher's, rather than the child's, needs. Clarence Beeby, who was the director of the New Zealand government's Department of Education that controlled the country's education system, and Sylvia's bête noire, said Anna's desires for her students' physical closeness made his "flesh creep" and he could not "help wondering what admirers of A-W would have thought" about Anna's confessions if they "had been spoken by a male teacher about a little girl" (Hood 1990, 241).

Lynley Hood suggests that Sylvia had been abused by two teachers as a child. These are shadowy events; Sylvia herself recalls one moment when she was about eight years old: "I did learn the strange excitement of being pressed close to a man's body ... he [a teacher at Hastings Central School] was picked up years later for this very sort of thing" (Hood 1988, 33). Sylvia's ambivalence about such "strange excitement" became thematic; touching seemed necessarily imbued with sexual overtones for her—and pleasure and fear were never far apart.

In touching them, Sylvia did not only cuddle her children; she also hit them. Of course, when she was in training in the late 1920s and right until the 1980s, New Zealand teachers were often expected to hit children, within reason. Sylvia was critical but initially admiring of the standard forms of teaching of the day. After one training practicum she wrote, "The clock and the strap did most of the teaching, successful teaching too, for their handwriting was copybook standard and no-one talked.... I thought, if only we could teach young children without the need to punish them all day" (*I Passed This Way*, 16). Sylvia's (partially successful) solution to punishment was to fully engage young children in a dramatic pedagogical adventure in which recalcitrance and boredom had no room to develop. But up until 1990, when corporal punishment became illegal in New Zealand, teachers routinely whacked children with sticks, leather straps, and the palms of their hands.

Throughout her career, Sylvia was ambivalent about the violence towards children so common in schools and in the children's homes. Even though corporal punishment was explicitly officially discouraged in Native Schools (Simon and Tuhiwai Smith 2001), Maori children were still regularly hit as the most common form of discipline. In *Teacher*, grappling with the question of physical punishment, Sylvia quoted with cautious approval D. H. Lawrence—"If a child annoys you, smack it and smack it hard. In its own interests" (in *Teacher*, 119)—as well as a neurologist friend who recommended smacking two-year-olds. But she was wary about hitting children herself because she almost always did it "in a temper," which meant she was in danger of overdoing it. More than one of her former pupils remembers bruises imparted by Sylvia's red stick: "If you didn't obey her instantly you got a hard whack on the back of the legs" (Hood 1990, 119, 141). She regretted her lack of control when she hit a child and usually sent children who needed punishing to Mr. Henderson, her husband, the headmaster:

> I wouldn't touch him myself, knowing my own temper. I thought of something less dangerous. "You go over to Mr Henderson, Matawhero" ... I crossed the room and took his arm ... But ... he sat down and broke down into loud crying.... I put my rage aside and began comforting him.... "Don't cry", I said, patting his leg.... In time I realised that I mustn't touch him in a rage ... I took him by the back of the jersey out the door, down the steps, across the grass. (*Teacher*, 117)

Upon her arrival in 1970 to teach at the Aspen Community School in Colorado, Sylvia's hosts were alarmed to discover that her means of gaining attention and obedience involved force, including the strap. These disciplinary methods had worked and were acceptable in rural New Zealand at the time, but they were quite unacceptable in the liberal confines of the "alternative" Aspen Community School (featured in *Spearpoint*). Sylvia's fans had not yet realized that pedagogical passion and physical intimacy in teaching had at least two faces for Sylvia. Violence and rage were not merely limited to the home or brought to school in the Key Vocabulary. Niceness was out; passion of all sorts was in play.

Erotics of Pedagogy

We have considered the question of sex in the children's vocabulary and in relation to Sylvia's accounts of her desire to be physically close to her pupils. But sex as a metaphor was most strongly present in Sylvia's wider pedagogical philosophy. She describes her very best teaching in terms of the seduction of a lover:

> When I teach children I marry them. I found this out last year when I began the orchestra. To do what I wanted them to do they had need to be like me. More than that. They had to be part of me.... I found that for good performances we had to be one thing. One organ. And physically they had to be near to each other and to me. (*Teacher*, 171)

> There is quietly occurring in my infant room a grand espousal. To bring them to do what I want them to do they come near me. I draw them near me, in body and in spirit. They don't know it, but I do. They become part of me, like a lover. The approach, little different. The askance observation first, the acceptance next, the

gradual or quick coming, until in the complete procuration, there glows the harmony, the peace. (*Teacher*, 172)

All the rules of love-making apply to these spiritual and intellectual fusions. (*Teacher*, 173)

Sometimes, sex was more than merely a metaphor for her pedagogical approach: it seemed to describe her practice in a straightforward way. That is, it was not simply Sylvia's *descriptions* of her teaching that were imbued with erotic imagery. Some of her pupils recalled her pedagogical style in those same terms. Here is Greg Tata, who remembers extraordinary music lessons from Sylvia:

Every day Mr Henderson warmed up our voices and Mrs Henderson would come in as if she were making love to the air around her. She'd look up at her husband and flutter her eyelashes and say "How are you getting on dear? Are the children ready?" We'd stare at this flirting in amazement. Then as Mr Henderson left she'd turn to us and convey that what had been going on with him was about to continue with us. (Hood 1988, 169)

Judging by her own accounts, Sylvia's flirtation with her pupils (let alone with the inspectors, parents, visitors, and so on) seems merely an extension or expression of her own particular personality and manner, where the turbulence of "love" ruled. But her flirtation is also pedagogically interesting. The notion of teaching-as-seduction is not entirely strange in the educational theory literature. It has been explored by some contemporary feminist educationists, most notably North American professor Jane Gallop (1992, 1995, 1997), whose infamous pedagogical style might very well be compared with Sylvia's, albeit in a university rather than a primary school setting. In brief, Gallop argues that the best education is a form of seduction. For Gallop, sexual desire and the desire to learn and to teach are interconnected. The desire of the good teacher is to enflame, to arouse passion, to be loved and attended to; the "good" student's desire is to be enflamed, to be aroused, to consume the knowledge of the teacher (Gallop 1992). It is in these eroticized terms that Sylvia described her own work: successful teaching was an excitement/incitement, a "lovely flowing" that she generated in her pupils and in herself. Standard teaching was typically dull, bland, safe; her teaching, like Gallop's, was erotic, passionate, and dangerous.

Gallop was considered literally dangerous by some of her students and, much to her intellectual stimulation, was charged with sexual harassment (Gallop 1997). The danger Sylvia's teaching in the 1950s and 1960s may have represented was not to the sensibilities of her pupils. Her creative practice was, she liked to imagine (as did Gallop), a danger to the standard pedagogical ideals of order, logic, and rationality. By foregrounding the power of the irrational and the emotional in learning and teaching, she intuitively anticipated later educational theorists' arguments that seduction, desire, and pleasure are the suppressed others in accounts of teaching-as-usual (Hooks 1994; McWilliam 1999). Sylvia also obviously came to the view held by psychoanalytic theorists in education—a view almost entirely submerged in contemporary mainstream educational debates—that eros and the unconscious have a central place in teaching and learning (see Appel 1996; Britzman 1998; Gallop 1995; Jagodinzski 2002 for a range of psychoanalytic analyses of the pedagogical relationship).

For Sylvia, not only was the celebration of creative passion in classrooms a challenge to standard, proper pedagogies, it was only inspired, erotic teaching that unleashed creativity. But what was the nature of this unleashing? And what did it give rise to? It cannot be assumed that Sylvia's energies actually produced free self-expression from the children. The ideal of individual creativity that was at the heart of her educational philosophy (Sylvia "inspired" rather than "taught") was often compromised in practice. Visitors to her classrooms noted that the pupils danced expressively *in certain ways*, they sang *certain sorts* of music, dressed in *uniforms*—and of course, produced vocabulary words from a *certain base* (exciting and transgressive personal moments). All of these activities were developed and closely managed by Sylvia: the creativity, in other words, was often hers (Hood 1988).

Despite her early view of herself as merely a loving facilitator unlocking the creativity in children, Sylvia dominated her classrooms. As she candidly and insightfully reported, "To do what I wanted them to do they had need to be like me. More than that. They had to be part of me" (*Teacher*, 171). Sylvia characterized her desires for her pupils to "be part of me" as a lover's seduction. Read more closely, Sylvia's unity with her pupils, as they expressed her will and her knowledge and talent, is not so much like two lovers in an embrace. It is more often like a patriarchal marriage, with Sylvia the wise, loving husband in absolute control. The paradoxical fact that the teacher's authority is at the heart of the generation of children's native imagery for the key vocabulary became explicit in Sylvia's account of teaching in Colorado. There she was unable to seduce the articulate and smart North American children: their passions were rooted in a soil that Sylvia could not understand. They would not be passionate lovers or obliging, productive wives for Sylvia. Her firm, even hectoring, authority was required to get them to read and to "behave."

Feminists have been active in attacking traditional models of pedagogy centered around the dominating, all-knowing (male) professor (Culley and Portuges 1985). Not only is pedagogical domination now unfashionable and unacceptable, but it has become unprofessional for the excessive personality of the teacher to be expressed in classrooms, as Sylvia's clearly was. Once, the eccentric professor may have been intriguing, irritating, rousing, controlling; now teachers must behave within strict ethical and behavioral limits or risk losing their jobs. In popular understandings of schooling and education, teachers must be motivated (but not overexcited), interesting (but not obsessive), disciplinary (but not overbearing), inspiring (but not seductive), and satisfied (but not pleasured) (see McWilliam 1999). These limitations are based in social demands for children's protection from despots, abusers, sadists, fanatics, laissez-faire practitioners, and all manner of individual styles that once were allowed freer (and sometimes inspirational) expression in classrooms.

Considering the complex passions Sylvia bought to her teaching—the kaleidoscope of brilliance, violence, love, control, creativity, excitement, success, and failure—it is clear that separating out what was "good" and "bad" in her teaching is not easy, or even possible. McWilliam and Jones (1996) point out that moves to separate the good/ethical bits from the bad/unethical bits in teacher practice need to be sensitive to what students stand to lose as well as gain, if eros, physicality, and abuse are conflated as all of a pedagogical piece. When we ban domination, we may also ban certain sorts of learning; when we tone down eroticized teaching, we may also suppress certain forms of inspiration.

While she has largely faded from view in the halls of academia in New Zealand, as the new owner of Sylvia's Selah said of her ghost, "She's still around." In the foyer of the teachers' college library that bears her name is a large photograph of Sylvia, captioned with her own native imagery: "What a dangerous activity reading is; teaching is." These words likely mystify most teacher-trainees trudging past to find books on classroom management, reading assessment, educational policy, and child safety. Perhaps one or two reflect on the myriad dangers of reading and teaching—the dangers of surveillance, of inspiration, of domination, of dreaming.

Notes

[1] As with other colonized countries, New Zealand's official record of its past (such as that taught in schools) is characterized by a "forgetting" about the history of the indigenous peoples and their relationship with the colonizers, especially as told from the perspective of the indigenous peoples.

[2] According to Hood's (1988, 81 and 180) carefully researched account, the "victim" stories Sylvia told about herself were not borne out by the historical facts—her grades were not consistently poor, her books were not deliberately burned, New Zealand education officials did not reject her ideas. She certainly had her critics in New Zealand, but "the whole place" was not against her, despite her assertions to the contrary.

[3] "Selah" was the name given by Sylvia to her private space in or near her various homes, where she withdrew to write, paint and think. See chapter six in this volume by Nancy Thompson and Judith James.

[4] The version of *Teacher* referred to in this chapter is that published by Penguin Books in Great Britain in 1966. *Teacher* was originally published by Secker and Warburg in 1963.

5 "Pakeha" means "white settler" in New Zealand. Originally a Maori term, it is a word that many white New Zealanders use to describe ourselves (as did Sylvia).

6 The official policy of the Native Schools system was to assimilate Maori into Pakeha culture (a form of British culture), including the English language (Simon and Tuhiwai Smith 2001).

References

Appel, S., ed. 1996. *Positioning subjects: Psychoanalysis and critical educational studies.* Westport, CT: Bergin and Garvey.

Ashton-Warner, S. 1960. *Spinster.* London: Secker and Warburg.

———. 1963. *Teacher.* Repr. Harmondsworth, England: Penguin, 1966.

———. 1972. *Spearpoint: "Teacher" in America.* New York: Knopf.

———. 1979. *I passed this way.* New York: Knopf.

Britzman, D. 1998. *Lost subjects, contested objects.* Albany, NY: State University of New York.

Culley, M., and C. Portuges, eds. 1985. *Gendered subjects: The dynamics of feminist teaching.* New York: Routledge.

Freire, P. 1972. *Pedagogy of the oppressed,* translated by Myra Bergman Ramos. Harmondsworth, England: Penguin.

———. 1976. *Education, the practice of freedom.* London: Writers and Readers Co-operative.

Furedi, F. 2002a. *Culture of fear: Risk-taking and the morality of low expectation.* Rev. ed. London: Continuum.

———. 2002b. *Paranoid parenting: Why ignoring the experts may be best for your child.* Chicago: Chicago Review Press.

Gallop, J. 1992. Knot a love story. *Yale Journal of Criticism* 5, no. 3: 209–18.

———, ed. 1995. *Pedagogy: A question of impersonation.* Bloomington: Indiana University Press.

———. 1997. *Feminist accused of sexual harassment.* Durham, NC: Duke University Press.

Hood, L. 1988. *Sylvia! A biography of Sylvia Ashton-Warner.* Auckland, New Zealand: Viking.

———. 1990. *Who is Sylvia? A diary of a biography.* Dunedin, New Zealand: John McIndoe.

hooks, b. 1994. *Teaching to transgress: Education as the practice of freedom.* New York: Routledge.

Jagodzinski, J., ed. 2002. *Pedagogical desire: Authority, seduction, transference and the question of ethics.* Westport, CT: Bergin and Garvey.

Jones, A. 1991. *"At school I've got a chance." Culture/privilege: Pacific Islands and Pakeha girls at school.* Palmerston North, New Zealand: Dunmore Press.

———, ed. 2001. *Touchy subject: Teachers touching children.* Dunedin, New Zealand: University of Otago Press.

———. 2003. Touching children: Policy, social anxiety and the "safe" teacher. Special issue: Childhood and cultural studies. *Journal of Curriculum Theorizing* 19, no. 2: 103–16.

———. 2004. Risk anxiety, policy and the spectre of sexual abuse in early childhood education. *Discourse* 25, no. 3: 321–34.

Levine, J. 2002. *Harmful to minors: The perils of protecting children from sex.* Minneapolis: University of Minnesota Press.

McWilliam, E. 1999. *Pedagogical pleasures.* New York: Peter Lang.

McWilliam, E., and A. Jones. 1996. Eros and pedagogical bodies: The state of (non)affairs. In *Pedagogy, technology and the body*, ed. E. McWilliam and P. Taylor, 127–36. New York: Peter Lang.

Middleton, S., and H. May. 1997. *Teachers talk teaching 1915–1995.* Palmerston North, New Zealand: Dunmore Press.

Scott, S., S. Jackson and K. Backett-Milburn. 2001. Swings and roundabouts: Risk anxiety and the everyday worlds of children. In A. Jones, *Touchy subject*, 15–26.

Simon, J., and L. Tuhiwai Smith, eds. 2001. *A civilising mission? Perceptions and representations of the New Zealand native schools system.* Auckland, New Zealand: Auckland University Press.

Tobin, J., ed. 1997. *Making a place for pleasure in early childhood education.* New Haven, CT: Yale University Press.

———. 2001. The missing discourse of sexuality in contemporary American early childhood education. In *The annual of psychoanalysis, vol. 23: Sigmund Freud and his impact on the modern world*, ed. J. Winner and J. Anderson, 179–200. Hillsdale, NJ: Analytic Press.

Walkerdine, V. 1981. Sex, power and pedagogy. *Screen Education* 38: 14–23.

CHAPTER THREE

"I My Own Professor": Ashton-Warner as New Zealand Educational Theorist, 1940–60

Sue Middleton

The invitation to contribute to this volume addressed me as a New Zealander who had written about how Sylvia Ashton-Warner's fantasies, theories, imagery, and life-history narratives threaded their way through my own. I had written of my youthful encounters with her work in *Educating Feminists* (Middleton 1993), in which I looked back on reading *Spinster* in 1960 at age thirteen and reflected on my teenage dreams of life as an artist and beatnik in Parisian cafés and garrets: confined to an Edwardian boarding school hostel in a provincial New Zealand town, I had plotted my escape to what Ashton-Warner described in *Myself* as "some bohemian studio on the Left Bank in Paris or over a bowl of wine in Italy, me all sophisticated and that, with dozens of lovers, paint everywhere and love and communion and sympathy and all that" (*Myself*, 212). When, in the early 1970s, I began secondary school teaching and read *Teacher*, that book built bridges between the frightening urgency of classroom survival, the enticing theories but alien classrooms described by American deschoolers and free-schoolers, and "what I believed myself to be when a girl on the long long road to school, a vagabond and an artist" (*I Passed This Way*, 307). As a young teacher I, too, had poured my impassioned soul into writing journals and poetry, painting, and playing the piano. Like Ashton-Warner, I had hoped that artistic self-expression could keep the mad woman in my attic at bay, for "asylums are full of artists who failed to say the things they must and famous tombs are full of those who did" (*Incense to Idols*, 169).

I had read Ashton-Warner's other books in the 1980s while juggling the conflicting demands of motherhood, doctoral research, marriage, university teaching, and artistic dreams. Four decades before me also in her thirties at the time, Ashton-Warner's conflicts had been similar.[1] In *Myself*, she wrote, "This programme I have set myself, or rather that has set itself upon me like an invisible aggressor, this pace at which I live: wife, mother, lover, teacher and what I call my 'work'" (81). Despite her frequently expressed hatred for teaching, Ashton-Warner created a beguiling image of it as a romantic adventure that could, albeit with difficulty, be accommodated in such a multifaceted life: "Not just part of us becomes a teacher. It engages the whole self—the woman, man, wife or husband, mother or father, the lover, the scholar or artist in you as well as the teacher earning money so that a worthwhile teacher is one of the blooms from the worthwhile person" (*Myself*, 10). Although Ashton-Warner would never have used the term "feminist" to describe herself or her writing (Pearson 1984), in effect she provided me with the subliminal beginnings of such an analysis. The style of educational research and writing I crafted in my 1980s doctoral thesis—analysis of life-history interviews and policy texts—was influenced by her mode of writing (Middleton 1985). Then as now, I explored how educational theories do not spring from other people's books or disembodied ideas but rather are rooted in all dimensions of our experience.

My earlier readings of Ashton-Warner's work laid down the strata that underpin my twenty-first-century re-reading of it for this chapter. But I am no longer the wistful teenager, the frustrated high school teacher, or the conflicted mother-wife-teacher-artist and novice writer. Now a fifty-five-year-old professor and grandmother, I find my earlier readings quaint and not very interesting relics of a remote past. The vicissitudes of romance and the conflicts of the working mother are no longer my personal concerns, and they no longer absorb me as a researcher/writer. Re-reading Ashton-Warner now, I feel exasperated by her compulsive infatuations and flirtations when young (*Myself*) and her addictions and cantankerousness when old (*I Passed This Way*; Endeavour Television). As I have aged, my own research has become less directly concerned with questions of embodied femininity, and my writing is increasingly theoretical and conceptual. My initial impulse here was to engage in a postcolonial critique of her work. But Ashton-Warner disliked the language of late-twentieth-century educational writing and feared her work falling "into the jaws of academic analysis in the unintelligible multisyllabic jargon by which so much living [in North America] is programmed to die from verbose manhandling" (*I Passed This Way*, 471). In accordance with her wishes, I shall resist the temptation to express my ideas in the lofty tones of poststructuralism or postcolonialism, although these lurk in the background of the following analysis. If my revisioning of Ashton-Warner's youthful work is post-anything, it is postmenopausal.

When the invitation to contribute to this volume arrived, I had just completed a study of the PhD in education in New Zealand (Middleton 2001). I did not expect that project and this one to coalesce. But the projects suddenly came together when I found the following passage in *I Passed This Way*, in which Ashton-Warner described her book *Teacher*:

> [It was] a thesis though I was the last to know it. I had, after all, studied a great deal since Horoera [her first school]: Rousseau, Herbert Read, comparative religions, the Bible, Gerald Manley Hopkins, Blake and Coleridge; the English poets, French literature, history and poetry; Russell, Freud, Jung, Adler, and Fromm: Maori mythology, history, culture and the language; the lives of the musicians, music textbooks, and even ploughed through Havelock Ellis, believe it or not. (*I Passed This Way*, 354)

She continued, "My level of learning, experiment and engagement as I see it now, but did not then, probably could not have been too far below a doctorate, with *Teacher* my inadvertent thesis, though it hadn't crossed my mind" (*I Passed This Way*, 354).

When she wrote that, Ashton-Warner had recently returned from a period as a visiting professor at Canada's Simon Fraser University. This was her first, and only, sustained formal experience in a university. She did not hold a university degree. She had trained as a primary school teacher in New Zealand in the 1920s; a period as a pupil teacher in the Hutt Valley (Wellington) had been followed by two years at Auckland Teachers' Training College and a period of probationary teaching. Ashton-Warner said that in formulating her educational theory (her published teaching scheme), she had read "*everything but education*" (*I Passed This Way*, 354, italics added). I was intrigued by her retrospective positioning of *Teacher* as a quasi-doctoral thesis, presumably in education. What would it mean to study Ashton-Warner as an academic writer of her time and place—a *New Zealand* writer of educational theory?

Educational theory is multiply located. It is a body of academic knowledge—a formal "subject" taught and examined in universities. It may also be an object of political contestation, such as in policy-making. Educational theory both emerges from, and gives shape to, teachers' professional knowledge: the sets of rules, maxims, guidelines and hunches that guide everyday practice. Researching the nature and history of educational theory brings into focus what Foucault (1980) referred to as "the union of erudite knowledge and local memories" (83). He asked, "[H]ow are the human sciences possible, and what are the historical consequences of their existence?" (in Gordon 1980, 236). What has made education as a "human science" possible, and what have been the historical consequences of *its* existence? What is the nature of, and what have been the conditions of possibility for education as a field of academic inquiry and professional understanding in New Zealand? What was the nature of Sylvia Ashton-Warner's educational theory, and what was involved in its creation during the years she lived and worked in New Zealand? To what extent did it struggle against, or flow with, the tides and currents of educational thinking and practice of her time (the 1940s to late 1950s) and place (New Zealand)?

My discussion falls into four sections. "I'm Not a New Zealander!" discusses the common belief that Sylvia Ashton-Warner's educational theory was "in confrontation … with the time and place in which she lived" (Clemens 1996, 90). "I Am My Own University" places Ashton-Warner's theory in the context of education as an academic subject. In "The Essentially Liberal Spirit," I study the curriculum documents and other professional knowledge available to teachers in New Zealand at the time. In "That Phantom of the Profession," I examine Ashton-Warner's perceptions of, and encounters with, educational authorities. My conclusion draws the threads together by means of a discussion of the transitional readers.

"I'm Not a New Zealander!": Myths and Counternarratives

Sylvia Ashton-Warner often claimed that her works were produced despite New Zealand, where "everything is respectably factory cut" (*Incense to Idols*, 164). Michael Firth's movie *Sylvia* (Reynolds and Firth 1984), as did Sylvia herself, painted a picture of an heroic, isolated, and maligned battler for progressive education in a colonial educational system that stubbornly resisted all progressive influences. At her most vitriolic, when interviewed in 1977 by Jack Shallcrass for a program produced by Endeavour Television, Sylvia went so far as to claim persecution and "spiritual murder" by New Zealand's literary and educational establishments. In that interview, she cried, "I'm not a New Zealander! I'm a landed immigrant of Canada!"

Yet New Zealand writing and teaching folklore include many alternative accounts. Sylvia's brilliance at what today is termed "spin-doctoring" prompted her authorized biographer, Lynley Hood (1990), to describe her as "a wonderful, profound, charismatic, two-faced con-artist" (282). Neglected and persecuted by the literary establishment? *Spinster*, which took the nation by surprise, was much acclaimed in New Zealand literary circles and popular media (Stevens 1961). Ashton-Warner won several of New Zealand's prestigious literary awards yet usually refused interviews or to meet her New Zealand public. Saintly teacher persecuted for unorthodox methods? Former colleagues and students have described her as frequently absent from school, increasingly dependent on alcohol and prescription drugs, dependent on teaching assistants and others to cover for her, and frequently losing her temper and even hitting children (Hood 1988). Addictions, cantankerousness, paranoia, and professional unreliability do not, however, undermine her importance as a writer of educational theory.

It is not my intention to investigate or evaluate the "truth" of the various Sylvia myths. Lynley Hood has already done so in her biography (1988) and research diary (1990) (see Brookes, this volume, for an examination of Hood's work). But myths themselves have truth *effects*—they provoke and continue to provoke. My own analysis here has been provoked by the fact that, despite evidence to the contrary, the myth of Sylvia as persecuted martyr persists, and she continues to be portrayed internationally (especially in the United States) as a lone light shining in New Zealand's educational darkness. A notable example of this is the 1996 American book, *Pay Attention to the Children*, by Sydney Gurewitz Clemens, a Californian teacher and founder of America's Sylvia Ashton-Warner Society. Describing Ashton-Warner's New Zealand background as an unfortunate impediment, Clemens struggles to understand how such brilliance could have emerged from such a colonial backwater: "Sylvia felt all of the pressures we [American women] felt, and had the additional burden of living in an outpost of the British Empire, expected to do one's duty and conceal one's emotions. Astonishingly, it was in conventional, dutiful New Zealand that Sylvia Ashton-Warner began a lifelong habit of listening to her inner voice, embarking on the journey toward abundant life in 1940!" (1996, 23). Determined to reinforce the myth of Sylvia as persecuted heroine, Clemens dismisses Hood's meticulously researched biography: "Lynley Hood reads Sylvia in a journalist's terms. By contrast, I am trying in this book to examine the texture of Sylvia's life for clues to how we can be sure Sylvia attempted to say the things she must—to tell her stories—but *what was their relationship to facts? Did she report accurately? Should we care?*" (Clemens 1996, 90, italics added)

By "we," Clemens is presumably referring to American teachers. For Clemens, the "texture" of Ashton-Warner's life matters more than its historical, biographical, or cultural "facts." I have never been an apologist for the New Zealand—or any other—education system. But this statement by Clemens rallied me to its defense, provoking me to argue that "our" (i.e., New Zealand's) Sylvia Ashton-Warner—as a person, as a teacher, as a novelist and as a writer of theory—could not have emerged from any other place. In Grumet's (1988) words, an educational theory "grows where it is planted, soaking up the nutrients in the local soil, turning to the local light" (14). Sylvia Ashton-Warner—as a person, a teacher, and a writer—*did* "grow" in New Zealand. Clemens's cavalier dismissal of New Zealand and its schools of the time led me to the archives at the University of Waikato: the New Zealand Collection, where I pored over curriculum and other education policy documents, and the Education Library, which contained New Zealand teachers' magazines of the 1930s–1950s. I realized that while biographers and literary critics had explored Ashton-Warner's "inner" conflicts as woman, wife, teacher, mother, and writer, they had done little analysis of the "external" conditions of possibility—historical, political, cultural, discursive—that enabled and constrained her *educational* thinking and writing in the 1940s and 1950s. What was it about New Zealand in general, and its schools in particular, that made Ashton-Warner's early educational works possible?

"I am my Own University": Writing and Publishing Theory

In 1963, *Teacher* was reviewed for the New Zealand Department of Education's *Education* magazine, a monthly publication issued free to schools (Ausubel 1963). In a tiny country with a population of less than three million, there were at that time few publishing venues for high-level intellectual engagements with educational issues. There was no academic education journal; the *New Zealand Journal of Educational Studies* would not be established until 1966. Until then, demand for such a journal would have been low since the nation's four university education departments employed a combined total of seventeen academic faculty in 1950 and twenty-two in 1960 (Middleton 1989). By 1963, only three PhDs in education had been awarded by New Zealand universities. Educational research was still in its infancy, centered on the New Zealand Council for Educational Research (NZCER), a progressive organization established in 1934 with a grant from the Carnegie Foundation. Educational research and researchers had not yet splintered into disciplines and paradigms. Masters theses and other publications often addressed broad philosophical, historical, or organizational questions and increasingly engaged with the ideas of the new developmental psychologies. In New Zealand education in 1963, hard-edged empiricism was beginning to rise but had not yet gained ascendancy (Middleton 2001).

The review of *Teacher* that appeared in *Education* magazine, however, was written from such a perspective (Ausubel 1963). The reviewer was not a New Zealander but a visiting American, Professor David Ausubel of the University of Illinois. Ausubel had a medical degree and a PhD in psychology. The titles of his books, such as *Ego Development and the Personality Disorders* (1952), give some indication of his medical-scientific orientation. In 1956–1957, Ausubel resided in New Zealand as a visiting Fulbright Fellow, and he wrote a book, *The Fern and the Tiki* (1960), about his largely negative impressions of the country and its inhabitants. Ausubel's review of *Teacher* was scathing. He described it as little more than a "patchwork of scattered impressions, fragmented vignettes, and miscellaneous comments about teaching and Maoris that provides neither a cogent account of her educational philosophy nor an illuminating picture of the contemporary Maori cultural scene" (Ausubel 1963, 30). He scorned Ashton-Warner for her lack of credentials and for her notoriously volatile personality: "True, one could hardly have expected an academically sophisticated pedagogic treatise from a person of Miss Ashton-Warner's background and temperament" (Ausubel 1963, 30). Grounded in the empiricism of medical science, Ausubel asked:

> [W]ould it have been expecting too much to find a carefully reasoned and systematic exposition of principles, a clear statement of underlying rationale, and a more detailed description of the method, and some attempts at critical evaluation or comparison with other methods? Recast along these latter lines, the resulting document might have been less artistic, but would have constituted a more useful contribution to the literature of education rather than an exercise in impressionistic autobiography. (1963, 30)

But Ashton-Warner identified and wrote not as a scientist but as an artist. Her "experiments" were not formally structured, and her language was poetic. Music, dance, and the visual arts, as well as the printed texts of poets and philosophers, influenced her reading of children's feelings, thoughts, and bodies.

Ausubel's review was emblematic of a mid-twentieth-century splitting of genres in academic educational writing throughout the English-speaking world. In his introduction to *Teacher*, British educationist Sir Herbert Read wrote that "her reports are factual, and this new book is a sociological document rather than a pedagogical treatise" (in *Teacher*, 13). Parts of *Teacher* consisted of diary entries: descriptions of, and thoughts and feelings about, the classroom, community, and children. Descriptive sociological studies had been acceptable in New Zealand educational writing in the 1930s–1940s. For example, Somerset's (1938) *Littledene* was a participant's account of everyday life (including education) in a small New Zealand rural town. But the ascendancy of scientific empiricism in the social sciences and associated struggles to gain status for education as a "proper" academic subject rendered such descriptive accounts unscientific and therefore academically illegitimate. As New Zealand's university education departments grew in size and number, the educational research community began to fragment into "increasingly separate worlds with their own professional identities, journals, conferences and vocabularies" (Watson 1978, 12). There was no room for "impressionistic autobiography," poetry, or fictional writing in the newly specialized fields of educational psychology, philosophy, history, sociology, and administration. In academic writing, the languages of art and science became incommensurable. Autobiographical writing was not allowed in theses until feminist research gained recognition in the 1980s.

In *Sylvia!* Hood (1988) notes that Ashton-Warner did not approach the NZCER as a possible (academic) publisher for the manuscript of her teaching scheme. Instead, she first published it in one of the New Zealand teachers' professional journals. Two years before her first book, *Spinster*, was published in

1958, Ashton-Warner published a series of eight articles in *National Education*, the journal of the New Zealand Educational Institute (NZEI), the primary school teachers' union/professional association. These were published under the name "Sylvia" (1955, 1956a, 1956b, 1956c, 1956d, 1956e, 1956f, 1956g). Like most primary school teachers, Sylvia and her husband Keith were members of the NZEI, and in a rare acknowledgment of the intellectual life of other teachers, she later alluded to the stimulation of social evenings after NZEI meetings in Ruatoria: "Cascades of music in some poky little residence to the domed silence of night. Philosophy in and out of the hours, metaphysics on the beach and sensational tales of inspectors" (*I Passed This Way*, 323). Barring one brief section on the Maori transitional readers, the significance of which I shall explore later, the manuscript that would (in a slightly edited form) be published in 1963 in the United States as the first half of *Teacher* (the teaching scheme) was serialized in *National Education* in 1955–1956. These articles were the first systematic exposition of her theory.

As a published educational theorist, Sylvia Ashton-Warner also left us with a remarkable record of the biographical or experiential affinities or underpinnings of her theory—what Britzman (1998) refers to as the processes by which educators "come to attach ourselves as well as to ignore particular ideas, theories and people" (16). For example, Ashton-Warner's book *Myself* was published in 1967. An edited version of the diary she had kept a quarter of a century previously in 1941–42, during World War II, this account of "the care of the self" (Foucault 1985, 1986) records her struggle to claim physical and mental space—away from her family and school—to dream, create, or obsess over her latest romantic obsession (she "ceased to exist when not in love" [*Myself*, 9]). She wrote:

> I mean to recover and keep the things I did while single; I mean some time to be what I had meant to be—in the first place a worthwhile person, not just for myself but for those who love me. I mean to so organise my loaded time that I'll retain some for myself to paint, do music, read and even learn to write. I'm not one of those people who were born for nothing. (*Myself*, 20)

In *Myself*, "It isn't art that matters so much as the life of art, the process" (Stead 2002, 102). Learning to write involved struggles between the warring facets of her life and personality, between "wife, mother, lover, teacher and what I call my 'work'" (*Myself*, 81). As Foucault (1985) described it, the crafting of the scholarly self involved "processes and events that took place between oneself and oneself. The adversaries the individual had to combat were not just within him or close by, they were part of him" (66).

The "adversaries" Ashton-Warner had to "combat" included children and teaching. Often these appear in her text as an obstruction to art. They "intrude on my inner thoughts, hack at my inner feeling," she writes (*Myself*, 100); later she describes teaching as "sending down stiff taproots into my heart" (150). Ashton-Warner began to connect what she read in her hard-won private space ("everything but education") with the vibrancy of her "intrusive" pupils and classroom. She could reconcile the artist and the teacher (as she much later, in 1977, admitted on Endeavour Television) by conceptualizing the children as the raw material for her art and the classroom as a kind of living canvas. Sometimes she also represents her "work" as academic: "tentatively, reluctantly, I'm becoming interested in no less than my infant room. From the reading I do in the early hours before the household wakes, how could I not become interested? Freud, Adler, Lipmann, Scheiner [sic],[2] Jung and Bertrand Russell explaining life and children, and all the poetry at night. I am my own University, I my own Professor" (*Myself*, 42).

During the early years of World War II, when she wrote the diary that would become the *Myself*, Ashton-Warner was in her second stable teaching job, as the assistant teacher at Pipiriki School up the Whanganui River. As was common practice in the Native School system of the time her husband, Keith Henderson, was headmaster (Simon 1998). She was recovering from the nervous breakdown she had experienced at their previous school in the roadless East Coast settlement of Horoera. As part of her treatment, her Wellington "neurologist,"[3] Dr. Allen, had urged her to write. He taught Sylvia that her own lack of concentration when reading resulted from a mind "too packed with native imagery to allow room for anything else in" (*I Passed This Way*, 283). Through self-expression—writing, music and the visual arts—she could "discipline dreaming" (*I Passed This Way*, 288).

In *I Passed This Way*, Ashton-Warner described how Dr. Allen had shown her "the nature of the mind as he put the pieces together again in their normal places" (281). It was, she said, her therapy with Dr. Allen that had taught her about the two major drives that lurked in the unconscious, "these two great powers in the personality which qualify all living: fear and sex" (*I Passed This Way*, 281). These "two great powers in the personality" became the core of her theory of organic teaching, as she learned to elicit from infants the key words that captioned them: "Out press these words, grouping themselves in their own wild order. All boys wanting words of locomotion, aeroplane, tractor, jet, and the girls the words of domesticity, house, Mummy, doll. The fear words, ghost, tiger, skellington, alligator, bulldog, wild piggy, police. The sex words, kiss, love, touch, haka" (Sylvia 1955, 392).

Her therapy taught Ashton-Warner that, by releasing her own native imagery, she could discharge the "violence that was in my character ever lapping and threatening near the surface, showing up in my nightmares" (*Teacher*, 9). Her own violence, she came to believe, was symptomatic of a universal law:

"Violence. The word beginning with a capital V widespread across the world. The violence I believe to be in all of us is subdued in the undermind, waiting, but which blasts out on occasion depending on how near the surface it is, or on the rigidity of the surface" (*Teacher*, 32). She formulated this idea during wartime and later wrote, "[T]he design of my work is that creativity in this time of life when character can be influenced forever is the solution to the problem of war. To me it has the validity of a law of physics and all the unstable, irrepressible emotion of beauty" (Sylvia 1956c, 295).

In essence, Ashton-Warner's pedagogy involved "taking the lid off" repressed emotions, giving vent to the destructive impulse through the alternative "crater" of creativity. In New Zealand, she taught in rural and at that time reasonably stable Maori communities. In *Myself*, however, Ashton-Warner muses about the teaching of the urban poor and, since the kind of scenario she is describing was not characteristic of New Zealand in the 1950s, one assumes she was referring to second-hand accounts of the United States:

> I suppose that schools in the big city slums ... If I were teaching there I ... And if I were allowed to I ... I mean children from criminal homes, starved and that. Throats cut in the night and that sort of thing, hungry, stealing ... I'd give them words like "knife" and "cutthroat" and ... "jail" and "police" and "blood". I'd give them words they lived with. (*Myself*, 110)

One wonders what might result in today's classrooms if "ordinary" teachers without training in psychotherapy attempted in this vein to "take the lid off" infantile traumas resulting from events such as terrorism, sexual abuse, or domestic violence (see Jones, this volume). In addressing her students' repressed emotions through her approach to key vocabulary, Ashton-Warner's pedagogy mimicked—was a reliving of—her own therapeutic process. Here it is useful to think in terms of the psychoanalytic notion of transference. Britzman (1998) writes:

> Transference is perhaps the most central dynamic of time and space that organises and stalls the practices of learning. The compromised and condensed time of transference catches the "then and there" of the past and the "here and now" of the present. As a mode of address, the message is derivative of something else, reminiscent of another scene but uncanny in its present urgency. (33)

During World War II, the time Ashton-Warner was formulating her ideas, official New Zealand government policy acknowledged the traumas of children and their families (Middleton 1998; Middleton and May 1997). "Taking the lid off" these, however, was regarded as a matter of professional judgment, and teachers were cautioned that their role was to "act as a buffer between the world of the child and the warring world of the adult, to pass on to the child only such of the jarrings and the jostlings of the adult world as he feels the childish mind can cope with at this stage. It is for the skilled teacher to say what burden of knowledge the child at each age can and should bear" (Beeby 1992, 129).

American teacher Sydney Gurewitz Clemens (1996) has argued that Sylvia Ashton-Warner developed her theories "not only in the fact of her own emotional undercurrents, but in confrontation, as well, with the time and place in which she lived" (90). I have briefly looked at her "emotional undercurrents," but they are not my central concern here (see Robertson, this volume, for further discussion). I am more concerned with contextual questions about "the time and place in which she lived." What were the tides and currents of educational thinking in the teaching profession at the time (1940s and 1950s) and place (rural New Zealand) in which Ashton-Warner lived, taught, formulated her ideas, and wrote her first educational texts? Were her ideas "in confrontation with" those of New Zealand's education academics, policymakers, and practitioners? To explore this, I now introduce some key New Zealand curriculum and other educational policy documents of the 1930s–1940s.

"The Essentially Liberal Spirit": Curriculum Policy

With few opportunities for high-level study or employment in education at universities, much of New Zealand's higher-level scholarship and theorizing tended to be "out there" in the wider education profession. Some leading educational thinkers and writers could be found among the ranks of school inspectors, education department officials, teachers' college lecturers, and classroom teachers. Therefore, some of the country's best educational thinking and writing surfaced in official curriculum or other policy documents. In 1928, the year Ashton-Warner entered the Auckland Teachers' Training College, advance copies of a revised primary school syllabus were distributed to all teachers, and the following year the New Zealand Department of Education gazetted its new *Syllabus of Instruction for Public Schools* (1929). This was popularly known, and still is referred to by historians, as the "Red Book." Written by a committee, this 223-page book, hardbound in red covers, included 63 pages of "syllabus," a 12-page bibliography, and 148 pages of appendixes written by inspectors.

I do not know if Sylvia Ashton-Warner ever read the Red Book, but it was the official curriculum until rolling revisions of the various school subjects from the mid-1940s to the 1950s replaced it bit by bit. These revisions retained what Ewing (1970) described as its "essentially liberal spirit" (209). Sylvia Ashton-Warner and Keith Henderson would have been obliged to comply with the syllabus, and the inspectors would have checked that their plans of work reflected its intent, if not its detailed content.

The Red Book and the postwar revisions that succeeded it were influenced by the core assumptions of the progressive educational movement of the 1920s–1930s (often referred to as "the new education"). The new education wove together psychoanalytic and psychological notions about the "normal" developmental stages of children with more "sociological" theories about the school's role in fostering democracy. The Red Book's twelve-page bibliography recommended many of the progressive texts of the time, including *The Dalton Plan*, five works by Dewey, a number of texts about Montessori methods, and Caldwell Cook's *The Play Way in Education*. (Ashton-Warner would later refer to Caldwell Cook in *Teacher*.) It also listed works by international authorities on "mental testing" such as Terman, Burt, and Thorndike. The technology of "scientific" testing was viewed as an adjunct to good "developmental" pedagogical practice (Walkerdine 1984).

The Red Book curriculum encouraged teachers to create their own curriculum and to tailor it to the "needs" of their pupils on the basis of their knowledge and understanding of the individual children and the wider school community. It was intended to provide guidelines rather than serve as a prescription:

> The Department particularly desires that the present syllabus shall be regarded both by Inspectors and teachers as mainly suggestive. Teachers are to consider themselves free to make any alteration or rearrangement of work they think desirable, and the Inspector will approve any reasonable scheme that appears to meet the needs of children of a particular type or of a particular locality. (New Zealand Department of Education 1929, 5)

Although the Red Book contained prescriptions for each subject, this "classification and framing" (Bernstein 1971) of school knowledge was not mandatory, and curriculum integration was encouraged:

> The teacher may with the approval of the Inspector base his instruction mainly on one subject. It is recognised also that the pupil as well as his teacher has a right to a certain measure of freedom, and that the most carefully planned schemes of work may not satisfy the pupil's desire to pursue a course of study that appeals to him. The Inspector will recognise that it is not always possible for a teacher to adhere closely to his daily plan of work. (New Zealand Department of Education 1929, 5)

Sylvia Ashton-Warner taught infants (the preparatory division). In light of Ashton-Warner's later claims about the "the rigid silence of the orthodox infant room" (1958, 199), it is useful to see how the "syllabus of instruction" for this level was conceptualized in the Red Book, which informed teachers, "No particular method of teaching reading is prescribed, but it is suggested that the reading material should consist at first of words as names of things or actions, then of simple sentences arising from the conversation lessons" (New Zealand Department of Education 1929, 9). Phonics might then be taught by means of "the interpretation at sight of words and sentences on the blackboard, on individual reading sheets, or in reading books" (9).

In the teaching of written expression, the Red Book noted:

[I]t is the custom to send the children to the wall-boards to illustrate stories, etc. Why should they not be asked to label the component parts of their drawings and write sentences about them? In both cases the children should be required to read to the teacher the sentences they have composed. Not only does the reading benefit the child but the teacher ascertains what is the actual vocabulary, and how far the command of language has grown. (New Zealand Department of Education 1929, 71)

The Red Book encouraged teachers to draw on a child's own vocabulary: "The labelling and matching of words associated with real objects and pictures illustrative of home and school interests and activities are always popular, and afford the necessary opportunities for recognising a large number of nouns" (New Zealand Department of Education 1929, 76). It argued that a child's interests should influence the topics and pace of lessons: "It is hoped that the new Syllabus will usher in a new conception of the oral lesson, and that the pupil and not the teacher will be the more active agent in the acquisition of knowledge" (70).

Other subjects were given a similar treatment. The Red Book's approach to the teaching of arithmetic in the preparatory division drew on progressive ideas about curriculum integration and learning through play:

In this class no formal instruction in number should be given. Pupils should, however, be afforded opportunity to develop some conception of number through stories and play activities in which there is free access to varied and suitable materials—e.g. blocks, beads, sticks, etc. To assist this development the teacher should take advantage of such opportunities as arise in rhythmic exercises, kindergarten games, nature-study, and other lessons. (New Zealand Department of Education 1929, 1)

Nature study aimed "To awaken and deepen the child's interest in nature, and to stimulate the curiosity which is characteristic of all children"; to achieve this, the New Zealand Department of Education noted,

It should be considered a fundamental principle that nothing should be regarded as Nature-Study in which the child is not observing by investigating Nature at first hand. From this it follows that work will be done mainly outside the classroom and it will be necessary in all cases for teachers to have a full knowledge of the possibilities of a district. School walks or rambles should be frequently arranged. (1929, 43)

While there was to be no formal instruction in history or geography until standard two (year four, or fourth grade in the American system) for infants, teachers were encouraged to explore and learn about their local area, for most parts of the country "are rich in historical incidents. And these both the teacher and the pupil should take a pride in seeking out and recording" (New Zealand Department of Education 1929, 31). Teachers were urged to become familiar with and to teach "tales of the Maori" in their classes. The purpose of school music was described as "to awaken the imagination of the children and widen their capacity for artistic self-expression" (57). Musical education in the preparatory division was to include "free bodily movement to music" as well as "listening without effort to music sung or played by teacher or gramophone" (9). The infant was also to engage in free drawing and handwork to help "express in concrete form his impressions of form, size, and beauty" and this would enable "him to realise not only the joy of using the creative power but also the satisfaction of doing something for others" (51).

The appendixes to the Red Book, written by inspectors, contain advice, examples, and rationales for the classroom practitioner. They are introduced with Carlyle's question, "How shall he give kindling in whose own inward man there is no live coal, but all is burnt out to a dead grammatical cinder?" and followed by a lament:

> There still survives in schools a great deal of the old-fashioned formalism that regarded education more as a mechanical process than as a means of securing for every child the fullest possible spiritual, mental and physical development. It is hoped that the present syllabus will give encouragement to those teachers—and fortunately there are many of them—who regard the child not as inanimate clay in the hands of the potter, or as an empty vessel sent them for filling, but as a soul, a personality, capable of being developed and trained for the wider service of humanity. (New Zealand Department of Education 1929, 65)

This was the "essentially liberal spirit" of the mandated syllabus of instruction at the time Sylvia Ashton-Warner completed her training. The text was liberal, but in practice, teachers' freedom was restricted by the requirements of a proficiency examination in standard six, the final year of primary schooling (year eight, or eighth grade in the American system). One of the first educational reforms of New Zealand's First Labor government (1935–1949) was to abolish this examination in 1936. Labor's agenda of educational reform was strongly influenced by the progressive educational theories of the day (Middleton and May 1997). In 1937 Labor supported the New Education Fellowship (NEF) Conference. Schools were closed for a week to allow teachers to travel to Auckland, Wellington, Christchurch, or Dunedin—the cities in which public sessions of the conference were held. Fourteen speakers from Britain, Europe, the United States, Canada, and South Africa included leading progressives such as Dr. Susan Isaacs from England and Dr. Harold Rugg from Columbia University, New York (Campbell 1938). The NEF public lectures had generated unprecedented interest among teachers and the general public and as Ewing (1970) notes, it "helped to revive the essentially liberal spirit of the Red Book, no longer subordinated to the demands of 'proficiency'" (194).

During the late 1930s and early 1940s, says Ewing (1970), most teachers "adapted themselves to the idea of giving less time to formal arithmetic, grammar, spelling and oral reading, and more to arts and crafts, music, nature study and physical education" (194). In an early issue of *Education* magazine, the progressive educator H. D. C. Somerset (1948) commented on the impact of the progressive and "scientific" theorists of the 1940s: "The best way for teachers to create a good school is by way of child study. The biggest change in education of late years does not lie in buildings or equipment but in the contribution to our professional knowledge through the work of such people as Dewey, Nunn, Burt, Susan Isaacs, Schonnell, Gates, Terman, Alexander, and Duncan" (171).

Others told of a gulf between policy and practice. In 1948, *Education* magazine included a symposium in which teachers wrote about their ideas on "modern education." A contribution from a junior teacher stated, "The new education, as yet, is still largely theoretical and exploratory" (Higgin 1948, 125). The explanation he offered was largely demographic: "Most of our inspectors, headmasters and older teachers developed their educational philosophies before the First World War. To them, the way out of the confusion is a return, in some form, to the stable formalism of the old order, with its emphasis on subject-matter rather than on the child" (Higgin 1948, 125).

Writing in the 1980s, Stuart Middleton (1982) commented, "The curriculum context with which Ashton-Warner worked, while having some claim to being liberal in intention was, in all probability as dull and, for Maori children especially, as disastrous as she puts it. Teachers in classrooms tend to be markedly more conservative than the curriculum they claim to serve" (29). However, more recent studies based on interviews with teachers who trained and taught at the time have supported the argument that the progressive ideas and practices as expressed in the Red Book and elsewhere were widely debated and that, while some resisted them, they were widely practiced in classrooms around the country (Middleton and May 1997).

So, although the grassroots culture in some schools was resistant to the new education, the dominant discourse of the wartime and postwar curriculum and other policy texts was in many ways consistent with Ashton-Warner's theory of organic teaching. Like her, they drew on psychoanalytic/ developmental theories of child development and also viewed schooling as a means of achieving a more just society. Ashton-Warner usually refused to acknowledge or engage with the works of other educationists. She insulated her program of self-study and her writing, locating herself within a literary/artistic, rather than an educational theory, genre. She claimed to draw on "[m]usic, art, philosophy, the mind and Maori mythology but nothing on teaching" (1980, 288). Sylvia's accounts of her encounters with the education profession—inspectors, academics, and publishers—were often tales of persecution. However, on other occasions, a submerged narrative of passionate attachment to educational authorities also surfaces in her texts, and to these I now turn.

"That Phantom of the Profession": Fear, Sex, and Authority

In *Teacher*, Ashton-Warner encapsulated her thesis as follows: "Education, fundamentally, is the increase of the percentage of the conscious in relation to the unconscious. It must be a developing idea. None of this is new, of course. It's the understood design of today's education" (207). Her statement is highly significant for two reasons. First, it encompasses the twin dimensions of mainstream progressive education: the psychoanalytic/psychological and the mastery of personally and socially relevant knowledge. Second, it acknowledges that *she knew* that her theory was consistent with this "design of today's education." Was she referring to overseas (British and American) education? Could she possibly have remained unaware that both dimensions of the international progressive movement—the psychoanalytic/ psychological and the sociological/political—were being *encouraged* at the highest levels of New Zealand education policymaking at the time?

To address this question, I need to return to my earlier discussion of the biographical underpinnings of Ashton-Warner's theory of organic teaching and the key vocabulary. Earlier I described how Ashton-Warner claimed that fear and sex, the two "great instincts," were the key to reading, psychotherapy, and education more broadly. In her infant room, they erupted to the surface by means of captions, the most powerful of which were "ghost" and "kiss," which represented "the two main instincts. Any child, brown or white, on the first day, remembers these two words from one look" (Sylvia 1956g, 11). She released her own pent-up native imagery through creative arts. Ashton-Warner claimed to have discovered a "law of physics," but her pedagogy can equally be seen as a projection of her own psychic conflict. Or as Britzman (1998) puts it, as a "teacher's own counter-transference of her or his childhood conflicts onto the screen of the student, the curriculum, and pedagogical strategies" (35). What were these "childhood conflicts"? How were these projected, or transferred, onto others? How were her encounters with authorities mediated by her own struggles with the twin drives of fear and sex?

In *I Passed This Way*, Ashton-Warner described how her mother had also been her primary school teacher. Caring for an invalid husband and nine children during the post–World War I Depression years, Mrs. Warner had struggled financially, professionally, and personally. As a child, Sylvia adored her invalid father and later described him as a fallen English aristocrat with literary leanings who told wonderful stories. As an adult, Sylvia always identified the artist in her as male. "Papa," however, also appears in Sylvia's writing (e.g., as Puppa in *Greenstone*) as a victim of his working-class wife's emotional and physical violence. As an adult, Ashton-Warner would always have difficulty relating well to other professional women (Pearson 1984). The family moved frequently, and the young Sylvia attended fourteen different primary schools in which she often also had to endure the "rigid orthodoxy" of her own mother's teaching methods.

As a child, Ashton-Warner learned that "inspector trouble" explained the family's financial instability and residential insecurity. The inspector was therefore to be feared, and this apparently external threat was inextricably blended with her childhood experiences of her mother's power. Ashton-Warner's mother had also suffered miscarriages and infant deaths. Sylvia herself had been named after one of the dead babies and felt, as she said in *I Passed This Way*, that she was named after, and sometimes felt like, a ghost. The "ghost" was therefore a key word not only in the "underminds" of the children she taught but also in Sylvia's own psyche. Years later, Anna, the protagonist of *Spinster*, would draw together Sylvia's childhood specter of the ghost with her adult terror of the inspector: "Just as in the minds of the Little Ones all goes down before the Ghost, so in my mind all goes down before this, this … shall we say … this Phantom of the Profession" (*Spinster*, 227).

As an adult, despite her therapy and her avenues for artistic expression, Ashton-Warner's childhood wounds continued to fester. In *Sylvia!* Hood (1988) argues, "As time passed she aired the old wounds under the more comfortable cover of fiction and found counterfeit relief in denying the old wounds in herself but discovering them in others. Such measures kept at bay the ever-present risk of emotional collapse, but the wounds never healed" (90). When manifested as the phantom of the profession, the inspector can be seen as a personification of Sylvia's fears. As Hood describes it, "this omnipotent being was not a real person but a monster from Sylvia's undermind; welded from the most fearsome qualities of Mama, God, and the inspectors of her childhood, he clung to her shoulders and tightened the grip of guilt around her throat whenever she defied him" (1988, 99). In Ashton-Warner's own writing, the "frightening inspector shade in the rafters, limiting and aborting all I do" (*Spinster*, 190) is occasionally acknowledged as a fantasy-figure, "a ghoul from the past that haunts, I think, all teachers of my generation, from those five-year-old days when we felt the tension of the teacher and the foreboding of the Inspector himself" (*Teacher*, 197).

As an object of fear, the inspector makes an early appearance in Sylvia's writing. In *Myself* she remembers Horoera School, where she had experienced her breakdown, as also a place that had afforded her freedom from inspectorial surveillance. In contrast, Pipiriki School could be reached by road: "Back on the coast I'd been getting somewhere, I think, far from the haunts of inspectors, out of range of the Education Department—out of reach of criticism. I even taught the Maori language there—O heresy! But here, with roads and bridges and no tidal rivers, an inspector could walk in any day" (*Myself*, 67). To use Foucault's (1977) metaphor, the nets of bureaucratic power could more easily enmesh her in their threads. The imagined threat of the inspector's panoptic gaze frightened her into teaching the way she thought "He" wanted her to: "One is obliged to return to orthodox methods" (*Myself*, 18). Similarly, in *Spinster*, her heroine, Anna Vorontosov, says: "In the safety of the world behind my eyes, where the inspector shade cannot see, I picture the infant room as one widening crater, loud with the sound of erupting creativity. Every subject somehow in the creative vent. What wonderful design of movement and mood!" (*Spinster*, 45); when confronted with an inspectorial visit, Anna exclaims, "[I]f only I had kept workbooks and made routine schemes and used orthodox timetables, and stood up and taught from the blackboard with a pointer, and insisted on silence like other teachers, then I should at least have the confidence of numbers" (227).

In her writing and in interviews (e.g., Endeavour Television), Ashton-Warner constructed a binary opposition between "the rigid silence of the orthodox infant room" (the New Zealand education system she taught in) and her own vibrant classroom: "this frightening, inspiring, beating of the child-heart in the raftered prefab" (*Spinster*, 199). As I've noted, this binary has been broadcast around the world in print (e.g., Clemens 1996) and on film. Hood (1988) argues that Michael Firth's film "shows her innovations taking place in a turn-of-the-century education system" (247). However, writes Hood, while this might have been inaccurate as historical "fact," the film "got it right" at the level of a psychological truth, since "the system Sylvia was really rebelling against was not the one she taught in but the one that was raked over by her harsh mother and a succession of rigid, petty and disapproving inspectors during her primary schooling in the early years of this century" (1988, 247).

Occasionally Sylvia herself glimpsed this insight. In *Myself*, she contrasts her mother's methods with those taught to her during her training. When young, she was taught "that strict traditional way: spare the rod and spoil the child and that"—but she goes on to say that "we didn't learn that at college. I've got to relearn what I was supposed to have learned" (*Myself*, 20). Learning to teach involved "beginning to extricate myself from the only conception of teaching I remembered since I resumed on the Coast—the manner in which I was taught myself" and "recollecting what I learned in college" (*Myself*, 42). Ashton-Warner claims to have taken little account of the academic side of teachers' college, although one essay she had written there on Rousseau had left a lasting impression:

> With astonishment I'd gathered that I agreed with the views of Rousseau.... He would take his pupil Emile roaming the countryside for his lessons in the way that we'd roamed when young: playing in the creeks, climbing the trees and examining the birds' eggs, carving steps in banks, exploring round corners, asking questions, answering them and talking about the creatures on our way. (*I Passed This Way*, 194)

When she had to repeat Education Two (now termed Education 200) after completing college and during her probationary teaching year—it was a compulsory course in order to become a qualified teacher—she had been "astounded to find education the most fascinating subject I had ever avoided. Now why hadn't I discovered this in college ... too busy chasing Keith Henderson I suppose. It concerned itself with my favourite interest, the minds of people" (*I Passed This Way*, 194).

So Ashton-Warner *had* encountered progressive educational theory by the time she started teaching. Progressive strands were threaded through the official school curriculum documents, many of them written by the inspectors. Inspectorial examination of teaching practice would result in a grading (a numerical score according to fixed criteria). As a process of monitoring, this exemplifies the disciplinary technology described by Foucault (1977) as "the examination that places individuals in a field of surveillance [and] also situates them in a network of writing; it engages them in a whole mass of documents that capture and fix them" (189). If inspectors were the surveilling eyes of the Department of Education, would they not be encouraged to read, evaluate and record teachers' work according to the current progressive rhetoric?

In *Myself*, an inspector's visit is described as an "enlivening breath from the outside world, the professional world, encouraging and giving us status to ourselves" (111). In an entry for May 1942, Ashton-Warner described how, after observing her classroom, one inspector commented that her teaching method was "what we go about trying to inspire other teachers to do" (*Myself*, 111). Here, as in many other passages, Ashton-Warner's own accounts of her encounters with education authorities are *positive*. For, just as with the key words that erupt as an infant's organic writing, the images of authorities (such as inspectors) in Ashton-Warner's own writing are generated from the *two* great drives or instincts, fear and sex. It is important then to explore how sex manifests itself in Ashton-Warner's educational writing, especially in relation to educational authorities.

Ashton-Warner seldom wrote directly about adult sexual intimacy, in the sense of bodily intimacy. However, as already noted, as a result of the ideas "taught" to her by Dr. Allen in the course of her own therapy, combined with her reading of psychoanalysis, she placed the "sex drive" firmly in the center of her educational theory. Of her own creativity, she wrote, "Inspiration is the richest nation I know, the most powerful on earth. Sexual energy Freud calls it; the capital of desire I call it; it pays for both mental and physical expenditure" (*Myself*, 168). Somewhat uncharacteristically she used a phallic metaphor in *Myself* to delineate the boundaries between "the phantom of the profession" and her own passionate pedagogy:

> Think of a room where we all come running in first thing in the morning to plunge into creativity! Ah ... tense orgasm! ... so that, detumesced, we could settle for number later. But you won't find that in my teaching scheme. The curriculum would be a wounded marine—it would die on its way to hospital. A teacher could be dismissed for such outlawry, sacked for sheer insanity. (168)

But this reference to the sexually aroused body is unusual. Matters of the flesh are given voice only off-stage, even in her flamboyant novel *Incense to Idols*. In this, a French concert pianist, Germaine de Beauvais, wreaks havoc on a small New Zealand city by living life according to her bodily desires:

> I still cultivate my depravities and venerate my idols to indulge every sense I've got. People like me need reality and dare not question it. We believe in the flesh and the appetites and the senses are our miracles. It is I who am divine inside and out and I make holy whatever I do. The scent of my hair is finer than prayer and my face more wonderful than churches, Bible or any creed. If I worship one thing more than another it is my own bamboo body. I'm mad on myself I'm so luscious. (*Incense to Idols*, 75)

While Ashton-Warner apparently remained faithful to her husband, the promiscuous Germaine is also a staging of one of Ashton-Warner's fantasized personae (McEldowney 1969; Stead 2002). De Beauvais acts out her fleshly fantasies, but like Ashton-Warner, she needs evidence of her own desirability reflected back from the eyes of her admirers.

Throughout her writing, Ashton-Warner's narcissism reveals itself in a constant need for approval. While her corporeal body may have remained technically faithful to Keith Henderson, she wrote quite openly about her (chaste) love affairs. In *Myself*, she explained that "it's a matter of note that after the years on the Coast the friendships I make harbour heartache. It seems I cannot love moderately or even singly, and I look for a mother in men and women the moment they reveal a regard" (72). In the introduction to *Myself*—the journal that she (perhaps) edited and published twenty years after it was written—she described:

> Love was my big trouble when I was young.... My need and dependence on it. I couldn't breathe without love in the air. I'd choke. I ceased to exist when not in love. The radiance within blotted out so that nothing would happen inside, nothing exploded into action. I can quite truthfully say that I never lifted a hand unless for someone: never took up a brush or a pen, a sheet of music or a spade, never pursued a thought without the motivation of trying to make someone love me. (*Myself,* 9)

Consummation of the affair would be, not intercourse, but a kiss. "Kiss" and "ghost" were her most powerful key words, or captions, for the two great drives that lurked in the/her undermind. So needy was she for positive affirmation from others that much of her time was spent wondering, "Does he love me, does he not." The merest perceived slight—a glance, a silence—could be read as a sign of betrayal. Her moods alternated between ecstasy and despair according to her loved ones' current conduct toward her. Like the other drugs she depended upon, addictive love kept fear and depression at bay (Hood 1988). It was this emotional dependency that made Ashton-Warner so vulnerable to inspectors. *Spinster, Myself,* and Firth's film depict Ashton-Warner's flirtations with and intense crushes on those progressive inspectors who encouraged her. As shown in Firth's film, Ashton-Warner was erotically aroused by "inspections" if the inspectorial eye reflected back an image of her own irresistible (physical, intellectual, artistic) beauty. The ultimate consummation, an inspectorial kiss, would set her world ablaze.

In *I Passed This Way*, Ashton-Warner positions herself as a wide-eyed child as she gazes adoringly up at Douglas Ball, "the new senior inspector of native schools," when he visited the isolated school on the roadless Pacific coastline at Horoera in 1940:

> He rode out on a mighty-boned horse, ploughing through rivers and signing the beaches like a Viking in the latest Jodpurs. He turned out to be very fair-haired and fair-skinned with extravagantly large blue eyes, all inquiry in them and comprehension, and when he dismounted and hitched his sweating horse, before me and my young Ash in arms, two at knee, he was so tall and so big that we nearly broke our necks looking up at his face. (273)

At the time he visited the Hendersons in Horoera, Ball was encouraging teachers in the Native Schools to work according to the liberal spirit of the Red Book curriculum. His personal philosophy of education was very similar to Sylvia's. Her classroom "loud with the sound of erupting creativity" (*Spinster,* 45) seems identical to Ball's "pulsating life of the classroom" (Ball 1948, 114). Like Ashton-Warner, Ball saw good classroom teaching as the product of three main forces—the child, the teacher and the subject matter, and the first two are the most important. Once the emphasis has shifted from subject-matter to personality, then the integrating bonds elude the pen of the curriculum-maker and cannot be set down in any printed syllabus of instruction. They are the intangibles of education, strengthened by the day-to-day relationships between teacher and children at what Glover calls "the point of contact." (Ball 1948, 115)

By the time he visited Horoera, Ball had introduced policies "to retain in the schools all those features of the old Maori culture which are worthy of preservation, thus developing a pride in their own race, whilst bringing to the pupils the best features of European culture" ("Historical Survey of Maori Schools" 1948, 75). In keeping with a shift from an overtly assimilationist racial policy, the Native Schools would be renamed Maori Schools (Barrington and Beaglehole 1974; Simon and Tuhiwai Smith 2001). Ashton-Warner was aware of Ball's ideas: "His view of Maori education accommodated racial temperament and characteristics and their particular needs in the curriculum and the daily timetable and he proclaimed there was a Maori culture worth preserving" (*I Passed This Way*, 272). Yet, one year after this time on the East Coast when she had gazed adoringly up at this Viking with his "extravagantly large blue eyes, all inquiry in them and comprehension" (*I Passed This Way*, 273), she could write, "Back on the coast … far from the haunts of inspectors, out of range of the Education Department—out of reach of criticism. I even taught the Maori language there—O heresy!" (*Myself*, 67).

Conclusion: Transitions and the "Inadvertent Thesis"

From her earliest years as a teacher, Sylvia Ashton-Warner had criticized schooling as a "plastering on of foreign stuff" (*Spinster*, 45). She sought alternatives to teaching's "homicidal intrusion of one upon the other … especially the reading, intrusion upon their inner thoughts and feelings" (*Myself*, 100). Organic teaching and the key vocabulary were techniques for educating from the "inside" rather than imposing from the "outside." Sylvia had "discovered" the key vocabulary while teaching at Fernhill School, near the small city of Hastings in Hawkes Bay (1951–56). Earlier I noted that one short portion of the scheme in *Teacher* had not been included in Ashton-Warner's first published version of her scheme in the eight articles published in *National Education*. This missing portion concerned the Maori Transitional Readers. The local omission of what had been an important component of her educational theory, and its later reinstatement for her overseas audience, is intriguing; I use this to tie together the strands of this chapter.

While lifting the lid off the child's repressed emotions and drives (fear and sex) was somewhat radical, since the 1930s New Zealand's highest educational "authorities" had encouraged teachers to experiment with methods and to draw on the child's "actual vocabulary" (New Zealand Department of Education 1929, 71). Many teachers in the Native Schools, as in other public schools, had made their own reading books (Middleton and May 1997; Simon and Smith 2001). In 1947, T. A. Fletcher, who had succeeded Ball as the senior inspector of native schools, wrote in his annual report:

> It must be admitted that the primer readers as supplied to the schools, have serious deficiencies, but so far there is nothing better available to supplant them as textbooks. They were not written for Maori children, and contain words that are unnecessary for a Maori child's vocabulary. The need is all the greater, therefore to supplement these books by suitable reading material. (as cited in Pearson 1984, 62)

Fletcher advised that "a study of the words needed by the Maori child should be one of the first points to consider" (as cited in Pearson 1984, 62).

From 1948, the locally produced Progressive Readers that had been introduced with the Red Book (as well as the American Beacon Readers used in some schools) were replaced by a locally revised version of the American Janet-and-John series (Price 1997; Wevers 1997). A handbook, *Reading in the Infant Room: A Manual for Teachers* (New Zealand Department of Education 1956), accompanied the Janet-and-John books and reminded teachers that "no reading scheme can anticipate the problems of every individual, or even of every class or every school" (2). Teachers were to "take account of differences" (2) and ensure that a child's reading matter contained "a large number of words from his spoken vocabulary" (3). A buzz of activity was envisaged in classrooms, since "freedom to move about, and freedom to talk, discuss and argue are essential preparations for reading" (15).

In *Teacher*, Ashton-Warner explained to her American audience, "The Maori Transitional Books are used not as a substitute for the American books but as a lead up to them. They condition a Maori child to be able to use the Janet and John series more wholly" (71):

> In word recurrence, sentence length and page length I have only open admiration for the American work. And I follow it respectfully and slavishly in the Maori books. The framework, like so much that is American, is so good. It's only the content that is slightly respectable for Maoris and me. (*Teacher*, 71)

The transitional readers were described as a bridge "out" of Maori culture and "in" to a Western worldview. There is a whole book yet to be written on themes of transition and race in the works of Ashton-Warner. In *Greenstone*, the published version of part of her first (unpublished) novel written in Pipiriki in 1941–42, Ashton-Warner had seen the radical potential of cultural hybridity (see Moeke-Maxwell, this volume). But twenty years later, when *Teacher* was published, she described schooling as a transition "out" of Maori culture. A deficit model of Maori was implied. Perhaps when she left the relatively insulated and intact Maori communities of Horoera and Pipiriki (early 1940s) and moved to the more urbanized areas of Hawkes Bay and the Bay of Plenty (1950s), Ashton-Warner witnessed the disintegration of Maori language, traditional leadership, and patterns of life (Sylvia 1956d). Maybe her ideas about cultural maintenance changed. Whatever the explanation, the section of her teaching scheme that had not been included in the original New Zealand version was reinstated in *Teacher*. How, then, did the two versions differ?

While the account written for Americans extolled the value of transitional readers as a "bridge" to Janet and John, the original *National Education* articles had adopted a very different stance. There the transitional readers were described as a failed experiment. In the article entitled "Organic Reading," "Sylvia" (1956a) described how she had

> tried to meet this division between the climate of a room and an imposed reading book by making another set of books from the immediate material, but all I did was to compose another dead vocabulary. For although they are closer to the Maori children than the books of the upper English middle class, their vocabulary is static too, and it is not the answer to the question I have asked myself for years: What is the organic vocabulary? (97)

Similarly, in "Organic Writing," she explained that no published text could take the place of a child's own writing:

> The drama of these writings could never be captured in a bought book. It could never be achieved in the most faithfully prepared reading books. No one book could ever hold the variety of subject matter that appears collectively in the infant room each morning. Moreover it is written in the language that they use themselves. (Sylvia 1956f, 54)

This attitude toward her transitional readers in the *National Education* articles was identical to that of New Zealand's educational authorities.

I have argued that, as an academic, professional, and administrative discipline, education in New Zealand constituted Ashton-Warner's theory and method as innovative, progressive, and "what we go about trying to inspire other teachers to do" (*Myself*, 111). Her work in Fernhill attracted considerable interest among the Hawkes Bay inspectors. The director general of the government Department of Education, Dr. Beeby, had stated that Ashton-Warner and her work were to be encouraged (Hood 1988). Her theory also came under academic scrutiny when the chief inspector of the region, Rowland Lewis, invited two professors of education, Fieldhouse and Bailey from Victoria University of Wellington, to review her methods. They found the children's levels of literacy impressive: "They could read like mad" (Fieldhouse as cited in Clemens 1996, 50). But what might be the wider social impact of "lifting the lid of the undermind"? Fernhill was in an urban area and, as Fieldhouse put it, their stories made public "all the gossip of the pa" (as cited in Clemens 1996, 55). Bailey wrote, "Their stories were full of violence and four-letter words" (as cited in Hood 1988, 143). What if one of the tabloids got hold of this?

A potential community problem arising from scandal-mongering and erupting violence was not the only reservation of officialdom. There seemed to be a contradiction between the practice of eliciting key words "from the inside" of a child and solidifying these into published readers for "other" children. Beeby commented that "the discrepancy between her theories and her insistence that we publish the books for wider use nagged at me" (as cited in Pearson 1984, 88). Similarly, Bailey told Sylvia "quite strongly that no reading books published in advance, and lacking the immediacy of the children's freshly remembered experiences and feelings, could take the place of her own method" (Hood 1988, 143). Beeby asked the Hawkes Bay senior inspector, Rowland Lewis, to discuss this with Sylvia Ashton-Warner. He wanted to see her theory and teaching method encouraged but was uncertain of the value of yet another set of "imposed" readers (Pearson 1984). In other words, would the key words of others, when congealed as commercially printed texts, become yet another "plastering on of foreign stuff"? (Ashton-Warner 1958, 45).

In her New Zealand *National Education* articles, "Sylvia" agreed with these ideas of the surveilling authorities—inspectors, university professors, and the director of the state education department. In her local publications, she agreed that the transitional readers contradicted her theory of organic teaching. But when writing for Americans in *Teacher*, she wrote of these as both a bridge to, and based on, the American material. All her life, Ashton-Warner had struggled against her own "incredible tendency ... to imitate those I admire," her habit of "patterning myself on other people" (*Myself*, 201). She tried, she said, to become someone "no longer enslaved by the fear of the responses of those I love to my intransigent ways" (*Myself*, 182). But throughout her life, Sylvia continued her narcissistic need for the kiss of authority and was inclined to put on a show for potential admirers.

In *National Education*, and later in *Teacher*, Ashton-Warner quoted Beeby, the director general: "[L]ife as a whole is too complicated to teach to children. The minute it is cut up they can understand it, but you are liable to kill it in cutting it up" (Sylvia 1956f, 54). Here, as in other occasional references, she was clearly aware that the thesis advanced in *National Education*, in *Spinster*, and in *Teacher* was in tune with the "understood design of today's education" (*Teacher* 1963, 207). Through her reading, her pedagogy, and her writing she explored connections between psychoanalysis, art, and (albeit to a lesser extent) social theory. These were also the threads of mainstream progressive education during the 1940s and 1950s, the time she taught in New Zealand primary schools. But Ashton-Warner did not engage in open discussion of her ideas: in *National Education*, she used a pseudonym. She saw herself as an artist, not a teacher, an artist forced by circumstances into teaching; she used teaching and children as "raw material" (Endeavour Television). When writing about education, she wrote in a literary style—novels (*Spinster*, *Bell Call*) or a combination of diary entries, poetry, reconstructed classroom scenes, and references to poets and philosophers (*National Education* articles, *Spearpoint*, *Teacher*). In the 1950s and 1960s her educational writing fell into the widening chasm between literature and science. The novels were didactic and her nonfiction fictional (McEldowney 1969).

During the 1970s, Ashton-Warner's work was read, particularly in the United States, as compatible with the more politically motivated progressivisms of the 1960s–1970s (see Connor and Radford with Robertson, this volume). But Ashton-Warner's ideas were not compatible with the "free schools" or "deschooling" favored by many 1970s activists (*Spearpoint*). She believed in compulsory attendance, and she believed in formal school discipline. In *Bell Call*, one of her lesser-known novels about education, Ashton-Warner defends compulsory schooling against a "hippie" mother who refuses to send a child to school: "Come ye wild ones, call the bells, and learn the true freedom of the spirit to be found only within the framework of discipline and order" (*Bell Call*, 231). Ashton-Warner's view of the purpose of schooling would sit equally comfortably within a conservative framework: "Come all children, call the bells, the length and breadth of the land. Come and receive education. Education to understand, to sort out the good from the evil, the truth from propaganda, and to preserve the heritage of the past" (*Bell Call*, 231).

As I conclude this chapter, I fear other women's responses to it. The narcissistic, "other-centered" personality so evident in Ashton-Warner is also characteristic of many of us who do academic work. In my interviews with PhD graduates, I heard many statements like "I've got my PhD, but I still feel a fraud" (Middleton 2001). Despite my years of experience I, too, am sometimes generally devastated by rejection by publishers or poor reviews. But my anxieties run much deeper than that. Will my chapter be an anomaly in an anthology of "other" women who celebrate and adulate Sylvia as one of feminist educational writing's international foremothers? Have I committed some kind of matricide? Am I an undutiful daughter? Have I been disloyal, and will I be pilloried by New Zealand colleagues for desecrating the reputation of one of our own? In late mid-life, have I become an ingrate, a traitor, a character assassin?

This was not my intention. My argument was fueled by indignation that Sylvia Ashton-Warner's claims of rejection by, and rejection of, New Zealand

and New Zealanders had been unquestioningly accepted overseas and that this international "bad press" had constructed a distorted view of education in my country. This pushed me into the unfamiliar and somewhat uncomfortable position of "devil's advocate" for New Zealand education in the 1940s–1950s. Accordingly, my central concern became the historical, political, cultural, and intellectual conditions of possibility for her theory's production at the time and place. In my work with student teachers, my emphasis is similar. I want them to understand the constraints and possibilities of the historical, political, geographical, and cultural settings in which they live and teach. In my classes, I sometimes use Ashton-Warner's writing as a model of "situated" educational theorizing. When I discuss questions of narrative "truth" with the students in research methods courses, I use as examples some of the conflicting accounts of Ashton-Warner's life in film, biography, and autobiography. And so her teaching and writing continue to enter mine.

But re-reading Ashton-Warner as an older woman, I have felt less sympathetic toward her personally than I did in my more youthful readings. I am irritated by a lack of generosity in her response to her literary success and by a denial of her encouragement by education officials. I become increasingly impatient with the tantrums, addictions, and bitterness that characterized yet were forgivable in her youth; they seem to have intensified and are no longer tolerable in her old age. When I re-read her final book, *I Passed This Way*, I wanted to shout, "Grow up!" On the basis of this postmenopausal reading, I no longer find her example or her fictional writing personally seductive. In fact, I intensely disliked her later novels. That would be another story, if I felt inclined to write it, but I do not. At last I have laid her ghost to rest. I doubt that I shall pass her way again.

Notes

[1] *Myself* was written in 1941 but not published until the early 1970s.

[2] Editor's Note: Sylvia means to refer here to Olive Shreiner, a South African socialist, antiestablishment radical, and also a writer. Shreiner's discourse against imperialism, colonialism, and women's oppression grew, like Sylvia's, out of arduous years of struggle with the writing establishment. Sylvia spelled Olive's name in her diaries as "Olive Schieinen", and this confused rendering from quick jottings and memory is clearly at work in a slightly altered form in the line from *Myself*. Her personal papers include diaries of quotable quotes from major theorists, and Olive had her own rather large section in this material, as evidenced in MS 3432 Commonplace Book 1942 in the Sylvia Ashton-Warner Archives at the Alexander Turnbull Library.

[3] There is a lot of informal (albeit usually unpublished) discussion as to whether Dr. Allen was a neurologist. Normally one would see a psychiatrist, but at the time there would have been few psychiatrists in the country.

References

Ashton-Warner, S. 1958. *Spinster.* London: Secker and Warburg.

———. 1960. *Incense to idols.* London: Secker and Warburg.

———. 1963. *Teacher.* New York: Simon and Schuster.

———. 1966. *Greenstone.* New York: Simon and Schuster.

———. 1967. *Myself.* Christchurch, New Zealand: Whitcombe and Tombs.

———. 1969. *Bell call.* Christchurch, New Zealand: Whitcombe and Tombs.

———. 1972. *Spearpoint: "Teacher" in America.* New York: Alfred A. Knopf.

———. 1980. *I passed this way.* Wellington, New Zealand: Reed.

Ausubel, D. 1952. *Ego development and the personality disorders.* New York: Grune and Stratton.

———. 1960. *The fern and the tiki.* Sydney, Australia: Halstead.

———. 1963. Review; *Teacher. Education* 12, no. 9: 27–28.

Ball, D. G. 1948. What does integration mean? *Education* 1, no. 3: 114–15.

Barrington, J., and T. Beaglehole. 1974. *Maori schools in a changing society.* Wellington, New Zealand: New Zealand Council for Educational Research.

Beeby, C. E. 1992. *Biography of an idea: Beeby on education.* Wellington, New Zealand: New Zealand Council for Educational Research.

Bernstein, B. 1971. On the classification and framing of educational knowledge. In *Knowledge and control*, ed. M. F. D. Young, 47–69. London: Collier Macmillan.

Britzman, D. 1998. *Lost subjects, contested objects: Toward a psychoanalytic inquiry of learning.* Albany: State University of New York Press.

Campbell, A. E., ed. 1938. *Modern trends in education: Proceedings of the New Zealand New Education Fellowship conference.* Wellington, New Zealand: Whitcombe and Tombs.

Clemens, S. 1996. *Pay attention to the children: Lessons for teachers and parents from Sylvia Ashton-Warner.* Napa, CA: Rattle OK.

Endeavour Television. 1977. *Sylvia Ashton-Warner.* Wellington, New Zealand: National Film Library.

Ewing, J. L. 1970. *The development of the New Zealand primary school curriculum 1877–1970.* Wellington, New Zealand: New Zealand Council for Educational Research.

Foucault, M. 1977. *Discipline and punish.* Trans. by A. Sheridan. Harmondsworth, England: Penguin.

———. 1980. *Power/knowledge: Selected interviews & other writings 1972–1977.* Ed. by C. Gordon and trans. by C. Gordon. New York: Pantheon.

———. 1985. *The use of pleasure: A history of sexuality.* Vol. 2. Trans. by R. Hurley. London: Penguin.

———. 1986. *The care of the self: A history of sexuality.* Vol. 3. Trans. by R. Hurley. London: Penguin.

Gordon, C. 1980. Afterword to Foucault, *Power/knowledge*, 229–59.

Griffith, P., R. Harvey and K. Maslen, eds. 1997. *Book and print in New Zealand: A guide to print culture in Aotearoa.* Wellington, New Zealand: Victoria University Press.

Grumet, M. 1988. *Bitter milk: Women and teaching.* Amherst: University of Massachusetts Press.

Higgin, G. 1948. Contribution to symposium on modern teaching. *Education* 1, no. 3: 125.

Historical survey of Maori schools. 1948. *Education* 1, no. 2: 75.

Hood, L. 1988. *Sylvia! The biography of Sylvia Ashton-Warner.* Auckland, New Zealand: Viking.

————. 1990. *Who is Sylvia? The diary of a biography.* Dunedin, New Zealand: John McIndoe.

McEldowney, D. 1969. Sylvia Ashton-Warner: A problem of grounding. *Landfall* 23, no. 3: 230–45.

Middleton, Stuart. 1982. Releasing the native imagery: Sylvia Ashton-Warner and the learner of English. *English Teacher* 10, no. 2: 16–31.

Middleton, Sue. 1985. Feminism and education in post-war New Zealand: A sociological analysis. PhD diss., University of Waikato, Hamilton, New Zealand.

————. 1989. American influences in the sociology of New Zealand education 1944–1988. In *The impact of American ideas on New Zealand's educational policy, practice and thinking*, ed. D. Philips, G. Lealand and G. McDonald, 50–69. Wellington, New Zealand: New Zealand–United States Educational Foundation / New Zealand Council for Educational Research.

————. 1993. *Educating feminists: Life-histories and pedagogy.* New York: Teachers College Press, Columbia.

————. 1998. Schools at war: Learning and teaching in New Zealand 1939–1945. *Discourse* 19, no. 1: 53–74.

————. 2001. Educating researchers: New Zealand education PhDs 1948–1998. *New Zealand Association for Research in Education State of the Art Monograph No 7.* Palmerston North, New Zealand: Massey University / New Zealand Association for Research in Education.

Middleton, S., and H. May. 1997. *Teachers talk teaching 1915–1995: Early childhood, schools, and teachers' colleges.* Palmerston North, New Zealand: Dunmore Press.

New Zealand Department of Education. 1929. *Syllabus of instruction for public schools.* Wellington, New Zealand: Government Printer.

New Zealand Department of Education. 1956. *Reading in the infant room: A manual for teachers.* Wellington, New Zealand: Government Printer.

Pearson, L. 1984. Challenging the orthodox: Sylvia Ashton-Warner, educational innovator and didactic novelist. Masters thesis, University of Waikato, Hamilton, New Zealand.

Price, H. 1997. Educational publishing. In *Book and print in New Zealand*, ed. P. Griffith, R. Harvey and K. Maslen, 144–46. Wellington, New Zealand: Victoria University Press.

Reynolds, D., prod., and M. Firth, prod./dir. 1984. *Sylvia.* New Zealand: MGM/UA Classics Release.

Simon, J. 1998. *Nga kura Maori: The New Zealand Native Schools system 1867–1969.* Auckland, New Zealand: Auckland University Press.

Simon, J., and L. Tuhiwai Smith, eds. 2001. *A civilising mission? Perceptions and representations of the Native School system.* Auckland, New Zealand: Auckland University Press.

Somerset, H. D. C. 1938. *Littledene: Patterns of change.* Wellington, New Zealand: New Zealand Council for Educational Research.

————. 1948. What makes a good school? *Education* 1, no. 4: 170–76.

Stead, C. K. 2002. *Kin of place.* Auckland, New Zealand: Auckland University Press.

Stevens, J. 1961. *The New Zealand novel 1860–1960.* Wellington, New Zealand: Reed.

Sylvia. 1955. Organic reading and the key vocabulary. *National Education* 7, no. 406: 392–93.

————. 1956a. The Maori infant room: 4. Organic reading. *National Education* 8, no. 409: 97–98.

————. 1956b. The Maori infant room: 6. Nature study and number: The golden section. *National Education* 8, no. 413: 248–49.

————. 1956c. The Maori infant room: 7. Organic teaching: The unlived life. *National Education* 8, no. 414: 294–95.

————. 1956d. The Maori infant room: 8. Tone. *National Education* 8, no. 415: 342–43.

————. 1956e. Organic reading is not new. *National Education* 8, no. 410: 141.

————. 1956f. Organic writing. *National Education* 8, no. 408: 54–55.

————. 1956g. Private key vocabularies. *National Education* 8, no. 407: 10–12.

Walkerdine, V. 1984. Developmental psychology and the child-centred pedagogy. In *Changing the subject*, ed. J. Henriques et al., 153–202. London: Methuen.

Watson, J. 1978. The widening research scene in New Zealand. Supplement: The ministerial conference on educational research. *New Zealand Journal of Educational Studies* 14: 1–18.

Wevers, L. 1997. Reading and literacy. In *Book and print in New Zealand*, ed. P. Griffith, R. Harvey and K. Maslen, 212–20. Wellington, New Zealand: Victoria University Press.

CHAPTER FOUR

Teaching's Intimacies

Cathryn McConaghy

In *After-Education*, Deborah Britzman (2003) poses what she suggests is "the novel question of our time": "how does one encounter one's own history of learning through the learning of the other?" (150). Such a question raises the possibility of fruitful encounters with both the intersubjective and intrasubjective experiences of learning. Similarly, we could pose the question with respect to teacher-becoming: how does one encounter one's own history of teaching through the teaching of the other? As with other teacher autobiographies, Sylvia Ashton-Warner's reflections on her teaching offer us the possibility of encountering our own teaching in new ways. Perhaps what is most distinctive about Ashton-Warner's teacher reflections is the intimacy of her writing. Through her narratives, the life and times of the teacher in difficult social contexts—the neuroses, fantasies, longings, crises, affirmations, and rejections—are made accessible. It is not so much her grand theories and successes as an educator that are compelling, although there was considerable interest in Ashton-Warner's philosophies and pedagogies at the time of her numerous publications between the late 1950s and 1980.[1] Indeed, some would argue that her attention to classroom conversations, children's creative energies, and the inner lives of children remain as important today as in the 1960s, when her organic pedagogy received widespread global interest. Rather, in revisiting her large corpus of fiction, nonfiction, diaries, and personal correspondence, it could be argued that what endures in Ashton-Warner's work are the numerous accounts of the fears, anxieties, and losses that cohere around the difficult work of teaching and living in remote rural communities. Her journeys through these traumas and anxieties, although far from resolved, speak to some more universal, at any rate more significant, experience of teachers and teaching in our time. What emerges in an analysis of Ashton-Warner's writings is a testimony of teaching as a form of consolation and survival, provoked by the challenges of both the psychic and social structures of teaching.

In an age of increasing accountability in schooling—in which teachers are required to attend to predetermined syllabus outcomes, rigorous organizational efficiencies, and detailed professional standards—the return of our attentions to the intimate life of the classroom and the complex dynamics of teaching and learning encounters provoked by Ashton-Warner's writings is like warm milk for impoverished teaching souls. This is particularly so in the contemporary context, in which accountability and trauma each want something different of schooling (McConaghy 2003). Ashton-Warner reminds us that teaching is messy work: chaotic, surprising, important, and impossible. Most of all she reminds us of our fantasy that the objects of teaching are other than our teaching selves.

As teachers, in acknowledging that our own histories and desires may be more central to our endeavors than we care to admit, Ashton-Warner's journey through the dilemma of narcissistic tendencies in teaching is instructive. As we follow her journey, a fascinating account of a psychic history of teaching emerges. In texts entitled *Myself* (a diary of her years of personal recovery teaching in Pipiriki), *I Passed This Way* (her autobiography), *Teacher* (an account of her teaching methods and philosophies), and *Spinster* (a fictionalized account of her "ideal" teaching type), a rich account of memories emerges in relation to teaching's objects, its ambivalences, anxieties, obstacles, selves and others, times and places, disclosures, deferrals, and failures and successes. These take place within a complex play of excitement and composure in the everyday lives of teachers and are rendered visible through Ashton-Warner's narratives. Together with her archived personal papers, which she gathered in the later years of her life, her published work testifies to the life and intimate times of the teacher as woman, lover, mother, artist, cultural interlocutor, intellectual, media icon, and exile.

In discussing the force of these testimonies, in identifying instructive aspects of Ashton-Warner's teaching history, it is also pertinent to explore what we may want of her as readers. Indeed, her contributions to both literature and education are significant and contested, as chapters in this volume attest. As readers we bring our differences to her texts; there are thus multiple Sylvias. Further, teacher narratives constitute partial (in a sense inadequate) accounts of the experience of teaching. In their discussion of the obstacles to representing teaching and learning, Pitt and Britzman (2000) observe that our narratives of teaching and learning are not the culmination of experience but rather are constructions made from both conscious and unconscious dynamics. The difficulty with representing teaching histories, following Pitt and Britzman, resides in the anxieties experienced over what coherence excludes. As biographers, we tend to look for patterns, causes, and effects. Importantly, we also tend to emphasize those aspects of our subjects that are most like ourselves (Young-Bruehl 1998). In our search for the idealization of our subjects we tend to underestimate the force of our own desires and the influence of our own "family romances" (Freud 1908). The challenge, writes Young-Bruehl, is to find difference and to disrupt the mirroring effects between subject and biographer. However, in this chapter I am less interested in recapturing some lost meaning about Sylvia Ashton-Warner—her differences—and more interested in what her life illustrates of the life and work of educators in difficult social circumstances. The chapter unashamedly seeks connection and thus is more about theory than biography.

In Ashton-Warner's memories of teaching we encounter confusions, contradictions, repetitions, and workings across multiple landscapes of meaning. The challenge from a social psychoanalytic perspective is identified by Jacqueline Rose (2003): "How to understand the link between public and private worlds, between our collective histories and the innermost, hidden, components of lives and minds" (preface). Rich and provocative, powerful in their symbolism and psychic force, Ashton-Warner's texts are above all testimonies of teacher-living. In encountering her texts as such, we give form to our desires to bear witness, as women or teachers, to the lives of women teachers, to take pleasure in a more intimate connection with them, to console ourselves for our missed encounters.

Teaching's Testimonies

Sylvia Ashton-Warner was a woman of the twentieth century. In a century of theories of trauma (Felman 2002), her testimonies of teaching in difficult times and contexts constitute significant theories of schooling and trauma that continue to resonate with the difficulties experienced in schooling today. From 1939 to 1969 Ashton-Warner worked and lived in rural New Zealand towns, often in impoverished rural Maori communities, bearing witness to child abuses, family violence, material deprivations, and the hardships of rural isolation. She was raised in severe material and emotional deprivation and rural isolation ("I'm sure the family didn't love me, including Mama and Papa" (*I Passed This Way*, 77)). In many ways we can speculate that her crises as a teacher were, at least in part, the crises of witnessing the traumas experienced by her students and their families—crises that may have been felt as repetitions of her own (see Robertson, this volume).

Felman and Laub (1992) and Caruth (1996) have explored the crisis of witnessing other people's traumas, and although their work relates to the extraordinary task of bearing witness to the testimonials of holocaust survivors, the difficult work of teachers bearing witness to the traumas of the children they teach is an area of educational research that remains largely unexamined. Ashton-Warner's testimonials present us with accounts of her witnessing— accounts infused with her own fantasies of the ideals of the good teacher, her theories of "the natural order" of the Maori experience, and her own traumatic history of her early childhood and her experiences of learning.

Although by today's standards Ashton-Warner's social theories of learning in difficult contexts were impoverished (particularly in comparison with her psychological insights), nonetheless she was perhaps ahead of her time in attempting to link the two. Herbert Read remarked in the preface to *Teacher* that this book is a "sociological document rather than a pedagogical treatise" (13). He may have been referring to Ashton-Warner's reading of the social conditions of her students and of their everyday traumas—a reading that greatly informed her pedagogical responses to them. Hers was an organic approach to teaching— organic in the sense that it was situated within the psychic, less so the historical and sociospatial conditions of her students, conditions also in part her own. Thus it could be said that Ashton-Warner's narratives document this process of reading and responding, of active witnessing to traumatic schooling contexts, drawn both from her own difficult childhood memories and her empathetic observations of Maori experiences.

Ashton-Warner's pedagogies could be described as an explicit response to children in crisis. They were developed with an acute understanding of the significance of deeply felt and difficult emotional experiences in the lives of learners: "I got drowned"; "Mummie got a hiding off Daddy. He was drunk. She was crying"; "Nanny's in the coffin under the ground"; "Our baby is dead. She was dead on Monday night. When Mummie got it" (*Teacher*, 53). Such were the everyday life experiences of the children in Ashton-Warner's classes, experiences that are now echoed in many contemporary classrooms. At issue here are the challenges of bearing active witness to everyday childhood experiences of life in difficult contexts. However, it is also possible that Ashton-Warner developed her pedagogy not only as a response to the learning conflicts and everyday crises of the children but as a form of self-consolation. If her pedagogy and her writings were a form of self-soothing, what was it that her comfort pedagogies sought to console?

Ashton-Warner was often an unsentimental witness with respect to her student's writings: "What I feel about their work has nothing to do with it" (*Teacher*, 58). Ashton-Warner's teacher writings suggest as much about the possibilities of witnessing in education as they convey the limits to it:

The drama of these writings could never be captured in a bought book.... The books they write are the most dramatic and pathetic and colourful things I've ever seen on pages.... But they are private and they are confidences and we don't criticise the content. Whether we read that he hates school or that my house is to be burned down or about the brawl in the pa last night the issue is the same: it is always not what is said but the freedom to say. (*Teacher*, 52–54)

Ashton-Warner provides a dispassionate reading of the children's texts— texts that must have disturbed at the same time as they impressed. Threats to her own personal safety, the violence of the environment in which her own children lived, and Maori children's rejections and refusals, and the abuses of them, would have challenged the limits of her composure and compassion. At times she attempted to confront her students' traumas head-on. She writes, "Don't avoid the trauma—include it in the readers" (*Teacher*, 69–70). The challenge for teachers, she argued, was in creating an atmosphere, sentiment, and temperament in the classroom that mimicked the children's experiences of the *pa*. This she linked to a type of cadence, a continuation of the familiar from home to schools: teaching with the stream, not against it, recognizing the children's sorrow and tears, and allowing natural dialogue in the classroom in order not to delay meaning were key strategies in her teaching. She described the obstacles to meaning-making—the mandated syllabus and set reading schemes for New Zealand children—as leading to a type of "smoothing over," what would be described now as reproductive pedagogy.

The pitfalls in teaching, Ashton-Warner claimed, were "copying, mood, repression and crippling fears" (*Teacher*, 49). Her classroom methodology was not about gaining composure in the face of trauma but rather about naturalizing trauma. As the following sections suggest, however, her naturalizing of trauma could be viewed as a strategy to depoliticize Maori education, a strategy to erase the difficult sociopolitical questions at the heart of Maori schooling—questions to which she (as most of her colonial contemporaries) was ill equipped to respond. Trauma, of course, may be commonplace in some contexts, but as Žižek (1998) observes, it is never neutral. For Ashton-Warner, the value of trauma was in providing the fire for creativity to erupt. Her pedagogy worked against personal atrophy to avoid the problem of the unlived life: living life meant creating opportunities for venting creativity, for welcoming strife. Thus, in many ways these strategies allowed Ashton-Warner to witness her own childhood traumas and to avoid the ever-present danger of her own "dry and withered" noncreative existence.

Although seeming to welcome the opportunity to encounter her students' crises, Ashton-Warner's journey of witnessing was not without its own crises. In 1941, three years into her time teaching at Horoera in the East Cape region of the North Island of New Zealand with her husband Keith Henderson, Ashton-

Warner, at the age of thirty-three and with three young children, experienced a long and debilitating emotional and physical breakdown. We can only speculate on its origins, but it is likely that the demands of actively witnessing Maori poverty and family violence—reliving of many aspects of her own difficult childhood—played a part. Isolation, fear, and loneliness were probably also significant factors. Few of those who teach in remote and impoverished indigenous communities escape the debilitating impact of being a stranger "under the gaze" of strangers. Ashton-Warner describes her discomfort at living sandwiched between senior Maori families; despite her respect for them, she yearns for women of her "own kind" (*I Passed This Way*, 307) and freedom from the orderliness and conservatism of the community. Ashton-Warner also had fears for the safety of her children and fears of losing them—or rather, of her incapacity to rescue them: "If the buggy overturned, which child should I save" (*I Passed This Way,* 256). As with her own father decades before her, her mental illness became progressively more debilitating until she was bedridden for many months. Her crisis led to twelve months of recuperation in Wellington where, under psychoanalysis, she began to write her testimonies of teaching. As she noted in her biography, "I'd been dying of fear" (*I Passed This Way*, 281).

In many respects, Ashton-Warner's isolated teaching contexts and their connections to memories of her own childhood dramas help to explain her loneliness and anxieties about living in remote "back blocks" communities. And yet there is also the possibility that what Ashton-Warner was experiencing was the loneliness and anxiety of the beginning teacher. Teaching in the classroom beside the wonderful Keith, master teacher and gentleman, Ashton-Warner's crises and personal and professional failures loomed large in both her eyes and the eyes of the school inspectors. At Waiomatatini she received a grade of zero from a school inspector, a grade published in the teacher's gazette (*I Passed This Way*, 333). Such events helped fuel her growing persecution anxieties and her protestations about never having wanted to be a teacher, a member of the "bloody profesh" (*I Passed This Way*, 294).

Despite such public disavowals and her lengthy illness, Ashton-Warner was able to make the transition from the early experiences of anxiety, the loss of her dreams of teaching and salvation fantasies for the Maori children to find inspiration, self-consolation, love, and reparation. This shift occurred through an engagement with her writings and art and her relocation to Pipiriki, an entirely different and more chaotic Maori community than Horoera, one much more to her liking, precisely because of the opportunities for liberties in such chaos. Ashton-Warner flourished at Pipiriki. She fell in love with Joy Alley and wrote several diaries and the drafts of her manuscripts *Myself* [2] and *Greenstone* (see Brookes, this volume; see James and Thompson, this volume; see Moeke-Maxwell, this volume). Pipiriki, her relationship with Joy, and her successes in teaching Maori children appeared to provide Ashton-Warner with a form of transitional space in which to heal and live creatively (Winnicott 1972). As I shall argue, this particular place, Pipiriki, provided a psychic space for Ashton-Warner to negotiate her fraught relationship with two sources of difficult knowledge: knowledge of teaching in difficult colonial contexts and knowledge of her own homoeroticism in a time of intense homophobia. These difficulties are linked in important structural ways, as we shall see, but first, the issue of reading her testimonies to these difficulties requires some elaboration.

Ashton-Warner's testimonials are not records of the events of the past, but testaments to the felt force of the experiences (Caruth 1995 as cited in Felman 2002). It is precisely the power of the effects in Ashton-Warner's writing and their connection with our own anxieties and traumas that provoke important historical questions about education and teaching in our times. Trauma has the power to call forth considerable energy for social transformation through its repetition compulsion. Indeed, in *Moses and Monotheism*, Freud (1939) suggested that "historical trauma energy can be the motive force of society, of culture, of tradition, and of history itself" (as cited in Caruth 1996, 24). For Caruth, speaking and listening *from the site of trauma* "does not rely on what we simply know of each other, but on what we don't yet know of our own traumatic pasts" (1996, 24). Thus, "in a catastrophic age … trauma itself may provide the very link between cultures" (Caruth 1995, 11). Here we can substitute the notion of teacher generations for cultures. Trauma thus conceived is not a symptom of the unconscious but a symptom of history. The trauma we as readers consciously connect with, as well as the trauma we may have felt or suspected without understanding, draws us to Ashton-Warner's accounts of teaching. Ashton-Warner's testimonies of teacher-trauma thus constitute a powerful force in both the formation of intergenerational teacher histories and in our engagement with significant historical questions about schooling in colonial and heteronormative contexts. Put another way, the impact that Ashton-Warner's encounters with both Maori communities and heteronormativity had on her work and life raises important historical questions for our knowledge of teaching. To what was Ashton-Warner giving testimony; what loss was she mourning; and what meaning was she attempting to make of her loss? As Phillips (1997) argues, mourning is fundamental to human experience and speaks to the transience of life. But what meaning can we make of teaching as mourning; in what ways is the work of teaching what Britzman (2000) describes as "the interminable work of making a relation to loss" (28)?

Teaching's Deferrals (and the Problem of Teacher Knowledge)

The substance of Ashton-Warner's testimonies—forged in moments in which our most intimate personal histories intersect with various social, spatial, and professional positionings—provides important points of departure for a historical investigation of teaching histories. In remembering teaching, the principle of deferred action is significant. The principle of deferred action refers to the phenomenon in which the force of experience is *felt* before it is *understood* (Britzman 2000): our understanding of teaching is therefore deferred from the time of teaching. It is possible that Ashton-Warner was a better teacher after she left the classroom—that she understood more of the teaching-learning encounter with Maori children beyond the reach of the classroom. Thus in teaching, as with other areas of life, memory is the basis of social action.[3] Teaching is difficult work: the deferral of understanding—our memories of teaching—allow teachers to make meaning out of complex teaching dilemmas. Much of Ashton-Warner's best writing about teaching, including *Teacher*, *Myself*, and *I Passed This Way*, read as her memoirs of times spent teaching and working through the anxieties and affective tensions associated with such dilemmas.

As an infant's mistress (elementary school teacher) in remote Maori community schools, Ashton-Warner was faced with considerable challenges in terms of her professional knowledge. The impact of bi/multicultural and linguistic contexts, the social dynamics of the community, and the challenges of understanding the set syllabus, identifying optimum learning conditions, dealing with behavior and discipline problems, resourcing teaching and so on, all required teachers to develop their own understandings. In thinking through the demands of making meaning of pedagogy, of creating one's own professional knowledge, Pitt and Britzman's (2000) work on the relationship between personal relations and knowledge is instructive. In relation to learning, "the force of affect in learning is other to the work of locating the self in knowledge" (Pitt and Britzman 2000, 18). Thus, anxieties in relation to learning may mask a difficult relation with knowledge: "Within the working through of anxieties, questions of knowledge are lost and found" (Pitt and Britzman 2000, 8). Similarly, with teaching, personal relations and the affective realms of teaching may be other to the work of locating oneself in knowledge; thus the emotional life of teaching is other to the work of locating the teaching self within professional knowledge. Within the working-through of anxieties about teaching selves and others, it is possible that questions of knowledge about teaching are lost and found.

Ashton-Warner's texts convey rich accounts of the relationship between teaching's anxieties and knowledge lost and found. They convey with considerable insight the relationship between talking about teacher knowledge and acting out and working through conflicted emotional ties. Her organic teaching methodology entails lengthy descriptions of teaching-learning relations, encounters with children, dream work, and so on. Indeed, she was often drawn to speak of these things through Maori characters and her own versions of Maori creation stories (see *Greenstone*, "The Rainbow Schubert," and others). As Felman (1993) observes, "people tell their stories (which they do not know or cannot speak) through others' stories" (18). But if such anxieties—over knowledge of her own story and her relationship to the stories of others—suggest a difficult relation with professional knowledge, what precisely was the nature of Ashton-Warner's difficult relation with teaching? She professed many times to having not wanted to be a teacher, and yet she is known as one of the foremost educational theorists of her time. She was a reluctant teacher, an antiheroine of pedagogy. Many aspects of her childhood are suggested within her biography and autobiography as contributing to this aversion to teaching (as various chapters in this volume attest), not least being her witnessing of her mother's crises of teaching (see Middleton, this volume). However, in addition to her own childhood history of difficulty, Ashton-Warner's insertion within the difficult context of the postcolonial encounter as a teacher in a remote Maori school requires further consideration.

Teaching's Others: Sylvia's Postcolonial Sensibilities

God, the people I've garmented in glory unrelated to what they were.... But life was barren without someone to worship.[4]

Our ways of making the other are ways of making ourselves. (Fabian 1983, 1)

One of the observations made by Pitt and Britzman (2000) in relation to difficult knowledge is how relations with knowledge become enmeshed with past and present preoccupations with others. The crisis of the insufficiency of knowledge, they argue, leads to a primal helplessness and a sense of incapacity to respond adequately. Ashton-Warner's responses to her incapacity as a teacher included a series of passionate attachments and preoccupations with people she claimed were perhaps undeserving of such affections. It is interesting to speculate to what degree Ashton-Warner's breakdown at Horoera—her preoccupation with interpersonal relations—was a symptom of the insufficiency of her knowledge as both a beginning teacher and an agent of empire. Certainly, over time, Ashton-Warner's experience of Maori people and her encounters with their ontological systems were profound. After the difficult early years, during her seventeen years of living and teaching in Maori communities, Sylvia became fluent in speaking the Maori language.[5] Learning an indigenous language is more than an intellectual task. For one thing, learning the language of the school community involves the teacher in role inversions—the teacher becomes the taught. Although the notion of teacher as learner is today widespread, in the 1940s it was somewhat unusual for those charged with ensuring proper civility and the spread of empire to also consider that they could learn from their colonial subjects. Indeed, Lynley Hood (1988) describes Sylvia's awkwardness around the colonial teaching-learning positions and their inversions.

The concept of the primitive has been central to psychoanalysis (Brickman 2003). Freud's (1913) work in *Totem and Taboo*, subtitled *Some Points of Agreement between the Mental Life of Savages and Neurotics*, seeks to establish a relationship between the libidinal developments of "the primitives" and childhood. Had Ashton-Warner read Freud on the nature of the "savage mind"? Certainly she developed her own colonial imagination and theories of the relationship between "primitivity" and aggression. Indeed, Sylvia constructed the notion of race usually within the tropes of the day. Her books preface her innovations in education as taking place "at the end of civilization" (*I Passed This Way*, 165).   She talks variously about the "challenges of racial development" (*Teacher*, 74); her desire to help construct "The New Race— literate and non-aggressive"; the need for "[l]iteracy for primitive people"; of Maori loss and the social failures of the Maori; the "neurotic Maori" (*Teacher*, 31); she wrote a fictionalized account of "Rangi, an emotionally disturbed Maori" and, curiously, suggests the need at times for what she describes as "the foot on the neck" pedagogy (*Teacher*, 102). At the same time Ashton-Warner was critical of the "colonisation of the mind" of much pedagogy, a trend she referred to as the production of the "mass mind" (*Teacher*, 96) and established herself as a cultural interpreter, capable of developing schooling that would contribute to the "[b]ridging [of] cultures" (*Teacher*, 31). She was critical of what she referred to as "the dead vocabulary" (*Teacher*, 59), which she described as "the vocabulary of the English upper middle classes" (*Teacher*, 41). Much has been written in recent years about colonial ambivalence and the contradictions of bourgeois liberalism: the colonial horrors committed under the banner of freedom and emancipation; the tensions between education and social justice; and the intractability of colonial logics and policies. It was within such colonial complexes that Ashton-Warner was required to negotiate her personal relations and her own ambivalent relation to teaching knowledge and the processes of knowing the other.

Despite her potential alienation (arising from an awareness of the children's dreams of violence toward her), one of Ashton-Warner's central projects was in "knowing the other" (*Teacher*, 67): "How they draw I draw and what they write I write" (73). Indeed, her numerous fictionalized mythologies—for example, *Songs from the River* and "The Rainbow Schubert" (published as *Greenstone 1– 7* [6])—were her testimonies to what she regarded as faithfully rendered observations of Maori people and knowledge. However, Ashton-Warner was not always so self-assured when it came to Maori schooling. She had her own voyage into teaching's heart of darkness:

> After leaving European Gisborne we found the colour of the people changing, the population thickening and darkening in an unnerving way as we penetrated Maori territory. To travel beyond civilisation was one thing but to abandon one's race was an other. The dream that had lured me had left this out. (*I Passed This Way*, 284–85)

Maori schools, she wrote frequently, were schools "beyond the frontiers of civilization … where the clock and the strap did much of the teaching" (*I Passed This Way*, 165). Indeed, Ashton-Warner describes her own use of corporal punishment and "foot on their neck" pedagogies (*Teacher*, 102). "Gone Maori teaching" was an expression levied at teachers who were lost to the world: "As the Great Depression ground on we'd hear of other couples of our year who had dropped out of currency and to hear it whispered of someone we knew, 'They've gone Maori teaching' was to hear of their doom and to register the professional stigma on us all" (*I Passed This Way*, 245).

In her earliest years in Maori communities during her own childhood, teachers were still largely subject to regulations regarding colonial relations.[7] Her mother would have been warned of entering into too intimate a relation with the natives. Ashton-Warner describes how she consoled herself in relation to the difficulties she encountered: "It's an arduous undertaking trying to turn one race into another, involving both force and failure, so for little reason other than to make teaching easier I plunged in and made hundreds of Maori infant reading books" (*I Passed This Way*, 327). Her reading scheme was thus a source of comfort, a consolation for the interminable work of developing the primitive mind.

Over time, Ashton-Warner imagined herself to have a relatively unproblematic relation with her knowledge of the Maori people. By contrast, the inspectors were portrayed as people challenged by the task: "pipsqueaks whose knowledge of their subject, the Maoris, wouldn't fill a cockleshell" (*I Passed This Way*, 272). Ashton-Warner carried the burden of saving the Maori from white schooling and the incompetence of her peers and the system. She both rejected and attempted to remake anew the legitimating conditions for colonial education. Thus, in developing a new type of schooling—schooling for trauma at empire's end—her pedagogy was designed to create a new "race" that was not only literate, but nonaggressive. As with many agents of colonial regimes, Ashton-Warner romanticized the losses of the colonial encounter in terms of the impoverished Western self. In capturing the sentiment of the *pa*—"the instinctive living drama, the communal sympathy and violence, tears and tenderness, brawls, beer, love and song, the tough but communal existence—it is the European whose losses are to be mourned" (*Teacher*, 67). Hence the targets of her pedagogy may have had less to do with the difficult work of colonial mimicry and more with the losses associated with colonial melancholy and mourning.

Teaching's Objects

If Ashton-Warner's explicitly identified teaching objects, the ostensible targets of her interferences, were aggression and the impulse to destruction, she framed them within the universalist frames of mid–twentieth century psychoanalysis (Brickman 2003). The aggressive instincts, in her analysis, were heightened by "race." Her organic literacy scheme was an approach designed to enable the force of children's creative vents to emerge and in so doing to enable them to counter the problem of "an unlived life." [8] When creativity dries up, she argued, a life is not lived, and destructiveness is the outcome.[9]

This understanding of the significance of both the creative and destructive impulses is, of course, the central idea in Freud's (1930) *Civilization and Its Discontents*. The possibilities for world peace, Ashton-Warner argued, stemmed from the approach taken in children's education: "I can't disassociate the activity in an infant room from peace and war" (*Teacher*, 93). Thus, in his 1963 preface to *Teacher*, Sir Herbert Read wrote: "This is an important book—as important as any book can be at this point in history…. Without exaggeration it may be said that the author has discovered a way of saving humanity from self-destruction" (13). Heady praise indeed! Ashton-Warner's "unassuming" and "un-pretentious" book, as Read referred to it, began as a teaching scheme for use with impoverished rural Maori children and entered mainstream education as offering something more universal. One hundred thousand copies of *Teacher* sold in North America when it was first released. Her novel, *Spinster,* was similarly successful before it.[10]

In her focus on recognizing the destructive and creative impulses, Ashton-Warner was critical of what she suggested were "pedagogies of symptoms" developed at "grandscale country-wide yearlong desperate conferences": "witness them floundering around with symptoms, symptoms and symptoms and not one glance at the causes" (*I Passed This Way*, 491). Such pedagogies were "dry pedagogies in which the vital juices disappear" (*I Passed This Way*, 467); within such approaches children were "sedated from the simple loss of living; imagination dulled, impulses blunted. No sign of the mind itself … no-one smiles except the teacher" (460). Here Ashton-Warner was referring to the schools she visited during her time in Vancouver. At the heart of the dilemmas of such schools was "the decay of fantasy … less attributable to the teacher than society itself" (*I Passed This Way*, 467). By contrast, in *Teacher* she advocated the enabling of the creative vent to guard against homogenization and interference in the natural persona of the child. Hers, she claimed, was a student-centered curriculum. But as Jones (this volume) and Robertson (this volume) argue, her key vocabulary was more her own than her students. What is at issue here is not so much the veracity of Ashton-Warner's claims, but the socio-structural dynamics of teaching and its ambivalences. Ashton-Warner was able to make good of Maori poverty and misery while demonstrating little understanding of the structural conditions of their poverty and poverty-related aggressions. Their poverty and losses were the sources of their imagination and individuality. Creativity and voice would emancipate the Maori, as it would Sylvia.

Teaching's Ambivalences

Judith Butler (1997) writes that ambivalence is the result of loss. Sylvia Ashton-Warner admitted to hating teaching. She entered what she termed the "bloody profesh" reluctantly and left it several times following crises of confidence occasioned by damning teaching assessments and "nervous breakdowns." She became a teacher when she could not become a professional artist and, like many working-class white women, ostensibly as a way of attaining some sense of middle-class respectability. As a married woman (she married at Teachers' College to a dedicated teacher, Keith Henderson), she was eligible to teach only in Native Schools. As a result, as a married female teacher, she returned to the impoverishment of rural New Zealand that she had grown up in as the child of a married female teacher. Her mother's teaching career was similarly difficult, marked as it was by frequent relocations, abject poverty, conflicts with male authority figures (inspectors, landlords and others), a "tribe" of dependent children, and a physically disabled husband. Sylvia learnt from her mother that teaching was, for a woman, an oppositional practice involving survival within patriarchal persecution. This she remembered and relived in her own teaching. Her passionate attachments to male school inspectors took the form of both love and hate objects—successful relationships with men required either their seduction or the survival of their persecution. She also confessed to her anger and violence towards her students, describing beltings given at Pipiriki in *I Passed This Way*.

In her writings Ashton-Warner constructs a persecuted history. Indeed, her persecutions became a lifelong driving passion, with rejections remembered long after the affirmations were forgotten. Although several inspectors and senior education department officials, including Beeby, the director general of education, were complimentary of her teaching innovations and her reading schemes, Ashton-Warner focused her attentions on the public rejections. Also targeted was her perceived rejection by the New Zealand Education Department, which refused to guarantee the distribution of ten thousand copies of her reading scheme that a New Zealand publisher required as an assurance. This particular New Zealand publication thus did not go ahead,[11] although a serialized account was published in a New Zealand professional journal. *National Education* published Ashton-Warner's "The Maori Infant Room" in four parts in 1955 and 1956 (Sylvia, 1955, 1956a, 1956b, 1956c; see also Middleton, this volume), despite the editor's recollections that although he was impressed by the vitality of the work, he was less enthused by the "confusion in the arrangement of her text" (Bond 1980, 115). It was, he recalls, "a semi-coherent manuscript of jumbled text and drawings" (Bond 1980, 115).[12] In the same article, Bond expresses surprise at Ashton-Warner's claims in her autobiography, *I Passed This Way* (1980), to have been rejected by New Zealand publishers and never been published there.[13] Although she claims to have been rejected, Bond writes that teachers in Maori schools seemed to like the way she taught (Bond 1980). She was, however, an unorthodox character in her frequent protestations about not wanting to be a teacher, and Bond suggests that the awkwardness in the responses from the New Zealand Education Department may have stemmed from their difficulties with such a position.

Ashton-Warner protested that she hated teaching: "As for hating to teach: that I believe. Writers hate to write too. The hardest and most painful thing is always the thing that means to oneself Truth; when you have to express your most inner meaning and express it directly" (*I Passed This Way*, 468). However, this assertion was commonly interpreted as more of a rejection than a problematizing of the work of teaching, an acknowledgment of its difficulties and frustrations. The discourse of the good and selfless teacher having a love of teaching was as strong then as it is in teaching today. Although many of us secretly confess at times to a hatred of teaching, Ashton-Warner was, of course, speaking the unspeakable. Perhaps more than their difficulty with a teacher who claimed to hate teaching, Bond (1980) suggests that the inspectors would have also been taken aback by the amorous intentions toward them of a young married woman. Ashton-Warner was always in love, usually with someone other than or in addition to her husband Keith. She imagined the objects of her affections to be also in love with her, despite a lack of reciprocal attentions. In numerous letters to her dear friend Barbara Dent over many years, she details these love attachments and her anxieties during times when she was without love objects.[14] Such adorations and crushes on senior male educators, Bond suggests, would have distanced them from her.

Despite the documented interest in her work shown by the New Zealand teaching profession and the department of education, Ashton-Warner felt and claimed rejection by the New Zealand establishment and the press, preferring instead to recall that her scheme was blind peer-reviewed at the instigation of the

Education Department by an Auckland infant's mistress who pronounced that if adopted, it would lead "to the end of the British Empire."[15] Perhaps the most painful rejection of all she recalls, certainly the one that arises time and again in her writings, was that the originals of her organic reading scheme, including 138 original full-color illustrations, were accidentally burnt by a careless school inspector. It is possible that she kept copies of these, even though she led us to believe they were lost. In her handwritten notes on the drafts of the manuscript of *I Passed This Way*, she writes, "But I still had my scheme in my hands."[16] Elsewhere she writes that upon hearing of their destruction, she set about reproducing the four books and only did two before abandoning the project. However, in correspondence in the 1970s between Sylvia and Dr. Gottlieb, the archivist at the Boston University libraries, she asks him to locate the carbon copies of the four books that she called the "Ihaka" books.[17] Whether the scheme in its original form was lost forever in the burning or another copy or copies existed, for Ashton-Warner the violence of the rejection cut deep, and some essence of the books, if not all trace of the books themselves, had been destroyed. The act certainly provided grist for her persecution mill. She remained forever ambivalently positioned, ambivalently positioning herself, in relation to New Zealand public education, acknowledging at times the affirmations of other New Zealand teachers and yet expressing to the Boston University library her wish for her archive to never fall into New Zealand hands, particularly those of the Department of Education.[18]

Ashton-Warner suffered from depressive anxieties throughout her life as a teacher and writer: "As time passed she aired the old wounds under the more comfortable cover of fiction and found counterfeit relief in denying the wounds in herself but discovering them in others. Such measure kept at bay the ever present risk of emotional collapse, but the wounds never healed" (Hood 1988, 90). Comfortable with her ambivalences, she lived a life of glorious contradictions. The author of pedagogical texts that demand more ethical and caring responses to children in crisis, she also admitted to using corporal punishment as a disciplining measure in her classes. She both loved and hated teaching, loved and hated male school inspectors, loved and hated her country, and was generally capable of extremes of passion on most things. Ashton-Warner's ambivalence to many things, her simultaneous fear and desire and love and aggression, should not surprise us. Indeed, the structural links between love and hate, fear and desire, morality and aggression were elucidated by Freud (1930) in *Civilization and Its Discontents*. Rarely, however, have we examined closely the manifestations and structures of ambivalence in teaching. As a profession that locates itself squarely within the realms of moral and social good, knowledge of the ways in which the fantasy of the good so often acts as a camouflage for aggression (Rutherford 2000) should alarm us as teachers. A retired teacher from New Zealand recounted that teacher mythology of Ashton-Warner over the last four decades constructs Sylvia as a "ratbag" who "chained her students to the leg of the piano," "attempted to seduce the local minister," "drank like a fish," and "kept a human foetus in a jar on the mantel" (Woodley, Keith, personal conversation, June 2003). Clearly considered an eccentric rather than a danger, traces of ambivalence are evident in her writings nonetheless. And she was good at holding a grudge. Freud writes that the instincts of destruction and aggression that emerge from the death drive should be viewed "not as monstrous anomaly, nor as demanding a successful repression, but as articulating the intimate truth of subjectivity" (as cited in Rutherford 2000, 25). The point to be made here is that as human beings, teachers have ambivalent relations with schooling, with children, with peers, and with aspects of themselves.

How this ambivalence manifests and how notions of good may disguise aggression deserve more analysis in the fashioning of teaching histories. As Lacan (1997) suggests, this masked aggression so often manifests in relation to alterity. Who then are the others to teaching, the focus of our aggressions? Who or what were the others to Sylvia's teaching? Despite her "successes," loss, loneliness, rejection, and disavowal figure as prominent suspects. The relationship between the personal nature of these (in Ashton-Warner's case) and the structural nature of teaching, in social and psychic terms, are at issue. Are loss, loneliness, rejection, and disavowal historical symptoms of teaching? In Ashton-Warner's case, these symptoms became heightened with her location in social contexts of abjection, in her experience in contexts of colonialism, heterosexism, and loneliness.

Teaching's Lonelinesses

Ashton-Warner lived in relative seclusion for nearly two decades during the years following the success of *Teacher*, *Spinster*, and *Myself*, refusing interviews and shunning the press and various speaking invitations. During this time she continued to write and teach. Britzman (2003) describes the productive potential of loneliness in education: loneliness can function as a type of transitional space in which to come into contact with the incoherence and the splitting that result from disavowal. In her foreword to the 1986 edition of *Teacher*, the writer and teacher Maxine Hong Kingston admitted to lying awake at night worrying about school. When she confided this to fellow teachers in the staff room, the only teacher to respond said, "You do? I never do that" (in *Teacher*, 8). Kingston continues: "I needed beside me Sylvia Ashton-Warner, who recognises 'professional loneliness'" (8). Although the contemporary literature on quality in teaching recognizes the significance of teachers being members of professional communities (for example, Newmann and Associates 1996), Ashton-Warner's writings have much to say about the significance of teacher loneliness.

Despite the success of her many publications and what could be regarded as a successful international career as a writer and educator, despite the various prizes and her award of an MBE (Member of the British Empire) and her central character in at least three feature films,[19] at the end of her life, Ashton-Warner was extremely lonely and fearful of depression. No longer able to write and express her creative energies—no longer sure she *had* creative energies—she feared the eruption of her obsessions and anxieties, the symptoms of an unlived life.

Ashton-Warner ended her life alone with a few boxes of her clippings, draft manuscripts, and personal correspondences. Throughout her life she had needed her work, her writing, to stay emotionally well. At the same time, she grew weary of it: "Dead, that monster, my work, I hope; but slumbering I fear."[20] Her creative output commenced in earnest following the emotional breakdown while in Horoera in the late 1930s. In letters to her friend Janet shortly after arriving in what she felt was a very inhospitable, remote, and wretched place, Sylvia writes of her sense of loneliness and the lack of women "of her own kind." Throughout her life and important to her sense of vitality and emotional health was intimate connection with women friends. The remoteness of the place was also significant, taking three days by horse and cart to reach the community only accessible at low tide.

The time at Horoera is different from the rest of her life in remote rural New Zealand in her attention to her creative life. She had periods of real loneliness and, like her fictional heroine Anna in *Spinster*, she would fortify herself for her teaching with a brandy in the morning and another at lunch. Her friendships with women, her romantic attachments, her writing, her art, and piano playing, together with brandy, enabled her to undertake the lonely work of rural small school teaching. She wrote to Barbara Dent, "I'm begging letters from you again. You don't write me enough letters."[21] Finding women of her own kind was central to her life and work.[22] Regarding her first fan letter, she wrote again to Barbara Dent that "it meant tremendous doors had suddenly swung open. It meant that I only had to pick up a pen to touch my own kind. My own dear kind. Which is sentimental and emotional—but for which I have no apology—only the explanation that at my age one gives up the idea of being perfect."[23]

What meanings did Ashton-Warner make of the relationship between women of her own kind and the loss of perfection?

What meaning has weaning,
Now,
That I love You—need you—
Tis the meaning.

That I see you, treasure you.
Tis the meaning.[24]

Teaching's Erotics and Disclosures: Post/Heterosexual Attachments

Sylvia Ashton-Warner was a serious flirt; as with all flirts, she tended only to flirt with the serious things in life—madness, failure, and other people (c.f. Phillips 1994, xvii). Her flirtations with women (or with the idea of women) began in childhood, culminating in a lifelong love of Joy Alley, and later in Vancouver, in a deep friendship with Selma Wassermann. She describes the force of her attractions to a woman in a letter to a friend: "I am violently stimulated by a woman. What have you got to say about that. No body in it. Violent is the only word for attraction. It has poured meaning over everything again. It's made me slightly sick."[25] And in her diary:

September 6-
All this intertwining
Of your legs and mine
Bare legs, talking, sensitive legs–
Whispering to each other
I don't want it when …
Not now.[26]

In her personal correspondences, Ashton-Warner was explicit about her love of women. But in keeping with the sensibilities of the day, in public, she chose not to disclose her postheterosexual attachments. Such nondisclosure and her own internal homophobias are arguably both symptomatic and causal of her difficult relations to knowledge of teaching. There are of course historical and contextual factors that help to explain the heteronormativities of 1940s and 1950s (indeed, contemporary) New Zealand and her positioning relative to them. Ashton-Warner was aware of these factors. Her archived personal papers contain a copy of a document called "Sex and the School Child" that clearly describes homosexuality as deviant and a form of illness.[27] Whilst such views are familiar to us, Sylvia's autobiography is difficult reading in its disavowals of her love for the key women in her life, notably Joy Alley. Lynley Hood's (1988) biography goes part way to addressing the absences, although it has also been read as dissatisfying, indeed offensive, in its explorations of Sylvia's sexuality (see Brookes, this volume on "the lesbian question"; see James and Thompson, this volume). However, the broader issues in relation to the difficulties in reconciling teaching selves with homoerotic selves that are raised in our reading of Ashton-Warner's life remain as significant structural issues in teaching today.

On the whole, Ashton-Warner was clever in disguise. However, one reviewer of her autobiography said he felt Sylvia's marriage to have been very unsatisfactory, recalling her husband Keith's claims that Sylvia should never have married: "Keith when interviewed observes, 'She should not have married'"; "the reader is convinced of this, without knowing why" (Moscoso-Gongora 1981). In portraying the "spinster" as the ideal teacher, Ashton-Warner is perhaps attempting to provide a solution to the difficult relationship between teaching, marriage, and homosexuality: as a spinster, one can be homosexual while subverting homoerotic desire in the pursuit of higher goals (teaching children and contributing to civilization and society). Sylvia was aware of Freud's explanation of sublimation as the process of substituting the sexual impulses for higher-order social pursuits.[28] In *Spinster*, the protagonist Anna yearns for love, but cannot bear the intrusion of a close relationship in her life. Ashton-Warner explained that she published *Spinster* because she could not get a publisher for her reading scheme. However, the book is more revealing of her fantasies of marriage to teaching[29] and her knowledge of the necessity of the sublimation of a teacher's eroticism in the formation of the teacher self.[30]

It is possible that her frequent protestations of rejection[31]—by her country, her profession, and the publishing world—were an armory against disclosure and her fears of exposure, a symptom of her own self-censure. Butler (1997) writes that "a loss in the world that cannot be declared enrages" (185). Sylvia may have used teaching as a disguise. Heterosexuality functioned in part to provide Ashton-Warner with a sense of composure and middle-class sensibility. And yet there were times when she allowed her radical otherness to emerge. In many of her writings she demonstrates a preoccupation with both excitability and its absence. Thus she writes of the dangers of both composure and censure (*Teacher*); of the significance of "tone and deep order" and the attainment of a "still center" (*Teacher*, 87); she recognized the strife of "the fire that on my bosom preys" and the "conscious chaos" of her classroom (*Teacher*, 87). She loved the sound of communication between children, the noise and movement, the passion and temperament, the stirring words and volcanic eruptions of creativity. She recognized the problems with a dead vocabulary and suppression, and (following Winnicott) the importance of creativity and the growth of the mind. At the same time, she wrote of the importance of teacher control and discipline, of reining in the latent energy that can oppose teachers. In later life she celebrated gaining composure:

> You'd never recognise me as that girl from the past habitually playing the limelight, talking too much, throwing round my music gratis and flaunting my art; I was becoming that someone I'd always been interested in—a self-contained impenetrable spinster, an indispensable unit of society ... [a] "Glorious Creature." (*I Passed This Way*, 411)

If Ashton-Warner had a tenuous relationship with heterosexuality (see Butler 1997), she also had a heightened need for affirmation. She writes in her diary: "Would I *ever* become accustomed to no applause."[32] Despite this need for affirmation, Ashton-Warner also had a strongly internalized sense of disavowal, of herself as abject. Perhaps this ambivalent relationship with heterosexuality and the difficulties around being able to perform her own homoeroticism are aspects of her loss. Butler describes "the ungrievable loss" (1997, 144) that is symptomatic of gay melancholia: "The prohibition on homosexuality preempts the process of grief and prompts a melancholic identification which effectively turns homosexual desire back in on itself. This turning back upon itself is precisely the action of self-beratement and guilt" (Butler 1997, 142). Indeed, Ashton-Warner acknowledged that she had to work at being liked and likable: "You never want to stay too long in a place, even Pipiriki. You use up the people. They get to know you and no poor human can survive being known" (*I Passed This Way*, 313). As a melancholic, Ashton-Warner became a consummate escapologist.

Teaching's Obstacles: Exile and the Art of Escape in Education

Writing in the *Chicago Tribune Book World*, P. Moscoso-Gongora's (1981) review of *I Passed This Way* is entitled "An Educator's Escape into Art." Escapism is a persistent theme in the book. The review quotes Ashton-Warner saying "I must escape from teaching" and "I retreated more profoundly into the consolation of imagination … to Maori settlements beyond the frontiers of civilization." Writes Moscoso-Gongora, "An autobiography spent in thwarted, improbable quests creates an obvious central problem." Moscoso-Gongora further argues, "She could not write better about Keith, though something is wrong; a distance from her husband, an increasing self-absorption, a desperation to flee. Her two nervous breakdowns make this necessary…. Her fascination with anything but teaching reaches irrational heights." In relation to the development of Ashton-Warner's reading scheme, Moscoso-Gongora notes, "No unmarred development this. Nervous illness and artistic instincts interrupt again." Interruptions, obstacles, avoidances, and daring escapes pervaded Ashton-Warner's life.

In his analysis of the psychoanalysis of escapology, *Houdini's Box*, Phillips (2001) demonstrates how Houdini compulsively re-enacted and reinvented his own confinement. Similarly, we could argue that Ashton-Warner constructed her life as a series of confinements from which she re-enacted, time and again, her own escape. Her classrooms, her homes, her marriage, her country were all sources of confinement from which she had to escape—to her Selahs, to North America, to other relationships, and to other thoughts. For as Britzman (2003) reminds us, "after the experience of education there is still the problem of thought" (171). Were Ashton-Warner's ambivalences and avoidances in teaching symptoms of her difficulties with thoughts of colonial pedagogy and her own sexuality?

Phillips (2001) also observes that people often feel most alive in the very moment of escape: "Getting free was the adventure, not being free" (17). It is possible, he suggests, that the source of pleasure is less about getting away *from* something than getting away *with* something. Our truancy stages for us a dilemma, erotic in nature, and linked to our ambivalence about whether we want our sexuality to intensify our self consciousness or release us from it (Phillips 2001). Thus escape and escape fantasies, he argues, are linked to both our fears of being found and of not being found. Ashton-Warner may have been escaping from being found out.

Despite being remembered as a teacher of international significance, for significant periods of her teaching career, particularly in the early years, Sylvia was often absent from the classroom. Her teaching strategies consisted in part of strategies to avoid teaching. Whether in her Selahs in creative pursuit or at home in bed, her autobiography suggests that she was more attached to her obstacles to teaching than to teaching (see Robertson 2001 on obstacles in teaching and learning). A large part of her teaching self consisted of an anti-teaching self, as she disclosed in a letter to her friend Barbara Dent: "a sherry before school in the morning and one after lunch … somehow the woman must keep going, whatever it costs in alcohol."[33] Regarding the inspector's visit, she wrote to Dent:

> They MUST have smelt my breath, but what have I to lose? When our reports came on Wednesday I made Keith promise me faithfully not to show me mine…. Keith knows that whether it is good or excellent it will still disturb me too profoundly, that they should rule on me at all. I'm an outlaw and at last I know it finally. That's the brandy story.[34]

And the Maori back-blocks story? Her location in Maori communities, although linked to the structural conditions of being a married woman teacher, may also be linked to a sense of marginality or fear of marginality. Ashton-Warner wrote of her friend Moyra Barrer, she is "at home among the Maoris, and so am I"; she noted, "[The Maori] don't hurt you like the Europeans"; "For a moment we were both hiding in the same retreat … among the Maoris. The 'bloody Maoris' who never hurt you in their supreme gentleness."[35] Sensing the power of the margins, her published schemas suggest strategies to avoid the curriculum of the day. Not only was she intent on escaping conventional teaching, she assisted her students in their escape from the conventional curriculum through her teaching scheme, the key vocabulary. That they were Maori students in a white schooling system is possibly both significant and incidental to Sylvia's interest in schooling and escapology. In his preface to *Teacher*, Sir Herbert Read observed her lesson to teachers that they must cultivate "negative capability," a form of absent/presence that, according to Ashton-Warner, she had developed into an art form.

Escape is both a symptom and an end in itself, Phillips (2001) suggests: a need to be able to escape the intentions and desires of others, while simultaneously a reaffirmation of our need for certain kinds of recognitions and reassurances. To escape—or to be unable to escape—is often linked to a sense of failure (Phillips 2001). Escapology lives out our fascination with risk and with playing out the drama of failure and success. An integral aspect of the teaching persona, success was important to Ashton-Warner. On being adored, and on being posted love, she wrote the following about Selma Wassermann:

> Later she told me that on that first morning of the seminar she'd come to my house before nine and had stood outside my gate in order to "savour the wonder" of being near A-W at last, on her own before she came in—and there she had been on that white fall morning listening to me practising Schubert. (*I Passed This Way*, 446)

In Colorado, Ashton-Warner reveled in the adoration: "two hundred teachers in the hall and a hundred waiting outside to get in … I have been *greatly* praised and appreciated" (*I Passed This Way*, 444). She contrasted her teaching in Vancouver at Simon Fraser University with her reception in New Zealand, describing the agony of the ousted child:

> Oh to be praised in the country of my youth, as my family had always praised me. At least I learn the hard way what it is like for a child not to be loved at home. Success can be hollow and lonely sometimes…. I'm permanently astonished at how people here love me. (*I Passed This Way*, 471)

In Godzone or New Zealand, however, there was only "hostility for and suspicion of an artist" (*I Passed This Way*, 471). She feared rejection and worked to stave off insults. As she wrote to her friend, Barbara Dent, later in life: "Please write a letter without insults as I am getting on now and take even longer to get over them."[36]

The fantasy of national rejection is an interesting trope in Ashton-Warner's writing. In part it may be linked to her identifications, her desires for representation, and her difficulty with being judged by others. Phillips (2001) writes, "If you are defined by what you can escape from—your country, your language, your poverty, your name—then you may need forever to seek out situations to release yourself from. To defy, in ever-greater feats of ingenuity and endurance, people's descriptions of you" (14).

In relation to her teacher gradings, she wrote that hers were "punitive beyond any teacher's professional recovery" (*I Passed This Way*, 362). She resented the denigration of the zero grading and on many occasions rejected the label of teacher: "I must escape from teaching" (*I Passed This Way*, 294). Pitt and Britzman (2000) observe how our memories of learning are closely tied to the fantasies of refusing to learn. Similarly, through Ashton-Warner we can read how our memories of teaching are closely tied to our fantasies of refusing to teach.

In relation to her identity as a New Zealander, Ashton-Warner writes of the "rigidity, timidity beneath the crinoline; stale mouldy air. Inbred thinking. And that goes for me when I'm there" (*I Passed This Way*, 414). But perhaps her crises were not only those of representation but also those more fundamental to the structural relations and contexts of teaching in our times. It is possible that the Selahs and North America were not an escape *to* but an escape *from*—from the crises of colonial witnessing, the prohibitions on teaching selves, and the psychic trauma of heteronormativity. In her diasporic tendencies, Ashton-Warner emerges as a reluctant and ambivalent witness to these phenomena.

What we avoid depends on the organization of the defenses of the individual: "we don't always flee from something because it is unacceptable; sometimes it is unacceptable to us because we flee it" (Phillips 2001, 31). Ultimately, though, fear always confers power on its subject. In our evasions, avoidances, elusions, our escapes are manifestations of the encoding of our histories. Phillips argues that we are only captured by what we have once been or wanted to be. Thus the only thing we escape is the past, or rather, our memories of the past. Linked to the psychic force of evasion is the power of memories. For Freud (1899), in his analysis of what he termed "screen memory," the significant memories of childhood are omitted rather than forgotten; we repress and replace. In such a scenario, escape is a form of consolation.

Teaching's Consolations

The loss of Opal [Joy] I couldn't stand... (*I Passed This Way*, 324)

We can read Sylvia Ashton-Warner's pedagogies not as ruminations on voice and creativity nor as better and better representations of the real but rather as performances of and consolations for loss, loneliness, and disavowal. Britzman (2003) describes the Kleinian notion of loneliness as functioning to provide a space for the giving up of idealizations of loved objects. Loneliness acts as "a fragile bridge necessary for thinking to cross from the emptiness of loss and anxiety to the poignant work of mourning" (Britzman 2003, 149). Perhaps Sylvia's idealization of Joy Alley was made real only as an enigma in her life; Joy Alley was a necessary focus for Sylvia's loss and grief and their missed encounter. Žižek (1998) notes that there is a "fragile balance between the sublime image of the beloved and her real presence" (164); in developing her dialogues with her students, Ashton-Warner opened up the possibilities of exploring connections and consoling herself for her missed encounters.[37]

For those learning to be teachers in rural and postcolonial Australia, my own place of pedagogy and connection, one encounters not so much the isolations, frailties, and vulnerabilities of students but rather the isolations, frailties, and vulnerabilities of the self. In Australia these teacher vulnerabilities tend to congregate in the rural schools and in tough inner-city schools. Whereas most books on pedagogy—the autobiographies of how one learns to teach—elide the complexity of the lived experience of the teacher in constructing coherence where doubt, anxiety, and uncertainty exist, Ashton-Warner's accounts of her life as a teacher are provocative and bold. Her accounts celebrate the notion of teacher vulnerability and imperfection. If Ashton-Warner's pedagogy was a form of self-consolation, it was also a source of great inspiration and productivity. Butler (1997) writes that "the critical agency of the melancholic is at once a social and psychic instrument" (191). Her truancies from her own classroom, her irreverence for authority figures, her failures and successes, her self-deprecations and admissions of neediness, her flirtations and excesses seem as wonderfully impressive today as they did in her own lifetime. Ashton-Warner's contributions to pedagogical histories—her insistence on attending to the intersubjective, her argument that the intersubjective is complex, problematic, and erotic—are valuable contributions to contemporary pedagogical dilemmas. Perhaps her inattention to politics was a recognition of the limits to what we can change (Phillips 1999).

A contemporary encounter with Ashton-Warner is a return to pedagogy, to the problematics of schooling as the problematics of teachers and learners; to the importance of the touch, dreams, fears, imageries, and imaginaries; to the importance of reading the slips, signs, symptoms, and symbols of pedagogical encounters; and, centrally, to the importance of teachers having conversations with children. Significantly, and although in her own imperfect way, Ashton-Warner was also able to mobilize pedagogy as a form of social action. She put personal ethics and the virtues at the forefront of difficult teaching, claiming in *Myself* that "to be a worthwhile teacher one must be a worthwhile person first" (18). And even though she was recognized in her own lifetime[38] in numerous ways and through numerous public awards, such praise was little consolation for Ashton-Warner. Indeed, in later life, she appeared to be inconsolable in relation to her losses.

Often described as "a difficult woman,"[39] Ashton-Warner admitted to her own excesses, although admitting that in later life she had begun to give them up.[40] Sylvia Ashton-Warner knew the trouble associated with being a clever girl: "it is not discreet to excel" (*I Passed This Way*, 301). Despite her obvious pleasure in her transgressions and excitabilities, she was also drawn to her own composures. They were her consolations. As teachers we console ourselves in different ways. Throughout her writings and life, Ashton-Warner appears to wrestle with her desires and consolations. She was an active witness to her own fears and psychic traumas,[41] to those of children, to the problem of undisciplined dreaming, to the dangers of repressed emotions, to the significance of fear and sex, the drama of the cast-off child, the unloved child, and the neglected, dried-up child, and she was a consummate witness to violence, aggression, and persecution in childhood. She went so far as to say, "My psychotic compassion is the one illness I've never recovered from" (*I Passed This Way*, 460). Despite her historical location in colonial regimes, she developed a "good enough" ethic of care for her Maori students and responded to their demands for loving and humanitarian gestures. She developed a willingness to tolerate both the loss of herself in her teaching and the repetitions of her own and other's historical anxieties—though such tolerances brought their own excesses. Such excesses may have been the source of her survivals, then and now. Žižek (1998) identifies the surplus pleasures of poetic excesses, in which the very "symbolic articulation of loss gives rise to a pleasure of its own" (156). One senses the great pleasure Sylvia had in what she also described as her poetic excesses.

Teaching's Survivals

The power imposed upon one is the power that animates one's emergence. (Butler 1997, 198)

What meaning is to be made of Sylvia's oppositional practices and transgressive stances in her teaching? Is it merely that in remembering her own teaching, she only remembered her deviations from the accepted script? As Ben-Peretz (1995) observes in her analysis of teachers' memories of teaching, it is precisely these transgressions that we choose to recall. What were her attachments to her multiple rejections—real and perceived—symptomatic of? In what ways is her ambivalence towards teaching mirrored in our own? What is difficult about teaching such that it calls forth powerful extremes of human emotion—and why are we surprised and affronted by emotional excesses in teaching? And what is it that survives in these testimonies of teaching—if fantasy is in excess of and prior to experience (Britzman 2003), what do we describe when we discuss students and lessons and schools? What belongs to the inside (the intrasubjective) and what belongs to the outside (the intersubjective) in terms of teachers' dilemmas? If teaching is about loss, what is "the historicity of [this] loss" (Butler 1997, 194)? And if loss, what is it that a teacher wants? What remains beyond loss?

Ashton-Warner's writings and life and our readings of her require an encounter with some significant historical questions in teaching. We can read her writings as monuments to her loss and mourning and to the difficult relationship we have as teachers with knowledge of colonialism and heteronormativity. In reading her testimonies, Felman (1993) suggests that we are recovering something the speaking subject is not—and cannot be—in possession of. Her losses were returned to us as testimonies to teaching's intimacies. Although we struggle to be in possession of our own intimate stories and histories of teaching, through Ashton-Warner's narratives we can recover something of these and in doing so be touched with the fever of it all again.

Acknowledgments

If there are any insights in this chapter they owe much to the many conversations and correspondences I have had with Judith Robertson since we met in Ottawa in 2000 and discovered that among our shared passions was the spiritedness and spirit of Sylvia Ashton-Warner.

Notes

[1] Among her successes, Ashton-Warner's book *Teacher* sold more than three hundred thousand copies. *I Passed This Way* was the winner of the New Zealand Book Award's best nonfiction in 1980. Ashton-Warner was elected President of Honour by her New Zealand PEN peers and was the winner of the 1980 Delta Kappa Gamma Society Prize, awarded by women educators in Detroit.

[2] In a review of *Myself* in the *Christchurch Star* (December 7, 1968) the reviewer wrote: "Frankness from a teacher—it makes good reading. [The book] describes her work as a teacher in small Maori schools and her attempts to improve herself in her vocation. But her frank description of her thoughts and feelings and her relationships with others gives much more to the reader." In a review of *Myself* (*New Zealand Listener*, January 17, 1969), Jack Shallcrass noted Ashton-Warner's admission that "poise is the first casualty in isolation." Shallcrass also comments on Ashton-Warner's anxieties, need for love and reassurance, her struggle for command of the mind, the imagination and emotions, her struggle to resolve conflicting demands and to discipline talents that were almost too generous. She was, he wrote, a woman of delicate and erratic sensitivity, acute insight, a gifted and unusual person and teacher.

[3] In an interview study of teacher's memories, Ben-Peretz (1995) observes that traumatic and uniquely significant experiences tend to leave stronger traces in teachers' memories. The content of teachers' memories from this research ranks interpersonal issues highest, then (in descending order) rules and principles, focus on students, the context, teaching alternatives, job difficulties, negative experiences, and lastly, positive experiences. Teachers tend to remember well the things they did that made a difference.

[4] Alexander Turnbull Library, Letter to Barbara Dent, MS Papers 5594–1.

[5] Ashton-Warner's approach to the teaching and her own learning of Maori language and culture was in step with the new thinking of the day. The *Education Gazette* (February 1, 1956) presents the resolutions of the Committee on Maori Education, headed by Mr. D.

G. Ball. This represented the first time that the Maori community had had input into an educational review. The committee suggested a number of principles, including that educational needs of Maori and Pakeha were identical; that when in schools as a minority group, the Maori should be helped to feel their own personal worth, security, and a sense of identity; and that the teaching of Maori culture, including history, legends, songs, art, and craft is necessary for the full personal development of the Maori. In addition, knowledge of the Maori culture was also considered necessary for the Pakeha child, in order that he may more fully appreciate the history, achievements, and intrinsic worth of the Maori; association between the Maori and Pakeha should be encouraged to the utmost; and the Maori child is in need of special assistance to learn the English language, particularly its written form. The committee supported the teaching of the Maori language "and recommends everything possible be done to implement it." Further, Maori were to be appointed to teachers' training colleges, and Maori parents were encouraged to take more active roles in education. The 1950s saw a change in attitude to the speaking of Maori language in schools (*Education of Maori Children*, 1953, report presented to the New Zealand House of Representatives, File E-3, New Zealand National Archives, Wellington) although bilingual programs for Maori were not established until 1978 in Ruatoki.

[6] "The Rainbow Schubert" (renamed *Greenstone 1 to 7* was typed on colored paper and published in the *New Zealand Monthly Review* in 1961: part 1 (violet) in June; part 2 (indigo) in July; part 3 (blue) in August; part 4 (green) in September; part 5 (yellow) in October; part 6 (orange) in November; and part 7 (red) in December (Sylvia Ashton-Warner archives, Alexander Turnbull Library, MS 4425–109). All archival sources in the endnotes that follow are to be found in the Sylvia Ashton-Warner collection of the Alexander Turnbull Library, Wellington, New Zealand, unless otherwise indicated.

[7] Regarding relations between teachers and Maori, the New Zealand Department of Education issued *Circulars to Native Schools* (New Zealand Archives E80/647, vol. 1, 1879–1894, Wellington): "Directions here given as to the relations between the Teacher and the Maoris—teachers will be expected to exercise a beneficial influence on the natives, old and young, to show by their own conduct that it is possible to live a useful and blameless life.... You are particularly cautioned against entering into close personal alliance with any clique or party of natives."

[8] Ashton-Warner drew the notion of an "unlived life" from Eric Fromm. Ashton-Warner kept three notebooks of quotes—on such topics as love, sublimation, genius, loneliness, truth, happiness, faith, education, sensuality, religion, beauty, time, fear, sin, work, sex, music, art, literary style, liberty, the Bible, and shapely living—in which she drew upon a number of writers, significant among them Sigmund Freud, Bertrand Russell, D. H. Laurence, Olive Schreiner, Omar Khayyam, C. A. Dinmore, Katherine Mansfield, Aldous Huxley, Mrs. Murray, and Eric Fromm. These date to around 1942 and were written at Pipiriki (Alexander Turnbull Library, MS 3432, 3433, and 3434).

[9] There is no evidence in Ashton-Warner's collection of notebooks that she was aware of similar theories put forward by Anna Freud and Dorothy Burlingham (see Britzman 1998).

[10] In explaining its appeal, and the appeal of her autobiography, *I Passed This Way* (1979), a New York reviewer, Judith Chernaik (1980), wrote,

> [T]he obsessed, minutely detailed novel of a teacher's life in a Maori infant school.... Hardly the stuff of best sellerdom, it instantly became the book everyone had to read, if only because it was as far as you could get from the packaged

glibness of New York life and letters. Ashton-Warner's autobiography has the same passionate ring, as well as an odd abrasive naivety, a product of her single-minded concentration on the subject, her own "unsophisticated heart." (Alexander Turnbull Library, MS 4425–122, published newspaper reviews)

[11] A fictionalized account of the pedagogy to accompany the scheme under the title *Spinster* (1958) was later published in London and the scheme itself was published as *Teacher* in the United States in 1963.

[12] In a review of *I Passed This Way*, Russell Bond (1980), who was editor of the journal *National Education* from 1948–1959 reflected: "I received from her a semi-coherent manuscript of jumbled text and drawings," with a note from Ashton-Warner saying her scheme had the ability "to ease problems of reading and of race and personality and to lessen delinquency; not only young Maoris and not only for young Pakeha but for people of any colour and age, including myself." Bond wrote,

> [A]t the time I was impressed by the vitality that infused her writing, though less by the enthusiasm that overflowed into confusion in the arrangement of her text. I published one article immediately and four more later.... [*I Passed This Way*] contains no reference to the publication of these articles. Yet there is so much about her efforts to win recognition for her teaching methods, so many expressions of anguish and frustration at the indifference of the educational bureaucracy.... Teachers in Maori schools seemed to like the way she taught.

[13] A letter from Carole Durix, dated April 12, 1979, asked Ashton-Warner to confirm that *Teacher* was ready for publication in 1953, that it was serialized in *National Education* using the book as a basis, and then published in the United States in 1963. Despite this correspondence and copies of the publications held in her own personal papers, Ashton-Warner maintained her stance in relation to not having been published in New Zealand.

[14] Alexander Turnbull Library, MS Papers 5594.

[15] Alexander Turnbull Library, MS Papers 5594.

[16] Alexander Turnbull Library, MS Papers 4425-057, notes and drafts of *I Passed This Way* (1965–1972).

[17] Sylvia Ashton-Warner, letter to Dr. Gottlieb, Boston University library (May 13, 1979), asking him to retrieve from the archive her "IHAKA Books (I think I called them). There are four. The carbon copies of the pages ... with text in handwriting ... are the four Maori reading books which were burnt by the NZ Education department Office. The pages you have are complete and I could resurrect them." Ashton-Warner also asked for the "TURI" books, two unnamed books with illustrations of Maori families and the four Pipiriki diaries, to be returned to her, so that she could publish them after *I Passed This Way* (Alexander Turnbull Library, MS Papers 4425–123, soft cardboard). Ashton-Warner died before doing so.

[18] Sylvia Ashton-Warner, letter to Dr. Gottlieb, Boston University library (October 29, 1976): "I don't want anything of mine left available in NZ." Sylvia Ashton-Warner, letter to Dr. Gottlieb (February 6, 1977), as she was assembling her collection for Boston and nearing the end:

> The big drive in me to send things away appears to be to prevent NZ hands getting at my things.... My most valued work you have, the small MS of the four Maori books the NZ Ed. dept. burnt many years ago. The drawings were in carbon outline and the text in rough script, in pencil, hard to decipher. Don't ever let NZ get hold of that. Half-size quarto paper, light weight.... I'd like to close this whole project now

and cease this mini-death and get on with my living. I have much to do. (Alexander Turnbull Library, MS Papers 4425–123)

Ashton-Warner then resumed sending another thirty parcels of personal papers. Several boxes not sent found their way into the Alexander Turnbull Library later.

[19] Films that drew upon Ashton-Warner's books included *Sylvia* (Reynolds and Firth 1984), starring Eleanore David, and *Two Loves* (Blaustein and Walters 1961), starring Shirley MacLaine and Laurence Harvey, which was released in Great Britain as *The Spinster.*

[20] "Songs of Exhaustion and Recovery," January 12, 1962; Coopers Beach, Northland and Bay of Islands, January 13, 1962 (Alexander Turnbull Library, MS Papers 0435-55).

[21] Alexander Turnbull Library, letters EL3 and EL4 in MS Papers 5594-1; see also MS Papers 5594–1, letter E7L3: "You can always picture me at Selah on a Saturday. Do send me a letter for every Friday's mail."

[22] Alexander Turnbull Library, MS Papers 5594-1, E2L:5. "I've been depressed this week—lonely for my own—of whom I see about 3 in a year. I need your letters. You belong to the company of Selah."

[23] Alexander Turnbull Library, letter E2L1P2 in MS Papers 5594–1.

[24] Alexander Turnbull Library, MS Papers 3431.

[25] Alexander Turnbull Library, letter EL9 in MS Papers 5594–1.

[26] Alexander Turnbull Library, MS Papers 4425-109.

[27] "Sex and the School Child" (circa 1944) by M. Edwards, psychologist, Department of Education (Sylvia Ashton-Warner Archives, Alexander Turnbull Library). Edwards wrote of deviant sexuality and the problem of homosexuality, "the deviant sexual fantasies and behaviours which can affect children." Further, he argues, "In the development of socially acceptable sexual behaviour, the most important factor is control" (4).

[28] Her notebooks kept in 1942 contain several entries under the heading "Sublimation," including quotes by Sigmund Freud (Alexander Turnbull Library, MS Papers 3432, Commonplace Book).

[29] Bernard T. Harrison (1981) says Sylvia Ashton-Warner writes that "when I teach people I marry them"; "her passion is consuming, ruthlessly concentrated on her chosen object, and her accounts of teaching contain much pain, distaste, even burning resentment at so impossible a marriage, as well as the returns of fine delight"; "finding meaning through interpersonal encounters, the marriage commitment"; "identifying with sharp clarity the extreme demands of marriage to teaching."

[30] In a review of *Spinster* (*Time*, March 16, 1959) the writer argues that the book conveys Ashton-Warner's view that teaching is a dangerous activity. For Spinster/teachers, love repressed in one area bursts out in another.

[31] Monty Simmons wrote in the *Roanake Times and World News* (February 3, 1980) in relation to Ashton-Warner's assertions that "to this day my work remains unpublished in NZ" and the tensions between hating and loving her native land: "her life, it seems, has been an extraordinary act of defiance." Simmons presents Ashton-Warner as "a lover, intangible, invisible, yet voracious and permanent."

[32] Alexander Turnbull Library, MS Papers 4425–049. Pipiriki, book 1. February 23–November 26 (either 1939 or 1940).

[33] Alexander Turnbull Library, MS Papers 5594–2 1953, E29.

[34] Alexander Turnbull Library, MS Papers 5594–2, 1953, E27, undated letter.

[35] Alexander Turnbull Library, MS Papers 4425–049. Pipiriki, book 1. February 23–November 26, 1939 or 1940, p. 5.

[36] Alexander Turnbull Library, MS Papers 5594–1, E19L2. See also her letter in MS Papers 5594–1, E19L4: "I have told Miss Alley to take her forked tongue and her familiarity somewhere else. The disagreement has made her more attentive but it is too late."

[37] Lacan (as cited in Rutherford 2000) writes that repetition is a missed encounter with the real, an attempt to find a lost object and in doing so, to miss it.

[38] A senior inspector wrote of her teaching in 1952: "Your enlightened outlook on education is producing some very fine results" (*I Passed This Way*, 329).

[39] "Difficult Woman," *New Zealand Women's Weekly*, August 20, 1962. The article also described Ashton-Warner as a "cranky, complicated, ultra-feminine, sensual woman."

[40] She was impulsive and keen for those around her not to fear this impulsiveness. Thus she wrote to her friend Barbara Dent: "I think I shall be writing to you a lot for a short time. I love to see an impulse run full. So seldom happens to be possible. Accept my ways, Sylvia"; and later, "Write to me a lot more. Relax in me. Accept my ways. My love, Sylvia" (Alexander Turnbull Library, MS Papers 5594–1, E2L6). In a piece marked '3.30pm Wed Selah' she writes: "dancing alone, drink to Beethoven—it makes for 'significant living'…how damaging is compulsion. Let it come when it is ready—at its own chosen time—not mine." And elsewhere she writes:

> I don't practice honesty strictly. It's so secure. And security is such an enemy. It clogs. Security in a friend. Security in love. It clogs. It's the insecurity of emotional honesty—of love that prods, spurs to action—stimulates. There is only one teacher besides fine art and that is torture. And torture comes from insecurity, in either the self preservation or the racial instinct. (Alexander Turnbull Library, MS Papers, 5594–1, E19L3)

> I found comfort in you and you ONLY because of your magnificent lunacy… O how lonely we can be among these monstrosities of drooling sanity. I'm so happy on my own with my pathetic work that possibly only you and yours will ever understand. (Alexander Turnbull Library, MS Papers 5594–1, E19L3)

[41] Ashton-Warner underlined the following passages in a review of Leon Edel's *Stuff of Sleep and Dreams, Experiments in Literary Psychology* (R. Z. Sheppard, "Secrets of Creative Nightmares," *Time*, May 24, 1982): "the unconscious of most writers remains a dark mystery of anxiety and chaos" and "an artist must care more about what he makes than what he is" (Alexander Turnbull Library, MS Papers 3437, exercise book dated March–May 1975; notes, quotations and loose leafed papers).

References

Ashton-Warner, S. 1958. *Spinster*. Repr. London: Virago, 1980.
———. 1963. *Teacher*. Repr. New York: Simon and Schuster, 1986.
———. 1966. *Greenstone*. New York: Simon and Schuster.
———. 1968. *Myself*. London: Secker and Warburg.
———. 1979. *I Passed this Way*. New York: Knopf.
Ben-Peretz, M. 1995. *Learning from experience: Memory and the teacher's account of teaching*. Albany, NY: State University of New York Press.
Blaustein, J., prod., and Walters, C., dir. 1961. *Two loves*. USA: MGM.
Bond, R. 1980. Review of *I passed this way*. *National Education*. 115.
Brickman, C. 2003. *Aboriginal populations in the mind: Race and primitivity in psychoanalysis*. New York: Columbia University Press.

Britzman, D. 1998. *Lost subjects, contested objects: Toward a psychoanalytic inquiry of learning.* Albany: State University of New York Press.

——. 2000. If the story cannot end: Deferred action, ambivalence and difficult knowledge. In *Between hope and despair: Pedagogy and remembrance of historical trauma*, ed. R. Simon et al., 27–58. Lanham, MD: Rowman and Littlefield.

——. 2003. *After-education: Anna Freud, Melanie Klein and psychoanalytic histories of learning.* Albany: State University of New York Press.

Butler, J. 1997. *The psychic life of power: Theories in subjection.* Palo Alto, CA: Stanford University Press.

Caruth, C. 1995. Introduction to *Trauma: Explorations in memory*, ed. C. Caruth, 3–12. London: Johns Hopkins University Press.

——. 1996. *Unclaimed experience: Trauma, narrative and history.* London: Johns Hopkins University Press.

Chernaik, J. 1980. A true visionary. *New Society* 54: 244.

Difficult woman. 1962. *New Zealand Women's Weekly*, August 20.

Fabian, J. 1983. *Time and the other: How anthropology makes its object.* New York: Columbia University Press.

Felman, S. 1993. *What does a woman want? Reading and sexual difference.* London: Johns Hopkins University Press.

——. 2002. *The juridicial conscious: Trails and traumas in the twentieth century.* Cambridge, MA: Harvard University Press.

Felman, S., and D. Laub. 1992. *Testimony: Crises of witnessing in literature, psychoanalysis and history.* New York: Routledge.

Freud, S. 1899. Screen memories. Trans. by J. Strachey. Reprinted in *Standard edition of the complete psychological works of Sigmund Freud*, vol. 3, London: Hogarth Press,1962, 301–322.

——. 1908. Family romances. Trans. by J. Strachey. Reprinted in *Standard edition of the complete psychological works of Sigmund Freud*, vol. 9, 217–52. London: Hogarth Press, 1959.

——. 1913. *Totem and taboo. Some points of agreement between the mental life of savages and neurotics.* Trans. by J. Strachey. Reprinted in *Standard edition of the complete psychological works of Sigmund Freud*, vol. 13, London: Hogarth Press,1964.

——. 1930. *Civilisation and its discontents.* Trans. by J. Strachey, The Penguin Freud Library, 1991. 243–340.

——. 1939. *Moses and monotheism.* Trans. by J. Strachey. The Penguin Freud Library, London, 1990, 237–386.

Harrison, B. T. 1981. Organic teaching: Sylvia Ashton-Warner. *Literary Review.*

Hood, L. 1988. *Sylvia! The biography of Sylvia Ashton-Warner.* Auckland, New Zealand: Viking.

Lacan, Jacques. 1997. *The seminar of Jacques Lacan, book VII. The ethics of psychoanalysis, 1959-1960,* Trans. by Dennis Porter, ed. by Jacques-Alain Miller. NewYork: W.W. Norton and Co.

McConaghy, C. 2003. Curriculum and accountability in an age of trauma. Paper presented at the annual meeting of the American Educational Research Association, Chicago, IL.

Moscoso-Gongora, P. 1981. An educator's escape into art. *Chicago Tribune Book World.*

Newmann, F. and Associates. 1996. *Authentic achievement: Restructuring schools for intellectual quality.* San Francisco, CA: Jossey-Bass.

Phillips, A. 1994. *On flirtation.* London: Faber and Faber

94   *Cathryn McConaghy*

94   *Cathryn McConaghy*

———. 1997. Keeping it moving. In Butler, *The psychic life of power*, 151–59.

———. 1999. *Darwin's worms*. London: Faber and Faber.

———. 2001. *Houdini's box: The art of escape*. New York: Pantheon Books.

Pitt, A., and D. Britzman. 2000. Speculations on qualities of difficult knowledge in teaching and learning: An experiment in psychoanalytic research. Paper presented at the AESA Conference, Vancouver, Canada.

Review of *Myself*. 1968. *Christchurch Star*, December 7.

Reynolds, D., prod., and M. Firth, prod./dir. 1984. *Sylvia*. New Zealand: MGM/UA Classics Release.

Robertson, J. 2001. Art made tongue-tied by authority: A literary psychoanalysis of obstacles in teacher learning. *Journal of Curriculum Theorising* 17, no. 1: 27–44.

Rose, J. 2003. *On not being able to sleep: Psychoanalysis and the modern world*. London: Chatto and Windus.

Rutherford, J. 2000. *The gauche intruder: Freud, Lacan and the white Australia fantasy*. Melbourne, Australia: Melbourne University Press.

Shallcrass, J. 1969. Review of *Myself*. *New Zealand Listener* 1527: 16.

Simmons, M. 1980. Review of *I passed this way*. *Roanake Times and World News*, February 3.

Sylvia Ashton-Warner Archives. Alexander Turnbull Library, Wellington, New Zealand.

Sylvia. 1955. Organic reading and the key vocabulary. *National Education* 7, no. 406: 392–93.

———. 1956a. Organic reading is not new. *National Education* 8, no. 410: 141.

———. 1956b. Organic writing. *National Education* 8, no. 408: 54–55.

———. 1956c. Private key vocabularies. *National Education* 8, no. 407: 10–12.

Winnicott, D. 1972. *Playing and reality*. London: Tavistock.

Young-Bruehl, E. 1998. *From subject to biography: Psychoanalysis, feminism, and writing women's lives*. Cambridge, MA: Harvard University Press.

Žižek, S. 1998. Love thy neighbour? No, thanks! In *The psychoanalysis of race*, ed. C. Lane, 154–75. New York: Columbia University Press.

CHAPTER FIVE

InSide/OutSide Cultural Hybridity: Greenstone *as Narrative Provocateur*

Tess Moeke-Maxwell
*(*Ngati Pukeko *and* Ngai Tai–*Umupuia)*

Toward evening—we know it is evening—a canoe puts off from the bank of That Side and sets off over the river. In it are Huia and Memory and Sire paddling back from That Side to This, all chanting a paddle song the old one has recently taught them, keeping instinctive time with the paddles, which is one sure time they know any instinctive rhythm. It is in Maori of course.

> Behold my paddle!
> See how it flies and flashes;
> It quivers like a bird's wing
> This paddle of mine....

But as they reach This Side landing an unrest stirs in Huia. Her allegiance to her Koro on That Side confronts her feeling for Puppa on This Side. In the crossing of the polished surface of the river is the crossing from the brown to the white, although she's too young to know it, and the emotional racial transition is not polished like the face of the river holding the gray of the sky in her waters and the glamorous gold of the trees; it is something with smudges on it, something with jagged angles. The racial transition is a sunken branch cutting the mirror surface. (*Greenstone*, 63–64)

In this chapter, I offer a rereading of Maori women's identity by utilizing Ashton-Warner's progressive ideas embodied in the biracial character Huia. By discussing the complexities and limitations encoded in Ashton-Warner's articulation of Maori women's identity, I will explore cultural stereotypes and notions of third space. Postcolonial theorist Homi Bhabha (1990) recognizes that hybridity "is the 'third space' which enables other subject positions to emerge displacing the histories that constitute it as well as setting up new structures of authority and political initiatives. The outcome is a different and unrecognizable area of negotiation of meaning and representation" (211). Conceptually, hybridity is liberating because it opens up a space to interrogate the way New Zealand colonial culture creates unequal subjects. It is emancipatory in that its construction and performance free the subject from a sense of dislocation, alienation, and partial participation within the culture/s of origin. Bi/multiracial women straddle two opposing cultures, making chameleon-like changes to hybridize. Theorizing the "third space" initiates insight and wisdom. Without being too utopian, I argue that bi/racial women have an advantage in reading/making sense of their cultural differences and ambiguities within the postcolonial nation. The hybrid opens up a new category of cultural location. It is inclusive in that it initiates new signs of identity and collaborative sites where new contestations occur (Bhabha 1994).

Accessing Huia's biraciality, I question a quintessential articulation of Maori women's identity in favor of a more complex reading through a feminist and postcolonial perspective. I highlight how Maori women are socially constructed and positioned spatially within the neocolonial nation through the deployment of a racialized and gendered axis that finds its roots in colonialism. In short, Ashton-Warner enables an alternative reading of Maori women's agency and emancipation through her insightful descriptions of Huia's biraciality and diaspora. Maori women, I suggest, are not merely subject to prescriptive unified racial and gendered identities but are agents in their quest to construct and mediate meaningful, albeit complex, subjectivities.

Presented in two sections, the first, "This Side, InSide, That Side, OutSide," contains the flow of my argument, utilizing Ashton-Warner's novel *Greenstone.* I demonstrate how Huia is positioned as a bi/multiracial hybrid while showing how the bi/multiracial female is constructed and positioned spatially within the neocolonial nation. I also show how cultural and gendered relationships are formed and how the bi/multiracial woman negotiates the tensions that arise between Maori and Pakeha/Other men, and Maori and Pakeha/Other women. This rereading demonstrates how the hybrid becomes discursively positioned to take up a borderland existence, living between, InSide, and OutSide the landscapes of This Side and That Side contained within her sense of self. The second and shorter section, "Embracing Maori Women's Hybridity," considers some of the current issues concerning Maori women's cultural hybridity in the new millennium. Ashton-Warner's relationship to cultural hybridity is also highlighted.

This Side, InSide, That Side, OutSide

Ashton-Warner's text recognizes the position of the hybrid through the character Huia, who became estranged from her parents when her Pakeha father left to fight in World War I; her Maori mother, Kaa, died after Huia was born. Ashton-Warner describes Huia as "not even half Maori but only a quarter" (*Greenstone*, 52). Both Maori and Pakeha, emphasized in the nurturing relationships she has with both her Maori grandfather and her surrogate father—portrayed in the character of her Pakeha grandfather—Huia lives most of her life as Pakeha in the landscape of This Side. She has white colonial genealogy, cultural history, and lifestyle. She lives with her Puppa (who adores her) and his Pakeha wife, Mrs. Considine (who hates her). They live in a small North Island rural settlement along with Puppa and Mrs. Considine's numerous children. Huia's female Maori relatives died during childbirth due to a makutu placed on them. Huia is the last female in their bloodline. Her Koro lives on That Side, the Other side of the river, in the traditional landscape of his *tupuna*. The makutu also manifests itself in the form of Puppa's illness. Both her Maori and Pakeha families are victims of an angry tohunga who resented the interracial intercourse between a Maori woman and a Pakeha man—Huia's grandparents.

Huia's hybridity is depicted in her constant coming and going across the river enroute to her two worlds (roots/homes) via the body of water that divides her whanau. Susan Friedman (1998) explores the homonym routes/roots to express a concept of cultural hybridity that takes into account the traveling between physical places of belonging/home. Identities are formed, she suggests, from a sense of displacement from home: home is recognized/known when absent. Huia's traveling between her dual homes brings a simultaneous sense of dislocation and rootedness.

Huia is torn between two worlds—her love of Koro and Puppa. An anxiety is created that needs to be acted out and simultaneously contained. Huia is split between This Side (living in the Pakeha world) and That Side (visiting her Maori great-grandfather). Her mother and father found love for each other in the rural landscape of the "ngati Te Renga Renga" people, Huia's iwi. Not permitted to marry, they would steal away to a small whare in the forest where Huia was eventually conceived.

Huia is defined by the paternal young male in the story, Togi, as "the next rangatira of the ngati Te Renga Renga and heir to all its lands" (*Greenstone*, 30). Ashton-Warner writes, "Returned at last from the First World War, [Togi] keeps both eyes on Huia" (*Greenstone*, 31). Huia is exoticized from infancy: "Her skin is almost as white as Flower's but her hair and her eyes give the Maori blood away. She is a very pretty child with a full top lip and eyes like canoes tethered at an angle" (*Greenstone*, 32). Huia loves her Puppa and identifies with him in his pain/anxiety. Ashton-Warner describes Puppa as follows:

He has one of these aquiline turned-down noses you find in the aristocracy, while behind his glasses his eyes can only be described as English blue. Possibly the term "English" can account for the whole impression; his face has the fine complexion and coloring often bred in the English climate, a fresh but fragile face. (*Greenstone*, 15)

Puppa is portrayed as a broken remnant of an aristocratic Englishman, highlighted in this description, "[b]ut look at his locked body. Rheumatoid arthritis as we know it but according to the Maoris in the valley it is the 'limb-withering' curse of the tohunga makutu" (*Greenstone*, 15). Again, Ashton-Warner notes: "He is locked at the hips too so that his whole thin body is a zigzag drawing of what a man's body should be, but you only see this when he gets up on his crutches, a far from graceful performance" (*Greenstone*, 16).

Further, Puppa's wife (Huia's surrogate mother) is referred to by Huia as "Flower's Mumma." Transferring the "mother" to her young Pakeha relative enables Huia to distance herself from a maternal relationship to the woman who has the responsibility to care for her yet despises her. Ashton-Warner reveals the surrogate mother's ambivalent attitude towards Huia when Mrs. Considine says to Puppa, "The less I see of that brown rat the better" (*Greenstone*, 22). She further expresses contempt for Huia to Puppa: "D'you expect me, a trained teacher, t'recognize a dirty little Maori? D'you expect me, a respectable woman, t'bow and scrape to a savage?" (*Greenstone*, 23). Ashton-Warner's attempt to explore the complex relationships between Maori and Pakeha women and the interplay of power invested in their respective gendered and racial status finds its expression in notions of brownness/native/Maori and whiteness/civilized/Pakeha.

As stated, Huia's biological mother, Kaa, is dead. In fact, all Maori women are absent from the story. Kaa is portrayed as a woman whose sexuality/femininity was out of control. Strong images of Huia's Koro appear every so often, representing the last of his people and the withering lands, subject of/to colonialism. His desperate need for Huia to reproduce the Maori race/iwi is etched in his every action toward her. He is presented as the emasculated noble savage and as the dying rangatira/nation. He looks to Huia to be the new hope/healer for his people's revival, to end the curse placed on Maori women during childbirth. She must save Maori from extinction.

River/Land Crossings and the Discourses of Colonialism and Nationalism

Colonization, imperialism, and assimilation positioned Maori as the disenfranchised other to the normative white masculine rational subject (Awatere 1984; Irwin 1992; Kelsey 1984; Orange 1987; Sinclair 1986; Smith 1998; Walker 1987, 1990). The invention of the New Zealand nation and national community relied upon a commonsense understanding of what it meant to be a

New Zealander (c.f. Anderson 1983). Nationalism required the subjugation of Maori difference in order to imagine a homogeneous community (Mohanram 1999). However, this white monocultural national identity needed the brown/Maori body to formulate its self against that body (Yeatman 1995). In a signifying chain of meaning, Pakeha could only come into representation as the universal subject if Maori were to carry signification of difference (c.f. Hall 1997). Ann Stoler (1995) states: "Nationalist discourse drew on and gave force to a wider politics of exclusion. This version was not concerned solely with the visual markers of difference, but with the relationship between visible characteristics and invisible properties, outer form and inner essence" (8).

The insidiousness of colonialism can be metaphorically related to Ashton-Warner's mysterious river. Her thoughts on biculturalism were most likely inspired through her experiences of living near the Whanganui River, which she traveled by canoe, enroute to her respective destinations. No doubt Ashton-Warner's relationships with local Maori functioned as a precursor to her ideas on cultural hybridity. Certainly, her insight into Huia's world/s would suggest a personal experience of Maori culture, highlighted in Huia's cultural vacillation. During her formative years, Ashton-Warner traveled between the relatively simple rural Maori lifestyle of Pipiriki to the Western landscape of the schoolhouse located on the Other side of the river. The combination of competing landscapes provided the crisscrossing of cultural experiences, which ensured her interest in both Maori and education. Her ability to speak te reo Maori and her participation in Maori rituals while teaching in Pipiriki from 1941–1945 no doubt deepened her own sense of Pakeha/Maori hybridity.

Ashton-Warner provides an inspired gendered reading of Maori identity, which was probably informed by her early exposure to biraciality and cultural hybridity through her observations and experiences/merging of/with local tangata whenua. Having been situated as an interlocutor between Maori and Pakeha during the 1940s, she was well placed during the 1960s to understand Maori's desire to challenge the national myth that suggested that Maori and Pakeha are "one people." The insights she gained enabled a provocative reading of colonialism that pre-empted postcolonial articulations of Maori cultural hybridity by nearly half a century (Collins 1999; Meridith 1999a, 1999b, 1999c; Moeke-Maxwell 2003).

Ashton-Warner's attempt to invoke a cautionary relationship between biracial Huia and the river highlights the discursive tensions Huia confronts in the colonial relationship: "The racial transition is a sunken branch cutting the mirror surface" (*Greenstone*, 64). These tensions find their roots in a sense of alienation that accompanies the cultural diaspora highlighted in *Greenstone* via the use of dominant binaries: pre-colonialism/colonialism; modernity/post-modernity; rural/urban; brownness/whiteness; masculinity/femininity. These binaries are encapsulated by imagery contained in and between This Side and That Side. The sense of mystery and force that Ashton-Warner attaches to the river finds its origins in the colonial condition, whereby the discourse/s of colonialism masquerade normatively as progress and development while upholding the imperatives of individualism, imperialism, and capitalism. Such imperatives are symbolized in Pakeha nationalism, practiced in monoculturalism, and signified by white bodies. Symbolically, a baby of potential prosperity suckles at the breast of colonialism while cradled in its discursive arms of progress. The river's mystery is realized in New Zealand's future body. Whose body is being suckled? Whose body will grow/develop normatively in the new nation, and who will benefit?

Simultaneously, river/colonialism must conceal the violence it levies at a communal Maori people in its forceful colonizing trajectory. Ashton-Warner recognizes that the brown tribal body must forgo its collectivity, its communalism, and its tribal resources if colonialism is to prosper in Aotearoa/New Zealand. In this difficult landscape, hybrid Huia must live, in the treacherous and dichotomous terrain of capitalism versus collectivism, individualism versus tribalism, whiteness versus brownness, and masculinity versus femininity. To survive, she must find a way to move beyond her biracial and bicultural difference. She must evolve beyond the respective racialized and gendered cultural prerequisites contained within notions of Maoriness and Pakehaness embedded deep within colonial nationalism.

Huia must negotiate the essence of the river/colonialism's current to make her Maori and Pakeha/Other border crossings possible. Enroute to her respective bicultural roots/landscapes, she is confronted with the undercurrents directing the river/colonialism. An undercurrent of fear pervades traversing over water. How deep/engulfing is it? How swift/violent is it? Will Huia drown, be swept away? Will the "New Race" become extinguished before the colonial offspring have a chance to thrive? Danger lurks as the children (the future nation) manage to negotiate the unknown danger. River/colonialism's point of departure symbolizes the beginning of colonization. Its flowing body carries a new history of Aotearoa. It glides into the future seen, yet unseen; known, yet unknown; recognized, yet unrecognized.

River/colonialism moves swiftly, with cold intent. So natural, it almost appears disinterested, innocently masquerading as a detached observer of all that is performed on both sides of its banks/borders. Colonialism calls Pakeha and Maori into being (prescribes identity) through its discursive practices (such as the discourse/s of education) by recognizing, naming, and placing subjects according to their race, gender, and class. Judith Butler (1990, 1993) illuminates the place of discourse as interlocutor in the social construction of gendered subjectivity when she suggests that subjects, once called into being, perform the very subjectivities they are subjectivized with. Highly specific identities are prescripted based on gender, race, and class specificities.

Nationalism's agendas must ensure the ongoing re/production of its national body, signified in white majority Pakeha culture. But in order for the colonial nation to reproduce itself, it must firstly have a definable body to reproduce itself against (Mohanram 1999). Hence, dominant subjects (colonial/Pakeha/white/male) require subjugated identities (colonized/Maori/brown/female) to form their difference against. Like mainstream New Zealand nationalism, river/colonialism needs a (di)vision (This Side and That Side) to flow through, in between its body, to determine identity. Nationalism relies upon an identity that is formed through notions of sameness forged through Pakeha difference to Maori (Sinclair 1986); it survives on the division between Maori and Pakeha cultures and their respective brown and white bodies. To survive, the separate landscapes/bodies must not touch. To merge would bring a withering, a drying-up, and a winding d-o-w-n to river/neocolonialism. River winds down toward and past the present (This Side and That Side), toward its confident (perhaps unstoppable) future trajectory. It is a constantly changing yet consistent current/flow. River/colonialism ensures This Side/Pakeha/white and That Side/Maori/brown are separated—condemned to view each other across a deep divide of make-believe (and yet real) difference.

New Zealand's shift to biculturalism during the 1980s was influenced through counternationalist efforts to argue for Maori sovereignty, in a bid to reduce Maori socioeconomic disadvantage (Awatere 1984; Mohanram 1999; Walker 1990; Yeatman 1995). A quintessential Maori identity was invoked to resurrect the Treaty of Waitangi (a peace treatise between iwi and the Crown). In 1840, over five hundred chiefs/iwi representatives and Crown signatories signed the four treaties that circulated the country. One version of the treaty was written in English and was semantically different from the second, Te Tiriti, which was written in Maori. Te Tiriti expressed the Crown's commitment to honor Maori self-determination and governance over tribal lands and resources. However, racial tension grew during the mid-1800s, as the Treaty of Waitangi gave authority to the Crown's agents to govern Aotearoa without respecting tangata whenua's rights. Eventually, the treaty was legally nullified, and Maori lost their legal right to protest against the injustices they faced. Consequently, iwi lost the majority of their lands, fisheries, and natural resources (Walker 1990). The impact on Maori infrastructures and communities was devastating. Maori counternationalists sought no less than the reinstatement of the principles encoded in the Treaty of Waitangi, which they hoped would provide some recourse to the injustices.

The development of the Waitangi Tribunal provided an important role in the Crown's recognition of iwi grievances by advising the Crown on reparative justice issues (Christianos, Tepania-Carter and Te Whanau O Waipareira 2001; Pearson 1990, 1991; Sharp 1995). Maori represented themselves in essentialist terms through citing genealogical links to tupuna and their lands, thus highlighting their unchanged status over time as tangata whenua (Christianos et al. 2001; Mohanram 1999). Emancipation was sought through economic development initiatives alongside Pakeha (Sharp 1990, 1995). Through Chatterjee's (1990, 1993) ideas on Indian women and nationalism, it can be argued that the task of reproducing the timeless Maori national community became the responsibility of Maori women, epitomized in their reconstruction as traditional and the cornerstone of Maoridom. They have been imagined as synonymous with nature/reproduction and timelessness/spirituality, while Maori men, as liberated disembodied agents, have been allowed to vacillate across cultures, thus enabling them to negotiate the changing terrain of the material/marketplace.

Inscribed with brownness, this revamped Maori identity mirrored Pakeha rationality, progress, and development: an identity symbolized by whiteness. The racial tensions of the 1970s and 1980s diminished as Maori men/iwi forged new relationships with Pakeha men in the marketplace. Women were left to carry the responsibility of reproducing the Maori community and its culture. The Crown needed to defuse the tension in the nation, while *iwi* needed to position themselves as corporate players in an environment of neoliberal capitalism (Mohanram 1999). Both were locked into a market-driven relationship. Within this new patriarchal alignment, the bi/multiracial woman was and is unrepresented in narratives of what it means to be a Maori woman in the early 2000s.

As in Ashton-Warner's character Huia, bi/multiracial women's voices differ from those women positioned solely as Maori or Pakeha. Through Huia, Ashton-Warner exemplifies a different subjectivity to traditional Maori women. Further, Huia's character shows that bi/multiracial women's subjectivity is different from Pakeha/Other women by virtue of their mixed racial ancestry and cultural hybridity. Ashton-Warner highlights how bi/multiracial Maori women become located in multiple landscapes and become subjected with dual cultural identities.

Huia provides a rare opportunity to read biraciality and cultural hybridity through a Pakeha/female lens. Through her diasporic positioning as a Pakeha female crisscrossing the Maori/rural landscape of the Whanganui River enroute to school/home, as well as observing and associating with her Maori peers, Ashton-Warner's sense of dislocation produces her own experience of cultural hybridity. This intrudes upon the historical landscape of the text and uncannily disrupts the neat cultural borders popular after World War II, concealed in New Zealand's national rhetoric "we are one people." Ashton-Warner's ability to play with time exposes a dual cultural positioning via hybrid Huia, allowing a reading of the third space to emerge.

Hybridity exists in the in-between spaces between the colonized and colonial culture. Bhabha (1990) claims the third space holds the possibility of emancipation in that this liminal space provides room for the hybrid subject to act outside the colonial authority. This, he suggests, enables the hybrid to have some agency, by turning the colonial gaze back to the colonizer. Bi/multiracial Maori women like Huia are able to perform their excess difference in ways that are unrecognized by the colonial authority. Like others, Huia usurps the bicultural imperative for pure Maori and Pakeha subjects. She is the excess that exceeds the colonial relationship.

Ashton-Warner presents an uncomfortable terrain when she invites the reader to journey into Huia's world. The bi/multiracial woman's identity is a familiar yet foreign landscape. The language, representations, characters, and cultural symbols are provocative in their ability to disrupt the boundaries between the conceptual categories of Maori and Pakeha. In essence, she questions who gets to be Maori and Pakeha in the postcolonial nation and pre-empts current articulations of Maori identity and authenticity.

InSideness

My efforts at engaging with the text are directed toward pushing against the imagery and metaphors evoked by Ashton-Warner to explore the possibilities and limitations of the third space as a place of emancipation. My desire in positioning myself on the bi/multiracial borderlands, between Maoriness/ Pakehaness and brownness/whiteness, is to create a space where my own Maori/Pakeha racial and cultural formations greet Ashton-Warner as narrative provocateur. The intention is to excite a reading of *Greenstone* through deploying a lens of liminality and narrative representation informed by a bi/multiracial Maori, feminist, and postcolonial conceptual lens.

Located on the border between Maori and Pakeha/Other cultures, bi/multiracial women negotiate new forms of colonialism emerging out of newly formed bicultural relationships and patriarchal alliances. This reconfigured wave of power is symbolized by Ashton-Warner's river flow. In her plurality of cultural difference, the hybrid is positioned with the skills to operate in multiple discourses—her conversations collapse the binary myths upon which colonialism/river sustains itself. As Linda McDowell (1999) writes:

> Instead of the identities of "oppositional" or "minority" groups being constructed as different from a "norm," it is now asserted that all identities are a fluid amalgam of memories of places and origins, constructed by and through fragments and nuances,

journeys and rests, of movements between. Thus, the "in-between" is itself a process or a dynamic, not just a stage on the way to a more final identity. (215)

The bi/multiracial woman speaks in multiple voices and hears multiple conversations via her location as Maori and Pakeha/Other in both the national and Maori community (Moeke-Maxwell 2003). She interprets, translates, negotiates, and mediates between That Side and This Side through the conduit of her InSide corpo/reality (c.f. Foster 1996). With her "eyes like canoes tethered at an angle" (*Greenstone*, 32), hybrid Huia has the advantage of seeing both sides of the river simultaneously as she crisscrosses between competing landscapes. Her peripheral vision (seeing with two sets of eyes) gives her insight and advantage. By the nature of her InSideness, the bi/multiracial's body functions as a place that cannot be incarcerated to That Side, This Side, or any Other side.

Her InSideness (sense of internal coherence) is only possible if she can mediate her OutSideness—multiple spatial positionings and cultural contradictions. Her unique racial differences (presence/absence of whiteness) signify her as either Maori (absence of whiteness) or Pakeha (presence of whiteness). The bi/multiracial mediates her dual/multicultural signification and the stereotypes associated to raced and deraced bodies by locating herself in either Pakeha or Maori color-coded cultural spaces. But the biracial woman is more than This Side or That Side (Maori and Pakeha) because she is an excess of both. She experiences herself as *both* Maori and Pakeha—albeit at different times and within different cultural contexts and landscapes. As such, she has the ability to move beyond the binary categories embedded within the stereotypes (and cultural landscapes) that accompany signifiers of Maori difference (brownness) and signifiers of Pakehaness (whiteness). She engages with the stereotypes and the spatial locatedness that accompany her raced/deraced body. The biracial woman usurps the cultural imperative contained within notions of Maori and Pakeha identity by refusing to align with a singular cultural identity. Her dual subjectivity prevents her from coming into representation as solely Maori or Pakeha. Huia exemplifies how the biracial female survives colonization and interracial contact by embracing her difference.

Ashton-Warner acknowledges the disenfranchisement of tangata whenua. She links the changing face/identity of Maori through her articulation of Huia's identity. Ashton-Warner recognizes (through the makutu placed on child-bearing women) that as soon as Maori women come into representation via the symbolic birthing process, the mother/landscape dies—is taken away. Thus, Maori become emasculated, disenfranchised, and agency-less (Awatere 1984; Walker 1990). Traditional Maori women function as a metaphor for the land symbolized in the earth mother, Papatuanuku, and emphasized in the dual meaning of the word "whenua," which means both "land" and "placenta." The message is clear:

landless Maori cannot survive in colonized Aotearoa. Huia is cleverly positioned as the leader of an evolving postcolonial culture. She is the excess of her respective whakapapa.

Positioned between Maori and Pakeha/Other cultures, the bi/multiracial woman functions as the new body/landscape upon which the Pakeha and Maori nations construct their identity. Symbolically, her body is the landscape where both Maori and Pakeha exist separately yet remain connected. Her difference plays a critical role as the body that gives identity/meaning to the reconfigured, tribal, and settler cultures. By extension, her difference (racial impurity) provides the borders that give Pakeha/Other men, Maori men, Pakeha/Other women, and traditional Maori women their cultural meaning. Her difference is subjugated and her existence denied, yet both the Maori and colonial nation desire her cultural "impurity" to construct themselves (via the traditional Maori woman's body) as culturally thriving entities (Mohanram 1999). Dead cultures cannot compete in corporate development! The bi/multiracial provides the departure from all that is essentially essential to Maori and Pakeha culture. In a signifying chain of cultural meaning, founded upon notions of sameness and difference, she is the difference that Pakeha and Maori construct their respective difference against (c.f. Hall 1997). She is the difference that must be subjugated in order for Maori to come into representation.

The bi/multiracial woman is an uncanny interlocutor who calls both Maori and Pakeha into being, thus permitting a new patriarchal alliance to sustain itself. The uncanny arouses a sense of the familiar while simultaneously invoking dread and terror (Freud 1955). In her ability to carry the mark of difference/duality, the biracial functions as a place that is recognized/known and signifies that which is familiar/home. However, the desire to return to that which is familiar/home (precolonial time, racial purity) haunts and evades the dissatisfied observer. The desire/necessity for the bi/multiracial woman's body of difference must be denied in order to ensure that the recently placated cultural tensions of the 1970s and 1980s continue. Contained within the capacity to carry a double semantic, the biracial woman's body becomes a site that invokes ambivalence. Her femininity and Maoriness is recognized/familiar, but her biracial hybridity is unknown/feared. An uncanny response is produced in the nation. Her presence (excess of difference) provokes that which ought to be repressed—evidence of racial impurity caused through the social intercourse between Maori and Pakeha.

Pathologized Other

Bi/multiracial woman can only come into representation through the dominant narratives available to her, either traditional narratives or their pathologized cousin, epitomized in a colonized identity. This is evidenced in the passage where Huia's father associates her brown body with badness:

> "If you don't behave yourself", gently enough from Daniel, "I'll send you back to the pa. It strikes me, young lady, that you've got more of your great-grandfather's melancholy in you than is good for you. You seem to have more *Maori* in you than *appears in your face*. Now pull yourself together, my lady, and behave yourself. If I come this way again and find you misbehaving I'll take down your pants and smack your bottom and send you back to the pa." (*Greenstone*, 81, italics added)

In this quotation, two dominant cultural representations of Huia are invoked to highlight the tension between stereotypical narratives of Maori and Pakeha identity. Ashton-Warner indicates the embodied place of race/color in cultural stereotypes through statements like "she hangs her black head" (*Greenstone*, 81), where Huia's black head emphasizes Maoriness/badness. Huia's black/Maori head is symbolized in pathological terms; she is constructed as melancholic/lazy, out of control, and has bad behavior. Butler (1990) explains "the culturally dominated suffer a paradoxical oppression in that they are both marked out by stereotypes at the same time they are rendered invisible. Their essence is attached to their bodies quite naturally" (59).

Huia achieves proximity to being a Pakeha girl (associated with whiteness) the more desirable her behavior is. Ashton-Warner illustrates that Huia must be good/Pakeha if she is to become liberated from modernity. If not, her father's intention is to incarcerate her in premodernity along with her Maori grandfather and his waka. Caught on the racial and cultural borderlands between Maori and Pakeha, Huia suffers the effects of racism. When the bi/multiracial woman comes into representation via these two narratives (the premodern/traditional and the modern/Pakeha), she is without agency. Relegated to the landscape of a traditional Maori woman's subjectivity (with all the cultural norms that seek to regulate and control her body), Huia is without agency to be positioned in alternative cultural contexts. A Maori identity requires that the specificities of her multiple identities are excluded (Collins 1999). For the bi/multiracial hybrid, either/or cultural stereotypes deny the subject her unique experiential differences as female, Maori, and Pakeha/Other.

The contemporary "Maori nation" promotes itself as a homogeneous community that has the responsibility to protect its disparate members by ensuring that iwi develop normatively through the conduit of the capitalist corporate economy. The success of the newly reconfigured, upwardly mobile iwi/corporations underscores the fact that the discursive processes of colonialism have historically disenfranchised all Maori, including those not represented by their *iwi* (Christianos et al. 2001). I return to Huia's story to illustrate the exclusion of bi/multiracial women.

Huia is caught between her Koro's desire of her (focused on saving the Maori community/nation from extinction) and her Pakeha Puppa's attachment towards her. A symbolic war is waged inside her body as it shifts and changes landscapes to accommodate the needs of the emasculated paternal figureheads, symbolizing precolonial times epitomized in the dying Koro/noble savage and his counterpart, the British patriarch. Neither can survive the new world that has intruded upon them and ended their respective glory days. Hybrid Huia is the Maori nation's only hope of surviving the ravages of colonialism. Her spirit is fed by the wise old Chief; she is the promise that her people will replenish Aotearoa through her reproductive potential (c.f. Anthias and Yuval-Davis 1989). Positioned as an interlocutor in bicultural hot spots, the bi/multiracial woman is torn between loyalties to Maori and Pakeha communities and to those who represent them (Moeke-Maxwell 2003).

White Women, Bi/Multiracial Women, White Men

"But, what is this? Huia's heart is tuned to her Pakeha grandfather [...], her mind is full of Puppa and the touching image of him. Is he all right? she wonders." (*Greenstone*, 64)

Huia finds herself caught between the white man and his wife. The ailing white patriarch is juxtaposed against the strong white Pakeha woman. Ashton-Warner writes: "'Mumma, he's at the door', from the children diving under tables and beds. Not 'Puppa, he's at the door'; in the final count it is she who is the protector as well as the breadwinner" (*Greenstone*, 75). Huia wants to protect her emasculated grandfather from losing his power to his wife's strong, articulate, able-bodied, reproductive, white, educated authority. Huia rushes to disrupt the beating Puppa receives. A dichotomy is formed between the prolific prowess of the white woman (she produces baby after baby, thus creating the new Pakeha national community) and the Maori woman who dies in her reproductive moment. Caught between these polarities, Huia stands full of reproductive potential. She challenges the dominance of Flower's Mother (that is, the Pakeha nation) to stop killing Puppa (former British dominance) when she states, "Don't hit Puppa, Flower's mother" (*Greenstone*, 65). Huia presents as the future, a synthesis of Maori, British colonial, and Pakeha history—an antithesis to the gendered and racialized war waged on the belly of Papatuanuku.

The British man's metaphoric castration is laid at the feet of his Pakeha/white wife. But remember his withering was caused by the tohunga's makutu; his immobility/paralysis finds its origin in the curse. His Pakeha wife's disdain of him is a projection of her own sense of castration/lack of power. His body is immobilized, ugly. The white woman violently beats against his brokenness. She is angry; why does she have to be responsible for producing (giving birth) and reproducing (working, parenting, teaching, nurturing) the new nation of his white children? Silently, he dreams of the day his mobility/agency will return. But his children, the future nation, know it never will. His body, symbolic of his once-proud British culture, can never be again. His aristocratic bloodline cannot prosper in this new landscape. The decline of British nobility/authority is symbolized in his withered legs. In the landscape of Aotearoa he lacks his own turangawaewae.

Huia functions as an interlocutor not only between brown and white peoples and landscapes, but also between white men and women. The white woman has hatred and jealousy toward her. It is Huia's responsibility to *perform* the brown/dirty, pathologized body upon which the white woman constructs her own sense of gender/identity. Huia is positioned to save Maori from the plight of colonialism/extinction. But what is less obvious is that she is also positioned as the one to save white men (the dying patriarchy) from white women, who function as the female authority, the reconfigured dominant cultural signifier. Somehow Hybrid Huia's brown/white corporeal presence is needed to interrupt the violent conversations among white/Pakeha men and women. Her tinana is needed to placate the tension of the white woman's authority over the white man and to simultaneously reflect the white man's authority over the white woman and brown Maori Other. But the white man is emasculated and entirely dependent on the white woman for survival. The virility of the new colonial nation depends on the white woman's gendered performance (reproduction and domesticity) to provide the nation with labor, while demarcating the boundary between the public and private worlds of its citizens. The colonial nation is crippled, illustrated in the f/ailing patriarch, Puppa. Maori have used the only resource left to retaliate against their colonialist perpetrators, makutu. It is up to Huia to traverse the river, heal the divide, and remove the makutu.

Huia's Koro is stuck on the Other side (That Side) of the river, where he is incarcerated by his disenfranchisement. Trapped in the past along with his dying women/nation, tied to the flora and fauna of his traditional home, he is immobilized, nativized, fixed (c.f. Appadurai 1988). Similarly, on the Other side of the river (This Side) the white children (new colonial nation) are tied to their New Zealand rural landscape and cultural traditions. Only Huia's body/waka can negotiate between these points of difference; her mind and soul belong, breathe, and are at home in these two different worlds, now related via the processes of colonialism.

It is not accidental that Huia lacks a relationship with living Maori women. Rather, it symbolizes the death of the old world—the bones of its mothers lie deep in the soil of Papatuanuku. This mysterious absence is explained in Huia's ability to reproduce a new hybrid nation. This new nation must be able to contain the flaxen essence of the past, as well the new woolen fiber of the present. But who is this young patriarch Togi, who shows interest and adoration towards the young Hybrid Huia? Healthy and strong (virulent), he protects Huia the baby, cares for her as a toddler, watches over her as a child, and is fascinated by her exotic beauty. Huia's youth/beauty is a metaphor for the new nation's evolution and potential development. She is watched over and coveted by many men; a f/ailing white patriarch, a dying Koro, and the future patriarchy symbolized in Togi. It is Togi who will take over redefining Huia to suit his/nation's desires. Her transformative abilities (cultural hybridity) are a source of desire for the white and brown, old and new patriarchs, and act as a constant thread that binds them into commonality. Her body is the affinity they share, the focus of their desire, the necessity of their mutually exclusive success.

InSide the OutSide

Represented without recourse to agency, is Huia condemned to dance like a monkey to the tune of her brown/white patriarchal organ grinders? This phallocentric imagery conjures up her feminine vulnerability and her passive penetrability. Yet is the female Maori hybrid merely a victim in patriarchy's desirous interplay of power, or does she find a way to transport herself to another time and another place deep within her "self"? Bi/multiracial women, like other Maori, seek an *affinity* in the form of a narrative of wairuatanga, which is resilience forming (Kohu 1997; Pere 1991; Tai 1997). Hybrid Huia finds her answer in her visits to the ancient wharenui abandoned in the bush. It is a place that has known life and love. The "meeting house" is the place that witnessed Huia's conception as the aroha between her Maori mother and Pakeha father found an affinity in each other and became joined in spirit and one body. The result of this biracial union: Hybrid Huia. Ashton-Warner highlights Huia's return to her roots:

> It was here in this deserted meeting house that Huia was conceived. [...]
>
> As Togi makes his unerring way along the forgotten track, weaving like a tunnel through massive trunks overlaid with delicate creeper and between the frothing ground ferns, Flower and Sue trail him [...] he steps upon the veranda of this haunted place, lowers his head for the Maori door opening and penetrates the odorous gloom. And sure enough, just as in one of Puppa's stories, here they find Huia sleeping, tucked in a ball like a forest creature all but covered in hair. You can see little more beyond the hair than two bare feet [...]
>
> Flower and Sue do not run to the carved panels of the ancestors on the walls with their eerie paua-shell eyes; the gloomy atmosphere terrifies them. They remain together, touching each other, surveying [...] all but brushing off physically the spirits of the ancestors crowding invisibly around them. (*Greenstone*, 31–32)

Huia, like other bi/multiracial females, locates her difference via the construction of her own real (and metaphysical) turangawaewae. This is achieved through a reworlding of themselves via their intimate, spiritual relationships with tupuna. In Huia's case, her whanau of origin are symbolized in the presence of her dead mother and her beloved tupuna. In the absence of the nurturing Maori mother (Kaa)—an absence juxtaposed against the presence of the alienating white surrogate mother, her dying brown and white grandfathers, and the new patriarch Togi—Huia finds a place to rest and a place to call home. Her discarded and abandoned ancestral home provides refuge and shelter from the coming and going to her roots. The meeting house is just that: the space where she stands face to face with her tupuna, her history, her future. It is a homespace away from her Maori and Pakeha colonial landscapes, away from the endless river crossings, away from colonial relationships fraught with the gendered and racial interplay of power between the old and the new patriarchs, between brown/Maori and white/Pakeha/Other, between women and men. This sacred (resilient) space is OutSide This Side and That Side: it is InSide. The meeting house is a private place, a silent place—a space filled with the happy voices of her people as they remember themselves to her, gather her up into their arms and whisper, "E kare, haere mai."

Embracing Maori Women's Bi/Multiracial Hybridity

The problem with postmodern conversations is that they work against a universal truth, an unquestionable reality. Postcolonial articulations on Maori women's cultural hybridity can be uncomfortable and challenging in their sense of instability and unfixity. There is a new anxiety over who gets to be Maori "enough" (Meridith 1999a, 1999b, 1999c) and a fear that in talking about "individual" experiences of Maori women's cultural hybridity, the mana of Maori women will be usurped. Bi/multiracial hybridity threatens essentialist-driven Maori identity narratives by illustrating a universal presence and participation in things "un-Maori."

In her uncanny familiarity, the bi/multiracial woman metaphorically resembles "home," a landscape that is recognized and loved. However, she disrupts the designated places reserved for marked/brown bodies through her agency to move across cultural spaces, thus destabilizing the idea of fixed cultural boundaries and spaces. Her diaspora means she has multiple homes. Enroute, she is out of her racially designated cultural place. Yet her difference is perceived as a threat—it horrifies both Maori and Pakeha. Thus terrorized, the observer has to deny the presence/reality of the bi/multiracial woman in an effort to deny her existence. But she refuses to be fixed or located by the new patriarchal demands placed upon her. If she is absent from her "traditional" kitchen, who will take care of reproducing the Maori nation and enculturating future offspring with Maoriness? Who will be metonymic of the marae/traditional landscape if she is out vacillating? Who will carry the required difference for Maori to fashion their traditional identities against?

Ashton-Warner resolves this problem by placing Huia firmly into the tribal landscape of the Te Renga Renga peoples after the death of her Koro when she states:

> By the end of the week when the time comes to send the spirit of the old one to Hawaiki it is old Niki who clothes the new rangatira in the ceremonial cloak to speak the last lament and who places in her ears the precious jewel-stones [...] When at last old Niki is satisfied with it [her hair] and not one strand strays from its place, she fixes a taniko band around her head, low across the forehead above the brows, and in it places the huia feather, the symbol of her rank. The traditional flax puipui is, of course, too big for her, wraps around her waist twice and reaches below the calves of her legs, while the ceremonial cloak of kiwi touches the ground in places. Yet as she stands with the sun on her head and the reflections in her eyes, barefoot before the bier, she is indisputably a rangatira. (*Greenstone*, 208)

Positioned thus, Huia is subjected with the status/identity of tribal leader. Coming into representation as the Maori nation's future hope, Hybrid Huia is required to forfeit her ability to be represented as anything other than quintessentially Maori. Her bi/multiracial hybrid performance/s and borderland existence are subordinated to the colonial agenda, in which her bi/multiracial difference/hybridity is regulated, controlled, and ultimately denied. Unable to live with the uncanny tension that Hybrid Huia provokes in the psyche of the nation, Ashton-Warner removes Huia's agency to perform her bi/multiracial cultural diaspora. Huia is forced to return to modernity and live in a landscape of timelessness and tradition. Ironically, Ashton-Warner has her Pakeha family vacillate towards other landscapes and postmodern possibilities: "But when the Considines take off down-river on the last morning of summer they leave one of their name behind them; Huia Brice Considine stands on the landing holding with both hands her greenstone [the symbol of traditional landscape]" (*Greenstone*, 213).

Was Ashton-Warner's articulation of Huia's renativized and singular cultural identity a product of her visionary genius? The author's insight into the subjugations that bi/multiracial women face in the wake of the new millennium is refreshing and significant. However, I am left questioning whether her own white Pakeha woman's uneasiness concerning Maori women's bi/multiraciality created an uncanny desire to deny Huia's hybridity/existence? Huia's hybridity was ultimately disavowed and negated to the tribal landscape and origin of her residual difference/brownness. Given that Ashton-Warner may have experienced herself as a bicultural (Pakeha/Maori) hybrid at a time when New Zealand was racially dichotomized into us/Pakeha and them/Maori, this may reflect her own transference as a bicultural hybrid woman living during the 1960s. Her own identity no doubt shifted to accommodate the changing landscapes she would eventually come to inhabit.

Ashton-Warner was obliged to negate her own sense of Pakeha/Maori subjectivity/hybridity in order to survive as a white Pakeha female at the time *Greenstone* was written. As such, Huia's subjugated difference (cultural hybridity) was merely a conduit in which Ashton-Warner could project her own identification with (and denial of) Pakeha/Maori difference. Given that bi/multiracial women still seek representation in Aotearoa in the 2000s, what possibility would there have been for Ashton-Warner to claim her own cultural hybridity during the 1960s? In order to be accepted within the monocultural nation at that time, it is probable that Ashton-Warner had to find a way to symbolically leave her Maori self/Huia behind. When a sense of Maoriness (spirituality via connection to landscape) is safely reserved in the subject's memory, the subject is symbolically free to culturally vacillate and return to his or her significant landscape at will. The ability to nurture a dual identity narrative enables an internal sense of cultural mobility and informs a sense of resiliency, well-being, and prosperity. Ashton-Warner found her own InSide in the OutSide of This Side and That Side through the character Huia.

Bodies Provocatively Placed

Through *Greenstone*, Ashton-Warner demonstrates that the social construction of the Maori woman's identity is not a simple process but is informed by the multiple discursive racial and cultural positionings she occupies and responds to. Her work reminds us that the gendered and cultural relationships between Maori and Pakeha (as well as within individuals), is subject to the ongoing complex reconfiguration of both Maori and Pakeha subjectivities. Further, the elaboration of Huia's biraciality provides a provocative reminder to respect the newly emergent ways in which Maori women are marked and spatially positioned (and position themselves) in society in accordance with their respective race, gender, and class status. What is even more significant about Ashton-Warner's work is that she makes the desire to reconfigure Hybrid Huia with a singular traditional Maori identity (through repositioning her within her native landscape) transparent. Reconstructing Hybrid Huia in this way suggests that she is expected to forego her biracial cultural difference. This functions as a reminder to resist the seduction of aligning Maori women's difference (race/brownness) with a singular and stable Maori identity; skin color does not equate neatly with cultural identity, and Maori whakapapa does not limit women of bi/multiracial ancestry from embracing other cultural identities and possibilities. As a protagonist of the ongoing colonial processes that seek to name, mark, and place Maori and Pakeha/Other in particular ways, the multiply-situated racialized woman negotiates the opportunities her bi/multiraciality and cultural hybridity bring. She does so in a way that promotes a positive outcome for not only herself but also for her whanau, hapu, and iwi. Her sense of being Maori is not diluted by the existence of her Other identities. Rather, they give her an internal referent against which she can constantly reaffirm her sense of Maoriness. By her spirit she is Maori.

A spatial and temporal metaphor is invoked in my concluding remarks to re-emphasize how biracial females like Huia and cultural hybrids like Ashton-Warner pursue their own sense of emancipation through accessing a dual/multiple cultural subjectivity. My own identity re/imagined and re/configured finds its resonance in Huia's story. Born Teresa Huia Lyons, I retrospectively deconstruct my present identification as a multiply-subjectivized Maori Pakeha/Other woman. Situated between the names "Teresa" (emphasizing my entry into modernity via my contemporary positioning as a first-generation urban Maori/Pakeha) and "Lyons" (emphasizing the colonial presence in my history and the fixity of this for my future), I retained the name "Huia" (that which denies the legitimacy of modernity and the processes of colonialism). Further, by formally reconstructing myself as "Tess" (a derivative of Teresa) when I was ten years old, I took the pieces back from modernity that suited me and fashioned a tool to work for me in the present/future, embodied in the name "Tess." I then added to this the names/voices of my Maori tupuna "Moeke-Maxwell" that sit protectively (in postcolonial presence) after "Huia" (continuity with the past) and beyond "Tess" (entry into postmodernity). The spirit of my tupuna positions me in this nation in a familiar way, despite my hybridity. I am at home in my tupuna, and they in me. My tinana carries the mark of their presence, connection, and relationship to Papatuanuku and to all peoples who live in Aotearoa/New Zealand.

Unlike Ashton-Warner, I do not require a fictional Maori interlocutor/Huia through which to narrate my hybridity. My bi/multiracial whakapapa provides me with a context to make sense of my cultural identities. My whakapapa binds me irrevocably to the landscape of Aotearoa and informs the experiences I have as a bi/multiracial Maori woman. Unlike Ashton-Warner, the bi/multiracial body/waka I negotiate across the new current of River Colonialism contains the residue of racial difference signified in the presence of my brownness. My difference is *real*, not imagined. The neocolonial racism I experience is not fantasy but actuality. However, like Ashton-Warner's, my diasporic (real and symbolic) comings and goings to the respective landscape/s of my tupuna/past are not romantic nonsense but a tool of emancipation and survival.

Glossary of Maori Words

Aotearoa:	Land of the Long White Cloud (New Zealand)
aroha:	Love; caring; concern; compassion
e hine:	Form of approach to a girl/young woman
e kare:	Darling; loved one; term of endearment
haere mai:	Welcome; come here
Hawaiki:	An ethereal realm where Maori return to after death
hinengaro:	Mind; heart; conscience
hui:	Gathering; meeting
huia:	Extinct indigenous bird prized for its feathers
iwi:	Tribe; extended family group; people
kaupapa:	Rule; agenda; idea; philosophy
kiwi:	Indigenous flightless nocturnal bird; New Zealander
koro:	Elderly man; grandfather
korowai:	Cloak woven of natural fibres and feathers
kotiro:	Girl
kuia:	Elderly woman; grandmother
makutu:	Supernatural power; black magic
mana:	Prestige; influence; authority
Maori:	Indigenous person
marae:	Meeting ground; traditional infrastructure
mokopuna:	Grandchild
Ngati (Nga/Ngai):	People of (used with tribal names)
pa:	Fortified village
Pakeha:	New Zealander of European/British ancestry
Papatuanuku:	Earth mother; the land
piupiu:	Traditional skirt made of flax leaves
rangatira:	Chief/tan (male/female)
rangatiratanga:	Chiefly; self-government; tribal independence
rangi:	Sky
raupatu:	Confiscation and theft of Maori lands
taha Maori:	Maori culture; the Maori side
taku:	My
tangata whenua:	Indigenous person/people; "people of the land"
taniko:	A woven design in flax fiber
taonga:	Property; treasure; artifact
tapu:	Sacred; spiritual ban; forbidden
tauiwi:	White colonial settler; foreigner; immigrant
te reo Maori:	The Maori language
tikanga:	Indigenous knowledge/practice; traditional custom
tinana:	Body

tino rangatiratanga:	Total self-government; national independence
tohunga:	Priest
tohunga makutu:	Priest who uses supernatural power
tupuna:	Ancestor
turangawaewae:	Living place/homeplace; "place to stand"
tuturu:	Authentic; original
wahine:	Woman
waiata:	Song; to sing
wairua:	Spirit
wairuatanga:	Spirituality; spiritual life-force
waka:	Canoe
wero:	Challenge
whakapapa:	Ancestry; genealogical links
whanau:	Family; community
whanaungatanga:	Kinship systems/relationships; relative; kin
whare:	House
wharenui:	Meeting house
whenua:	Land; placenta

References

Anderson, B. 1983. *Imagined communities: Reflections on the origin and spread of nationalism.* London: Verso.

Anthias, F., and N. Yuval-Davis. 1989. Woman-nation-state. In *Woman-nation-state*, ed. N. Yuval-Davis and F. Anthias, 1–17. Basingstoke, UK: Macmillan.

Appadurai, A. 1988. Putting Hierarchy in Its Place. *Cultural Anthropology* 3, no. 1: 36–49.

Ashton-Warner, S. 1966. *Greenstone.* New York: Simon and Schuster.

Awatere, D. 1984. *Maori sovereignty.* Auckland, New Zealand: Broadsheet Collective.

Bhabha, H. 1990. The third space: Interview with Homi Bhabha. In *Identity: Community, culture, difference*, ed. J. Rutherford, 207–22. London: Lawrence and Wishart.

———. 1994. *The location of culture.* New York: Routledge.

Butler, J. 1990. *Gender trouble: Feminism and the subversion of identity.* New York: Routledge.

———. 1993. *Bodies that matter: On the discursive limits of "sex."* New York: Routledge.

Chatterjee, P. 1990. The nationalist resolution of the women's question. In *Recasting women: Essays in Indian colonial history*, ed. K. Sangari and S. Vaid, 233–54. New Delhi: Kali for Women.

———. 1993. *The nation and its fragments: Colonial and postcolonial histories.* Princeton, NJ: Princeton University Press.

Christianos, B., E. Tepania-Carter and Te Whanau O Waipareira. 2001. *Te Whanau: A celebration of Te Whanau O Waipareira.* Waitakere City, New Zealand: Authors.

Collins, H. 1999. Nga tangata awarua: The joys and pain of being both Maori and Pakeha. In *Oral history in New Zealand*, vol. 11, ed. M. Hutching, L. Evans, and J. Byrne, 1–5. Wellington, New Zealand: National Oral History Association of New Zealand.

Foster, R. 1996. The bilingual self: Duet in two voices. *Psychoanalytic Dialogues* 6, no. 1: 97–98.

Freud, S. 1955. "The Uncanny." *The Standard Edition of the Complete Psychological Works of Sigmund Freud, Vol. 17.* Ed and trans. James Strachey. London: Hogarth, 217–256

Friedman, S. 1998. *Mappings: Feminism and the cultural geographies of encounter.* Princeton, NJ: Princeton University Press.

Hall, S., ed. 1997. *Representation: Cultural representations and signifying practices.* London: SAGE.

Irwin, K. 1992. Towards theories of Maori feminism. In *Feminist voices. Women's studies texts for Aotearoa/New Zealand,* ed. R. du Plessis et al., 1–22. Auckland, New Zealand: Oxford University Press.

Kelsey, J. 1984. Legal imperialism and the colonization of Aotearoa. In *Tauiwi: Racism and ethnicity in New Zealand,* ed. P. Spoonley et al., 15–44. Palmerston North, New Zealand: Dunmore Press.

Kohu, H. 1997. Hinewirangi Kohu. In *Faces of the goddess: New Zealand women talk about their spirituality,* ed. C. Kearney, 38–61. North Shore City, New Zealand: Tandem Press.

McDowell, L. 1999. *Gender, identity and place: Understanding feminist geographies.* Oxford: Blackwell.

Meridith, P. 1999a. Being "half-caste": Cultural schizo or cultural lubricant? *Tu Mai* 4 (July); 24.

———. 1999b. Don't you like kina bey? Et, you're not a real Maori! *Tu Mai* 3 (June): 4–6.

———. 1999c. Hybridity in the third space: Rethinking bi-cultural politics in Aotearoa/New Zealand. *He Pukenga Korero* 4, no. 2: 12–16.

Moeke-Maxwell, T. 2003. *Bringing home the body: Bi/multi racial Maori women's hybridity in Aotearoa/New Zealand.* PhD diss., University of Waikato, New Zealand.

Mohanram, R. 1999. *Black body: Women colonialism and space.* New South Wales, Australia: Allen and Unwin.

Orange, C. 1987. *The Treaty of Waitangi.* Wellington, New Zealand: Allen and Unwin.

Pearson, D. 1990. *A dream deferred: The origins of ethnic conflict in New Zealand.* Wellington, New Zealand: Allen and Unwin.

———. 1991. Biculturalism and multiculturalism in comparative perspective. In *Nga take: Ethnic relations and racism in Aotearoa/New Zealand,* ed. P. Spoonley et al., 194–215. Wellington, New Zealand: Dunmore Press.

Pere, R. 1991. *Te wheke: A celebration of infinite wisdom.* Gisborne, New Zealand: Ao Ako Global Learning.

Sharp, A. 1990. *Justice and the Maori: Maori claims in New Zealand political argument in the 1980s.* Auckland, New Zealand: Oxford University Press.

———. 1995. *Why be bicultural? Justice and identity.* Wellington, New Zealand: Bridget Williams Books.

Sinclair, K. 1986. *A destiny apart: New Zealander's search for national identity.* Wellington, New Zealand: Allen and Unwin.

Smith, L. 1998. *Decolonizing methodologies: Research and indigenous peoples.* New York: Zed Books.

Stoler, A. 1995. *Race and the education of desire.* Durham, NC: Duke University Press.

Tai, R. 1997. Ruth Tai. In *Faces of the goddess: New Zealand women talk about their spirituality,* ed. C. Kearney, 77–96. North Shore City, New Zealand: Tandem Press.

Walker, R. 1987. *Nga tau tohetohe: Years of anger.* Auckland, New Zealand: Penguin Books.

———. 1990. *Ka whawhai tonu matou: Struggle without end.* Auckland, New Zealand: Penguin.

Yeatman, A. 1995. Interlocking oppressions. In *Transitions: New Australian feminisms*, ed. B. Caine and R. Pringle, 42–56. New South Wales, Australia: Allen and Unwin.

CHAPTER SIX

Imagination on the Edge of Eruption: Sylvia Ashton-Warner's Volcanic Creativity

Judith Giblin James and Nancy S. Thompson

When Sylvia Ashton-Warner's memoir *I Passed This Way* was nearing publication, her New York editor suggested that the book include a map of New Zealand. Sylvia agreed, but only on the condition that Australia—the continent that dwarfs New Zealand on maps and in popular consciousness—be excluded.[1] Never reluctant to reconfigure geography or other physical facts when it suited her, she took equal license with the psychological landscapes that interested her more deeply. To speak of Sylvia as a mapmaker draws our own effort to map her creative process onto one of her central analogies: in *Teacher* (1963), she likened the mind of a Maori child to a volcano with two vents, one destructive, the other creative. Although Sylvia professed that turbulent emotions released through the creative vent would dry up the destructive one, volcanoes in nature tell a different story of the inextricability of destruction and creation. A satellite view of the equatorial islands of the Pacific Ocean reveals a pathway of volcanic eruptions, now fertile land masses, the archipelagos cartographers classify and subdivide with names like Micronesia and Melanesia. These small islands, born of violent upheavals, have given birth to cultures and peoples with cohesive identities.

Just as cartographers connect the dots of ancient volcanic activity in charting (and, admittedly, even in naming) such configurations, we acknowledge that our map of Sylvia's creative process in the following pages also comes from trained but inevitably subjective choices of which dots—which specific volcanic moments—to connect. Our narrative of Sylvia's development as a writer has the status of any narrative, though it achieves whatever authority a decade-long immersion in her life-documents can bring.

Why redraw a map that others have already charted? Sylvia herself gives a compelling account of her career in *I Passed This Way*, and biographer Lynley Hood has supplied a corrective atlas of Sylvia's omissions and distortions in *Sylvia!* (1988) and *Who Is Sylvia?* (1990). Our map puts Sylvia's relationships with women at the center of her creative development, focusing particularly on her lifelong obsession with the woman she called "my inspiration and my pain."[2] That revealing phrase suggests the creative eros and the destructive anger that were never far beneath the surface of this volcanic relationship. In mapping the details of Sylvia's passionate friendship with Joy Alley, our goal is to provide a more comprehensive guide than that given in either biography or autobiography; by including Joy's memory of the relationship, we clarify and extend received knowledge of Sylvia's creative appropriation of Joy's life. Letters, diaries, manuscripts of published and unpublished fiction, as well as interviews, reveal the patterns and consequences of Sylvia's dependence on and lingering attachment to Joy, the "soul mate" she called "all the ideal girls since childhood embodied in one, the woman I'd sought and had found at last" (*I Passed This Way*, 324). The history of this most volatile and influential of Sylvia's relationships with women yields fascinating insights into Sylvia's creativity and illuminates facets of the eccentric Anna Vorontosov, *Spinster*'s autobiographical protagonist, that have remained inexplicable until now. Although *Spinster* draws on experiences at Fernhill School, where Sylvia discovered and refined the key vocabulary, its origins can be traced to a period of exceptional creativity in the early 1940s in Pipiriki, where she recovered from a nervous breakdown by learning to write. This period of intense intellectual and artistic excitement was fed by Sylvia's fascination with Joy.

By the time Sylvia began to think of herself as a writer in earnest, she had learned that her mind could destroy her. In 1939, while she, Keith Henderson, and their three young children lived at the lonely coastal outpost of Horoera, where waves pounded relentlessly against the rocky shoreline and surging tidal rivers jeopardized access to the outside world, Sylvia succumbed to fears and desires she could no longer contain. A life-threatening breakdown incapacitated her for almost a year, separated her from her children, and required hospitalization in Wellington, where she was treated for a severe anxiety neurosis by Dr. Donald Allen, a neurologist trained in Freudian psychoanalysis. So deep was her depression and escape into daydreams that she found herself paralyzed, unable even to eat or read. When asked why she couldn't get out of bed, she replied, "My dreams are too heavy" (*I Passed This Way*, 276).

Before the image of a volcano with two vents became her standard explanation for bifurcating art and anger, Sylvia vacillated between destructive depression and ecstatic imaginative escape. At this crisis, pleasure and pain merged in regressive fantasies—illusions fueled by pent-up energies in what she came to call her "undermind."[3] While hospitalized, she wrote of her longing "to pull the bedclothes over my shoulders now and dream and dream and dream.… I want to live in my dream world alone but my specialist tries to drag me out & keep me out.… [I]f it was not for my babies & husband & the ones that love me I'd like to go mad & just lie & dream somewhere with someone to make me eat & keep me clean."[4] To comply with her neurologist's demand that she explore her "dream world," Sylvia began to read the works of Freud, transcribing or paraphrasing in a notebook the ideas that attracted her. In an entry distilled from Freud's (1907) *Creative Writers and Daydreaming*, she noted:

> The artist, like the neurotic, had withdrawn from an unsatisfying reality into this world of imagination, but unlike the neurotic he knew how to find a way back from it and once more to get a firm foot on reality. His creations, works of art, were the imaginary gratifications of unconscious wishes, just as dreams are, and like them they were in the nature of compromises since they too were forced to avoid any open conflict with the forces of repression. [B]ut they differed from the asocial narcissistic products of dreaming in that they were calculated to arouse interest in other people, and were able to evoke and gratify the same unconscious wishes in them too.[5]

By such reading, Sylvia learned that dissatisfaction was the source of creativity and, at Dr. Allen's suggestion, began to see the possibility that her own neurosis could be shaped into art.[6] Forever afterward she would trace the source of her art to the need to control her daydreams. If she wrote about her desires and fears, she believed, she could bring them under the discipline of craft. By the time she arrived at Pipiriki, still officially under Dr. Allen's care and still medicated with sedatives, she had begun to teach herself the arts of narrative by writing compulsively in diaries and in long letters to Dr. Allen—letters she never sent.

From her sessions with Dr. Allen and her reading of Freud, Sylvia understood her mind and her creativity in dichotomous terms. The volcano has two vents—creative and destructive. Such oppositions participate in the hierarchical system of binarity within patriarchal culture in general and within the set of psychological tenets by which Sylvia's fragmented mind had been taken apart and "piece[d] together again" (*I Passed This Way*, 281). This binary model, according to psychoanalytic theorist Jessica Benjamin (1988), is "the basic structure of domination" (48). Sylvia was fond of saying that she never picked up a pencil or wrote a word except out of love for someone. Creativity, she wanted to believe, was an act of love—one designed to express a passion that might otherwise lead to violence or anger or depression in the roiling waters of her "undermind." But her creativity was fueled by an idealized and possessive love, which, as Benjamin claims, "defends against something" (1988, 136). Volcanic passions are not so easily separated into productive and destructive forces. The exhilaration of learning to write was inextricable from the painful emotions Sylvia sought to control.

Sylvia's stockpile of Freudian ideas directed her thoughts into deep veins of imagery. Having become a voyeur of her own mental processes, she began to find the minds of others fascinating, especially when denied access to them. Like her desire to look into the innermost consciousness of the Maori children she taught, manifested in the key vocabulary, she wanted to learn the deepest secrets of a succession of women whose affection she sought in Pipiriki and afterward. From the beginning, these special women were often nurses allied with the district health programs for schools and communities that were a staple government service in New Zealand. In Pipiriki, the school teacher's residence was just across the road from the cottage usually occupied by nurses. Two of them figured prominently in Sylvia's emotional life; the second, Joy Alley, was alternately her muse, her teacher, her audience, her soul mate, and her nemesis.

When Sylvia called Joy Alley her "inspiration and [her] pain," she came close to recognizing the proximity of idealized love to loss, envy, fear, and hate (see Brookes, this volume, for further discussion of Sylvia's relationship with Joy Alley). The pattern that most typically characterized Sylvia's volcanic expressions of creativity (and certainly typified her relationship with Joy, about and for whom she wrote, painted, and sculpted obsessively during their first years together) can be seen in miniature in Sylvia's relationship with Molly Dorset, Joy Alley's precursor in the nurse's cottage at the river.[7]

Sylvia had known Molly Dorset when both were students at Wairarapa High School in Masterton in the 1920s. Molly remembered Sylvia favorably from high school, nursed her through mumps, and joined her in long soul-baring conversations Sylvia suggestively called "mind trysts." Between the first of April and the last of October 1941, Sylvia wrote copiously about falling in love with Molly, becoming disillusioned, developing feelings of jealousy, anger, and betrayal (alternating with attempts to return to her first ardent feelings), and examining over and over the signs of Molly's feelings for her and her own feelings for Molly—the gestures, the words, the silences. Such minute analysis was characteristic of Sylvia's intense imaginative involvement with the moods and motives of her muses:

> Was [Molly] really hurt from refusals and reserve, were they really responsible for the sudden breaking off of the lovely thing that had been between us or had she just naturally lost interest in a person that was uninteresting? Or did she still feel love for me? But was deliberately withholding it to punish me for hurting her?

Calculation marked every stage of courtship and disillusionment for Sylvia. At the beginning, she deliberately gave Molly "my gaze" because "I wanted her to feel that whenever she turned to me she would find my eyes steady and welcoming, like a haven to come to." Near the end, she contemplated revenge: "I knew that I wanted Molly's goodwill before she went in order that she would write to me, in order that I would have the opportunity of leaving [the letter] unanswered."

Sylvia understood that she "sought a mother in Molly," yet she tied this longing not to resentful feelings for Margaret Warner, her own mother, but to the neurologist who had mothered her through her breakdown. The following passage about Molly, in an unmailed letter to Dr. Allen included in Sylvia's "Pipiriki Diary," epitomizes the pattern of idealized love leading to vexation:

> The trip we [made] together to Whanganui was like a dream come true. I think I know the secret of it. I depended on her and was nervous. She mothered me at the hotel. Then she began taking me for granted and speaking in her brisk nurse's way. I began to be jealous of her other friends on the river and the invisible cord seems to have been severed. She hurts me too often and too much with her nurse's tongue and her gauche manners.

Hurt escalated to anger, and Sylvia began to imagine telling Molly her feelings: "Before I left the house I was explaining in fantasy to Molly how she had hurt me, ... and I was in a fine rage by the time I got [to school]." She took her emotions out on the children and later carried them home to Keith, crying in bed, provoking him until he agreed with her: "She's an ill-bred, ill-mannered little bitch."

One final incident suggests the extremity of Sylvia's emotional investment in Molly. On the eve of Molly's departure, Sylvia learned the nurse had been having an affair with Jack Templeton, son of the owners of the village store. In her diary, Sylvia railed, "God, wouldn't I like to take Jack from her from under her eyes. Rough, clumsy-handed plebeian." Jealousy fed the desire for revenge, revenge Sylvia took on Molly's last morning in Pipiriki, when she ordered the nurse to "get out of my house." Keith witnessed the dismissal and demanded that Sylvia apologize. Keith, she wrote, "was in tears at the thought that I had that in me. 'Such cruelty,' he called it. I hate the bugger and wish I had not sent the apology although it was only a few lines. I hate her and am having difficulty in getting her off my mind."

Into this turmoil, Joy Alley stepped. The youngest daughter of a respected New Zealand family of educators and social activists, Joy was thirty-three when she arrived in Pipiriki on October 12, 1941, to begin her duties as public health nurse in a district that included some two thousand Maori homes and fifteen schools. She met Sylvia and her family almost immediately. Sylvia was impressed; compared to Molly, the new nurse was a cultured aristocrat. "Miss Alley is soothing, courteous and poised and enthusiastic about her work, and .. wonder of wonders .. asks me down in writing .. us *all* down .. and seems to like me coming," Sylvia wrote.[8] Joy had an immediate influence on Sylvia's creativity. Her diary entries expanded, her work on the draft of a novel set in Pipiriki escalated, her passion for poetry and music flourished, and she resumed playing the piano in the dark, because Joy liked listening to her that way.[9]

In slightly more than a month after Joy's arrival, Sylvia had fallen for her. *Myself*, the autobiographical account drawn from her Pipiriki diary, gives an exact description of this change, though Joy has become the more acceptably heterosexual character Dr. Saul Mada:

> I can't believe that here I am loving someone again immediately after my vows to the contrary but it is so and I can only excuse myself in two ways: that I must have been made precisely *for* loving and that, in the casual way of miracle, Dr. Mada is probably the one person left in the world who could inspire it again. (55–56)[10]

By making her muse male, Sylvia publicly distorts but privately reveals her imaginative erotic investment in Joy.

Although Sylvia admired Joy's poise, the nurse's characteristic reserve challenged Sylvia's ingenuity in eliciting the praise she needed. Aligning herself with Joy's tastes and preferences in literature, music, and art buoyed Sylvia's mood and her creativity. She became a sparkling and frequent visitor at the cottage, where the two read voraciously, listened to classical music on Joy's phonograph, and engaged in long, probing dialogues while smoking cigarettes and drinking tea or beer or whatever was available late into the nights. Many years later, Joy recalled that Pipiriki was "a locale designed to feed the imagination" and her experience of it was indelibly rich. After long Saturday talk sessions "Sylvia sometimes stayed the night" at the cottage or in the deserted hut that became the first of Sylvia's two Selahs (studies or studios) in Pipiriki.[11] "I'd never had a friend like that before," Joy said.[12]

Sylvia's own retrospective account in *I Passed This Way* is equally vivid. She describes luxurious evenings together, boat trips upriver as Joy ("Opal Owen") made her rounds in the district, and a profusion of creative gestures inspired by Joy: chalk drawings of an exotic Egyptian water bearer captioned "Moon of My Delight" (after the phrase in *The Rubáiyát of Omar Khayyám*) and of "a great bird with wide-stretched wings and iridescent feathers" (*I Passed This Way*, 298); a crayon sketch of "brilliant yellow poplars spearing the forest ... reflected upside down in the green eyes of the River" (*I Passed This Way*, 302); a "replica of [Joy's] bronze Buddha" carved into a clay bank (*I Passed This Way*, 308); and even a sculpted bust of Joy, fashioned in clay special-ordered from Christchurch. "I secretly paint for Opal at times instead of learning to write," Sylvia confides (*I Passed This Way*, 302). She describes a day devoted to "painting for her a watercolour of the face of Beethoven to celebrate the symphonies and concertos on her Gramophone we have shared by lamplight and firelight":

> I do it in one sitting in a fever of obsession not entirely arisen from the thought of
> Opal but as much from the delirium of painting anyway, and when I pass her cottage
> on the way home and her car is not there I slip in the gate, down the path through the
> heavy scent of the old-time roses, into her bedroom and hide the portrait in the book
> she is reading which is D. H. Lawrence's *The Rainbow* so that when she returns
> from a heavy day on her rounds and sinks wearily into bed she'll suddenly come
> upon it in private and I won't be there to get the knock-back. Furtive tribute. (*I
> Passed This Way*, 302)

Sylvia predicts that Joy will cherish the portrait, even though "praise from Opal seldom takes the form of words": "If anyone knows where Opal is now, if she's still alive, you'll find that portrait framed on her wall" (*I Passed This Way*, 302). Sylvia had been dead for more than a dozen years when we visited Joy in her retirement cottage in Auckland, where the Beethoven portrait sat atop the television.

Sylvia found that Joy's reserve could be breached in conversations about the books they passed back and forth between them: works by Lawrence, Havelock Ellis, Bertrand Russell, Katherine Mansfield, Herbert Read, Carl Jung, Virginia Woolf, Olive Schreiner, Aldous Huxley, and modernist poets such as T. S. Eliot, Laurence Binyon, Robert Bridges, Gerard Manley Hopkins, and W. H. Auden, to whom Joy was especially attracted. Alongside her immersion in painting and music, Sylvia devoted herself to "Rangatira," the novel she was writing for Dr. Allen, developing idealized characters based on herself and Joy. Meanwhile, Joy began to write poetry at Sylvia's urging, feeling and expressing emotions she had never engaged before.

In the beginning, Sylvia's taste had seemed too sentimental for Joy, and Sylvia had vowed to "change myself somehow, educate myself out of this weakness till my mind is as clean as Opal's and she'll come to approve of me" (*I Passed This Way*, 298). Opal's name, in fact, may derive from Sylvia's admiration for Joy's mind, which she likened to "the inscrutable heart of the gemstone opal" (*I Passed This Way*, 309). In her writing and her art, seeking Joy's approval meant "escape from the representational" in favor of the "uncluttered symbol" (*I Passed This Way*, 309). Yet for her most substantial artistic tribute to Joy, Sylvia chose a traditionally representational medium. The bust she carved of Joy was inspired by a specific moment:

> I am standing at the school gate one morning in the bitter mist lifting from the River
> as she leaves for Wanganui for a few days, after a deep division yesterday over
> something unnecessary, irresponsible, and inexplicable, which is to say it was my
> offence, and she looks back over her shoulder at me, her face saying everything I've

wanted her to say, but which she has not said: a look that must be engraved on time. (*I Passed This Way*, 303)

Sylvia began work on the bust, hoping to represent the qualities she found beautiful in her muse: the aristocratic features, at once delicate and strong, and especially the look of connection and awareness between them that Joy projected in taking leave of Sylvia, looking back over her shoulder, holding Sylvia's gaze. Sometimes, looking into a mirror, Sylvia used her own face as the model "for important broad essentials."[13] When Joy herself sat for the sculpting, Sylvia felt deeply happy in capturing her friend's qualities in art: "I feel in the making of your head I'm having a high spiritual experience … one of the very high ones. I enter a world of inspiration where every desire and act is englamoured. I *feel* inspired."[14] Joy and the act of representing Joy gave her these peak creative pleasures. And it was within Joy's power to take them away—as she did when, exhausted by her responsibilities in the district, she declined to sit after a day's work. Sylvia took Joy's refusal as an affront to "Art," the direness of the act somehow magnified by the abstraction into which Sylvia elevated it.

As had been the case with Molly Dorset, tensions were inevitable with the growth of intimacy and Sylvia's need to sustain or deepen it. Sylvia visited Joy early one morning, expecting to be greeted as enthusiastically as during their evening visits. As it happened, Joy was preparing for a busy day when Sylvia intruded. In the first version of this scene in a manuscript called "Skylark," it is obvious that they have already experienced conflict. Not being welcomed as she had hoped, Sylvia speaks the words she wanted to hear from Joy, imitating Joy's manner: "I'm so glad you came round. I've been waiting for you all the morning. I heard you coming from through the cottage."

Joy, annoyed, replies, "No. You can't make me into that."

Sylvia responds, "I've given over making you into anything…. Any making over will be done on myself." But disturbed "to see [Joy] unhappy," Sylvia thinks, "I must let myself go and show you how much I love you so I put out my cigarette and say, 'Do you mind if I cuddle you like this?'" She concludes, "You allow it and seem to want it a bit so I lay my head on your breast under your chin, one hand on the back of your neck and one on your face. We don't speak at all but for my saying, 'You're my darling.'"[15]

Midway in the Pipiriki years, Sylvia, disenchanted with Joy as she had been with Molly, confronted Joy in a manner that Joy recalled as unbearably cruel: "I was labeled very clearly as selfish, unfeeling, intellectually lazy, emotionally immature, greedy…. Worse still, I didn't care a damn about anything, she'd say. I took these judgments very seriously and felt useless." Sylvia once wrote to Joy, "God curse you for failing me." Joy found this accusation a turning point in their relationship, comparing it to a frightening incident during her early nursing career: "In 1934 I had specialed a paranoid for six months who regularly hid knives in her bed and who would hide behind doors to frighten me. Sylvia's words were much more lethal and hurt very deeply. I had never been cursed before."[16]

Joy's retrospective understanding of the dynamics of her relationship with Sylvia was that Sylvia's need to control others was stronger than her need to be loved. The two needs—love and control—intersect in Sylvia's desire to locate the key to Joy's deepest secret self. Both are encoded in Sylvia's revision of the first of many poems Joy wrote in Pipiriki. Joy recalled,

> One spring morning when I was low with flu a child from the school came to my door bringing daffodils from Sylvia. Those flowers were the inspiration for four lines which seemed spontaneously to drop like petals to my lap:
>
>> Whose graceful words, whose lips
>> Have opened up the hidden crypts,
>> Deep down the crypts, heavy the chain
>> For you the key, for you the pain.[17]

To the bedridden nurse, the lips of the spring daffodils spoke the language, the graceful words that offered release from her misery. In return, Joy intended to offer Sylvia the key to her "subconscious, the opening up of that part of the mind" that Sylvia had been seeking, exposing the pain in the hidden crypts. "It has nothing to do with sex," Joy told us. The crypt had special resonance for Joy as an image of her claustrophobia, which she traced to a time in childhood when her brothers threatened to throw her into a trash bin.

Sylvia revised the poem in copying it into her exercise book and later in typing a sheaf of Joy's poems for possible use in *I Passed This Way*. Here is Sylvia's version:

> To Sylvia—
> Whose graceful hands
> Whose lips
> Have prised open the guarded crypts
> Deep down the crypts and heavy the chain
> Yours the key.
> Yours the pain.[18]

By providing a title that names her and changing "graceful words" to "graceful hands" and adding a layer of gothic suffering, Sylvia made herself more physically the martyred agent of Joy's liberation. If the hands and lips belong to Sylvia, Joy had good reason to insist that an image of lesbian sexuality was not her intention. Sylvia's revision of the last line—making "For you the key, for you the pain" into "Yours the key. / Yours the pain."— implies that in liberating Joy's secret, Sylvia causes herself emotional pain. The only person who benefits, in other words, is Joy. Sylvia will suffer in the long run for befriending Joy so deeply and intimately. The revision inscribes onto Joy's poem Sylvia's reading of her experience in befriending Molly Dorset: giving her heart (and her art) to another woman will lead to betrayal and loss. Although she had no compelling reason to believe so at the time, she was acutely right.

Sylvia and her family left Pipiriki less than two months after Joy, in March 1945, on their way to a bigger school at Waiomatatini on the East Cape. Joy had gone to an assignment at Wairoa in Hawkes Bay, some two hundred kilometers away. In August, during the celebration of the Japanese surrender that ended World War II, Joy began a love affair with a male physician eight years younger than she. Her passion for the man she refers to only by his first name, Tasman, or Tas, enraged Sylvia almost to the point of a second mental collapse. She never forgave Joy the perceived betrayal, but neither did she forget the love they had shared in Pipiriki. She wrote compulsively about both at the time of their break and through the 1960s, especially in the manuscript sequence that led to *Myself*. Even her autobiography records the bitterness but also calls Joy (Opal) one of "the three major formative loves of my life" (*I Passed This Way*, 316). The other two are Keith Henderson and an education official, Walter Harris (called Hilton Morris in the book), whose importance Sylvia began to inflate only after the intrusion of Tas made her "no longer first" with Joy. The events of the ten years of Sylvia's active enmeshment with Joy became a volcanic depth from which Sylvia drew throughout the remainder of her creative life.

As she had with Molly, Sylvia vacillated between desire for reconciliation with Joy and a need to vent her rage and hurt, which escalated dangerously after a visit to Joy in Wairoa in August 1945, when Sylvia was repulsed by evidence of Joy's lovemaking with Tas: an empty wine bottle still on the mantelpiece, a full ashtray, the unmade bed. During the visit Sylvia cried uncontrollably and forced Joy to listen as she read the Song of Solomon "to remind [her] of what in-loveness can be" and the book of Ruth to show "the dignity, ... the sanctity, courtesy and essential privacy" to be found in a proper marriage.[19] Sylvia's choice of the story of two women, a mother and daughter-in-law, as a homily on marriage is not surprising. Joy and Sylvia often affirmed their intimacy by saying that they felt married to one another.[20] The more meaningful connection for Sylvia, however, would have been Ruth's steadfastness. If Sylvia sought a mother in Joy, as she had earlier in Molly, and this mother abandoned her too, she could see herself in the role of the faithful daughter who teaches a lesson of loyalty. An angry twelve-page letter to Joy followed on the heels of Sylvia's visit.

Joy had known from the first that Sylvia would react badly to Tas's presence in her life. In the letter divulging her love for Tas, Joy pleaded to Sylvia, "Don't leave me. Don't—we have—I couldn't stand it. There is Buckets to say. Don't leave me—."[21] But Sylvia's behavior, when invited to meet Tas, offended Joy. Thereafter, Joy's letters began to recount incidents and plans focused on Tas. She excused herself from a scheduled visit to Sylvia in Waiomatatini; yet when an expected letter from Sylvia failed to arrive, Joy shot back, "Have you divorced me[?]"[22] Later, it was Joy who failed to reply promptly to Sylvia's letters.

Throughout the ordeal, Sylvia struggled to preserve her place beside Joy, even while criticizing her:

> Sharing is the worst word my darling.... These love affairs—we must accustom ourselves to them in each other[']s lives—allow them their necessary place—But there is only one you for me—and only me for you. Is that what you think—or—not now—there's only Tasman—and when he will touch you again—but later—later— when I haven't written for a long time—and you find that you are mine after all—is that what you will think[?][23]

Jealousy and resentment fed Sylvia's imaginative involvement with her rivals. Her immersion in Joy's desire for Tas has its parallel in Sylvia's fantasy of seducing Jack Templeton to avenge Molly's betrayal. Sylvia's reaction to Joy's betrayal, however, exceeded the narrative boundaries in which she sought to enclose it.

At the time of Joy's defection, Sylvia momentarily believed that the loss of Joy would destroy her. The short unpublished manuscript called "Thief" records a week of agony in October 1945. Sylvia addresses Joy: "I say with the tears dropping on my hands 'I am waiting for you to come back to me when you have learnt what I have learnt. But don't be too long. Don't leave it till my death-bed.'" When she wrote these words, Sylvia had been grieving uncontrollably, crying so profusely that she asked to be excused from school for two weeks. The raw emotions recorded in "Thief" persisted for more than two decades, even spilling over into "Tenth Heaven," Sylvia's 1967 revision of "Rangatira," the manuscript on which she had worked in Pipiriki. In a highly personal and revealing passage excised from that manuscript, the narrator says of characters based on Walter Harris and Joy Alley, "I know he is not important to me now because if he died I wouldn't care. But the day I hear Dette is dead ... even though I never see her, or hear from her [or] hear about her ... something in me will die also."[24] The "something" she believes "will die also" is revealed in the manuscript "Skylark":

> I found out today as I did the house and tidied my art-things in the music room that without you, alive, I could do no creative work. That it is ultimately, irrevocably for you, whether you love me or hate me. I knew this morning during that giving-crying time that I had indeed fused with you spiritually and that now, at this division, I was haemorrhaging and dying.... You will always be my inspiration and my pain and I

must live in your inspiration (spiritually) alone. With you dead I am dead and my work too.[25]

After Joy's affair with Tas, Sylvia's anguish transformed her perception of the sculpted bust from an image of Joy's beloved qualities to a representation of coldness, hauteur, disdainful rejection—most particularly Joy's betrayal by having turned her face away to another. As Sylvia's inspiration, Joy held the upper hand; as her pain, Joy was demoted to the status of despised crone. Though we might argue that in the capacity to cause emotional distress Joy still held the upper hand, Sylvia always had the power of representation, of interpretation—the power of assigning meaning.

For many months, all during its sculpting and casting, Sylvia had learned the sculptor's art as she went along. The bust of Joy was the organically articulated embodiment of Sylvia's desire—desire for idealized love, for fusion in "a love that … equate[s] itself with me, interflow[s] with my self."[26] On a narrative level, the story of the bust is a simple one of disillusionment turning what was once desired into something pitiably ugly, despised. On a symbolic level, where the most intense desire is often located, the bust suggests the mother-breast, even as it stops short of representing it. The process of its creation inscribes the desiring touch of the artist exploring, shaping, venerating the face, the hair, the neck, the shoulders. The hands pass over the malleable clay that still carries the smell of earth and leaves its impress on the hand that touches it. For Sylvia, who would take the faces of Maori children and American visitors in her two hands with such intimacy that each felt known, accepted, and loved, the act of sculpting must have held deep sensual gratification. To create the face of the beloved—the face that mirrors your own—suggests the perfect fusion of art and eros. Indeed, representing Joy became the enduring, often subterranean motive of Sylvia's writing career. No other intimate—not Keith, not her parents, not her children, not her other women soul mates—lived with such vividness in her imagination. *Spinster* is marked from start to finish by the memory of Joy and the language and motifs Sylvia associated with her dream of their fusion.

In July 1965, at the beginning of an ultimately aborted work called "Thee" in which diary material about Joy was to be treated as a "love affair … for a separate novel," Sylvia had a startling recognition: "I am writing the early life of Anna Vorontosov…. Saul is really Eugene. The whole thing falls into place. I'm shaken…. I'm frightened of the power in the book."[27] Saul of the "Skylark" manuscript and the later *Myself* was Eugene of *Spinster*. If Joy is Saul, as Sylvia made clear in her autobiography, Joy is also Eugene, the "dark-winged memory" of a first love to whom Sylvia as Anna longs to return—the home or the mooring in which she will feel safe.

Sylvia's discovery of Joy's presence in the prehistory of *Spinster* demands a new reading of this provocative novel. From this perspective, it is about the teacher as artist, haunted by memories of a past unresolved relationship. Creative interaction with her Maori pupils temporarily distracts Anna from the overtures of Paul Vercoe and her enduring attachment to Eugene, the lover she left behind in Kazakhstan. But the emotional and physical fusion she seeks with the children is marked by guilt, knowing that such intimacy would be considered unorthodox by the educational establishment. Following the suicide of the wayward and equally unorthodox Paul, Anna finds the key that opens the gates to the native imagery of the children and a psychological intimacy with them—a "mind tryst" in the sense Sylvia used the phrase with Molly and Joy.[28] With the encouragement of school inspector Abercrombie, whom she has foolishly romanticized, Anna begins to believe she is living fully in the present and making a contribution to Maori education that will allow her scope and influence in the teaching profession. When her annual evaluation is announced by letter, however, she learns that her creativity has made no difference in the way the establishment sees her. She reclaims her Maori primers and teaching scheme from Abercrombie and buries them in two tiny boxes side by side, like the adolescent Wharepita's miscarried twins, fathered by Paul. The grading letter arrives in tandem with its own twin—the longed-for letter that Anna does not open until she is already aboard the ship that will take her back to Eugene.

On one level, *Spinster* is an idealized self-portrait that excuses Sylvia's decision to give up teaching in the noblest terms: because she is not appreciated and because the shortsighted bureaucrats do not understand and are not willing to reward what she has done. When viewed as a story that emerges from Sylvia's love for Joy, we can see in Anna's commitment to an authentic artistic life the philosophy that Sylvia developed in thrall to her muse in Pipiriki. Allusions to Beethoven, Schubert, Lawrence, Russell, Read, and others—the influential figures of her studies with Joy—provide this link, as do scenes of the furiously diffuse creativity typical of that early period: Anna turns from the piano to the guitar to her chalks to paint to clay to setting the children dancing, moving expertly (if compulsively) from one medium to another. In such scenes, *Spinster* evinces a dedication to personal growth and deep immersion in the arts and emotions of the Maori people that marked Sylvia's years on the river.

Joy's presence is indicated more directly by three gestural and verbal motifs that unify the novel: tableaux of parental (mothering) comfort; images that encode a long-sought creative fusion between Sylvia and Joy in Pipiriki and after; and a recurrent emblem of the perverse underside of such fusion—symbiosis turned parasitical—in the novel's master trope of the Old Man of the Sea.

Spinster begins and ends with parallel mothering gestures linked to Joy: "What is it, what is it, Little One?" Anna asks at the start, comforting a tearful Maori child. She takes him on her knee and "tuck[s] his black head beneath [her] chin" saying, "There … there … look at my pretty boy" (*Spinster*, 3). Alone that night, remembering the incident, she thinks, "[I]t is I who am the Little One." Caressing the photograph of the face her "spinster heart craves," Anna sheds tears for the memory of the love she left in Kazakhstan: "No longer does Eugene take me on his knee, tuck my black head beneath his chin and say, 'There … there … look at my pretty girl'" (*Spinster*, 3). At the novel's conclusion, reunited with Eugene and prompted by his question, "What is it, what is it, Little One?", Anna tearfully expresses the hurt she has suffered from the New Zealand educational establishment in the very words of the Maori child she comforted at the novel's beginning: "That's why somebodies they tread my sore leg for notheen: somebodies" (*Spinster*, 269). In an identical act of consolation and comfort, Eugene "takes [Anna] on his knee and tucks [her] black head beneath his chin.… 'There … there … look at my pretty girl'" (*Spinster*, 269). Not only does "little one" echo Sylvia's pet name for Joy, "Tiny," but the gesture itself appears to derive from the static image recorded in Sylvia's Pipiriki diary of cuddling with Joy, her head on Joy's breast, tucked under her chin: "We don't speak at all but for my saying, 'You're my darling.'"[29]

In addition to such revealing tableaux, Sylvia's bond with Joy is evoked in Anna's ideas about fusion of the races and of individual bodies and souls. Fusion, *Spinster* suggests, is a sensuous but ultimately spiritual ideal, a higher order "communication" that participates in the divine. From the very start of their relationship in 1941, Sylvia and Joy drew from the poetry they mutually admired in vowing that "only utter truth can be between us." This phrase, from a poem by Mary Coleridge, defines the uncompromising candor that each promised the other in their intense mind trysts. Such moments reappear, strategically displaced onto the Maori children: "Steadily those evenings of reading, Beethoven, Schubert, thinking, working and remembering, move inland. Only in blood and by blood, claims my mind, can the races mix" (*Spinster*, 10). Fusion as a symbiotic merging, an interpenetration of two worlds, two states, two souls, is often possible for Anna in the infant room: "Sensuously and accurately I vibrate and respond to the multifold touch of my Little Ones.… I am made of their thoughts and their feelings" (*Spinster*, 24).

When Anna contemplates her response to the attentions of Paul Vercoe, she draws back, understanding the power of her need for fusion. The possibility of intimate communion (sexual, spiritual—each is implied) is weighed in words directly tied to Sylvia's love for Joy: "Only just in time have I recognized the 'Thee and Me' between us" (*Spinster*, 36), Anna thinks as she withdraws from feelings that attract her to Paul, a mere child by Anna's standards, a man in his twenties. "Thee and Me" derives from Edward FitzGerald's popular translation of *The Rubáiyát of Omar Khayyám,* read and recited repeatedly by Sylvia and Joy. FitzGerald's version of the poem resonates throughout the Pipiriki manuscripts and Sylvia's Freudian understanding of libido and longing:

> There was a Door to which I found no Key:
> There was a Veil past which I could not see:
> Some little Talk awhile of ME and THEE
> There seemed—and then no more of THEE and ME.[30]

In the manuscript fragment called "Thee," Sylvia uses FitzGerald's image of sexual fusion and obliteration in tandem with an epigraph quoting the favored line from Mary Coleridge, associating "utter truth" and "THEE and ME" just as she does in *Spinster.* Anna thinks, "Only utter truth will do in a crisis" (*Spinster,* 107). She is merciless in rejecting Paul and others—even the faraway Eugene—as candidates for the fusion of "THEE and ME." When, toward the climax of the novel, Abercrombie becomes Anna's inspiration, her feeling of release into creativity carries the verbal stamp of Joy's poetic response to the gift of daffodils Sylvia ordered delivered to the ailing nurse: "I hear in the world behind my eyes the sound of rusty hinges. As though some opening were taking place.... As though some lid, heavy with orthodoxy, tradition and respectability, were being prised open" (*Spinster,* 233).

In many respects *Spinster* seems to be a book Sylvia wrote to free herself from the still unsettling and painful love for Joy, but it is oddly the reverse—a direct engagement of pain and loss. Even the relationship between Anna and Paul is a veiled criticism of the relationship between Joy and Tas. The physical signs of their passion that Sylvia resented seeing in Wairoa, the ocular proof of losing Joy to Tas, echoes in Anna's pronouncement that "I cannot stand to witness the pulsing Thee and Me.... I cannot endure the contemplation of two lovers together unless one of them is I" (*Spinster,* 226). Anna, unlike Joy, maintains a mature perspective and rejects the younger man for his own good and for hers, even in the face of genuine desire. Barbara Dent, Sylvia's confidante in the 1950s, assumed that Paul Vercoe and Saul Mada were the same character.[31] She was close, but very little in Sylvia's description of Paul resembles Joy. Only the standards by which Paul falls short—that he is not someone who can be relied on for "utter truth" or for the fusion of "THEE and ME"—resonate with Sylvia's memories of losing her soul mate to the young doctor.

Spinster's recurrent motif tying Anna's guilt to the story of the Old Man of the Sea from the fifth voyage of Sinbad the Sailor in the *Arabian Nights* is likewise a vestige of Sylvia's relationship with Joy. The Old Man tricks Sinbad into carrying him on his shoulders and from this perch forces the sailor to take him to the ripest fruits of the island high in the trees. Each day the quest for the ripest fruits continues. Beneath the weight of the Old Man, the weary Sinbad picks grapes from low vines and ferments them to ease his suffering. The Old Man confiscates the wine, becomes drunk, and falls from Sinbad's shoulders, leaving his victim the opening to crush his skull with a rock. The caretaker, punished for his good deed, ultimately gains revenge. Anna frequently refers to this story as an explanation for feelings she attaches to her sense of failure as a teacher: "It is something you find on your shoulders with tight legs clasping your neck. I thought I had forgotten Guilt" (*Spinster*, 4). She vows at the beginning, "Slowly I will recover my lagging professional status and prove myself a thoroughly useful force in the service. Then maybe this Old Man Guilt will release my throat and I'll be one with others at last" (*Spinster*, 5).

At times, Anna's guilt is complicated by the fact that the only way she can face her professional challenges is to make herself "severely immune" by drinking "half a tumbler of brandy" before reporting to school (*Spinster*, 4). Both the guilt and the need for brandy, however, have another source—an attempt "to lose the past": "Do I actually want memory, as much as it wants me? Are Eugene and I still so engrossed that even time and oceans fail?" (*Spinster*, 8). The memory of Joy and the story of their early blissful bond and the crushing loss of it constantly assumes the role of the hidden, disguised, emotion—guilt, longing, anger, whatever name she gives it—that Sylvia portrays as strangling her.

Joy's association with the Old Man in Sylvia's mind dates to the Pipiriki years, as suggested by a diary entry written in 1942. One evening Sylvia arrived at the nurse's cottage with an armload of books, expecting to be welcomed even though she had come unannounced and at an inconvenient time. Sylvia wrote that Joy's refusal of her company "made me very sore and upset and I realised with dismay how much I depended on others for my source of energy.... Sometimes she seems heavy to carry."[32] In this complex statement Joy is the weight Sylvia carries (the Old Man), yet Joy, as the source of Sylvia's creative energy, is also a Sinbad figure on whom Sylvia (this time the Old Man) depends for sustenance. As played out in *Spinster*, the logic of the Sinbad plot is also violated. The adventurous and creative Anna (Sinbad/Sylvia) carries a burden of guilt connected with leaving Eugene (Old Man/Joy), yet Anna is permitted to sail away from the guilt and return to Eugene, who still loves her. Sinbad does, of course, prevail in the *Arabian Nights* version, but only with the Old Man's death. The Sinbad plot does not cohere in *Spinster* because Sylvia needed the wish-fulfilling fantasy of reunion with a beloved that, by 1958, she knew she could not achieve in reality. In manuscript drafts a decade later, Sylvia reverses the Sinbad roles again, portraying herself as an exceptional Old Man who has survived the retaliatory blows of Sinbad/Joy.[33] Sylvia's insistence on having her own way with the story (interpreting it in contradictory ways when it suited her) was the fundamental prerogative of her art: the use of storytelling to control the emotional crises of her life. Like Scheherazade, who spins this tale and a thousand others to save herself (and the women who would follow her), Sylvia's story is intended to ensure her survival by refashioning in fiction a reality from which she longed to escape.

The Old Man of the Sea is a paradigmatic plot embedded deep in Sylvia's imagination as the parasitical potential of the symbiosis she preferred to idealize as love or fusion. Apart from *Spinster*, one of the best illustrations of the centrality of these tropes comes from manuscript drafts of "Tenth Heaven," remnants of "Rangatira" that constitute Sylvia's oldest surviving attempts at fiction. At its core is the figure of the mixed-race Huia Brice Considine, the headstrong third Te Renga Renga and rightful leader of her Maori tribe. Huia, a famed concert pianist and artist, has succumbed to a crippling disorder that she believes is the result of a curse levied by a cruel *tohunga*, or shaman. Others in her community explain her isolation, her madness, and her paralysis as grief over "a woman-affair" with "a golden-haired princess" who had visited the tourist hotel on the river. This revelation was omitted from the last draft of the novel, as was a passage describing a reunion between Huia (Sylvia) and the golden-haired woman physician (Joy)—the meeting of Maori and Pakeha women of polar temperaments, capable of fusion and fulfillment: "two of the same sex free of it to love each other always"[34] (see Moeke-Maxwell, this volume, for an alternative version of Huia in *Greenstone*).

But it is not ultimately Huia's love-longing or a curse that has condemned her to madness. Rather, it is the fact that she is an Artist, a Genius, a God, whose "marauding imagination" has turned her mind "inside out," lured her attention inward. Another version reveals Huia's problem as a severe depression like the one Sylvia herself experienced. The past wraps "all its arms around your neck so that you can hardly lift your head from the pillow," Huia says.[35] With its imagery reminiscent of the Old Man of the Sea's strangling weight on Sinbad's shoulders, the passage is another version of the reply Sylvia gave to her inquirers in 1939: the depression is so paralyzing that she cannot leave her bed; her "dreams are too heavy."

The past replayed, revised, rewritten in purposeful fantasy, rather than idle daydreams, was Sylvia's solution. A slip of paper inserted in discarded fragments of "Tenth Heaven" and dated September 8, 1961, carries the confession, "When I wrote this tale the first time I believed in all these people. They turned over the guts in me." She wrote in order to "live out a plastic love together in mind."[36] Her motivation in part was to enjoy the fantasy of love with Joy and in part to bring that fantasy under the discipline of art. When her editor told her to burn "Tenth Heaven" and start over, she refused. "I love this book," she told him; "It comes from the deepest sources in me. I love everybody in it. I loved writing it."[37]

"Tenth Heaven" and the sprawling "Rangatira" from which it derives are apprentice pieces in which Joy's formative influence on Sylvia's creativity can be traced. They also show the importance of Joy in Sylvia's dream of a fusion of minds and spirits. At the end of her description of the Pipiriki years in *I Passed This Way*, Sylvia returned to the poet Mary Coleridge to sum up her relationship with Joy:

> Long suns and moons have wrought this day at length,
> The heavens in native majesty have told thee.
> To see me as I am have thou the strength;
> And, even as thou art, I dare behold thee.
> (*I Passed This Way*, 316)

Sylvia's concept of fusion is strikingly registered in the last two lines. "To see me as I am have thou the strength": the fearless gaze of acceptance is the "look that must be engraved on time," the loving backward glance that inspired Sylvia to sculpt the face of Joy. "And, even as thou art, I dare behold thee": to Sylvia, for whom posturing and playacting were lifelong survival skills, the highest tribute would be to entrust the "utter truth" about herself to one who could see her as she was and accept her unconditionally.

In their long conversations in Pipiriki, Sylvia and Joy tried to reach such a level of knowledge and acceptance, but the crypts never opened wide enough for Sylvia's satisfaction. The breach over Tas proved irreparable, though Sylvia tried desperately to keep before Joy's eyes the ideal of "THEE and ME" as superior to base physical desire. Out of her grief and jealousy over Tas, Sylvia wrote perhaps the final testament to what might have been: "Two human entities fuse, become one and die one death; not two.... This is the core of life and the heart of my philosophy."[38]

Even so, the role of Joy in shaping Sylvia's philosophy was substantial. She provided the motive and the themes of Sylvia's earliest writings and inspired images and emotions that give *Spinster* its depth and mystery. As Sylvia predicted at Wairoa, Joy remained forever the source of Sylvia's "inspiration"— if also, inevitably, a source of "pain." For Sylvia, creative and destructive passions were inextricable. In fantasy, muses are the pliable clay of the artist; in real life, they are objects of a combustible resentment. Contrary to the ideal of fusion Sylvia conceived, the two did not live one life or die one death. They saw each other for the last time in 1952, but neither ever erased from memory the passions discovered on the river. Sylvia died on April 18, 1984, in her final Selah overlooking Mt. Maunganui, an extinct volcano. The first flowers to arrive were roses from Joy.[39]

Acknowledgments

The authors wish to thank the department of English and the office of sponsored research at the University of South Carolina for travel grants that supported research for this project. We are also grateful to the heirs of Sylvia Ashton-Warner for permission to quote from unpublished manuscripts and to the Alexander Turnbull Library in Wellington, New Zealand, and the Mugar Memorial Library[40] at Boston University for permission to quote portions of manuscripts in their possession. We are especially indebted to Joy Alley and to Sylvia's children—Jasmine Beveridge, Elliot Henderson, and Ashton Henderson—for their willingness to be interviewed in 1998 and for their generous insights.

Notes

[1] Sylvia Ashton-Warner, letter to Bob Gottlieb, March 29, 1979 (Sylvia Ashton-Warner papers, Mugar Memorial Library, Boston University, uncatalogued box).

[2] Sylvia Ashton-Warner, "Skylark," draft 2, book 6, "Oct 27, '45, Saturday morning" (Mugar Memorial Library, box 16, folder 4), n.p.

[3] Sylvia's chalkboard drawing of a volcano (a photograph of which is printed in Hood 1990, xxiii) shows key vocabulary words blasting out through two vents, illustrating her idea that channeling strong emotional content from the "undermind" out through the creative vent of symbolic expression could help to redirect the vent of violent enactment. Long in her mind, this image resonates with a drawing in Herbert Read's (1943, 175) *Education through Art*. A volcano-like projection rises up from the "lower darker levels" of a "continuous stream" representing Jung's collective unconscious or Freud's archaic heritage, the regions of the mind comprising Freud's id. Our examination of Sylvia's personal copy of *Education through Art* reveals that Sylvia read and underlined passages on this page; thus, we can be fairly certain that Read's image, along with Sylvia's extensive study of Freud and Jung, is the impetus for what Sylvia called the "undermind," the source of the strong emotional images that she sought to free through taking the key vocabulary of Maori children and in her own creative process.

[4] Sylvia Ashton-Warner, "Horoera, June 1936–Feb 1939" (Mugar Memorial Library, box 4, folder 9), n.p.

[5] Sylvia Ashton-Warner, "Freud, March 42/Russell, May 43 (Pipiriki)," Education Department Exercise Book (Mugar Memorial Library, box 7, folder 1), n.p.

[6] Because Dr. Allen boasted of current and former patients who had published their writing, Sylvia determined not only that she would write, but also that she would win his admiration by publishing a bestseller (see Hood 1988).

[7] Molly Dorset is identified in Sylvia Ashton-Warner's earliest revision of her Pipiriki diary—"Pipiriki, 1936–39" (Mugar Memorial Library, box 4, folder 8)—and in the Pipiriki school log kept by Keith Henderson. She is called Jean Humphrey in Sylvia Ashton-Warner's *Myself* and Jean Humphries in Lynley Hood's (1988) *Sylvia! The Biography of Sylvia Ashton-Warner*. All quotations related to Molly Dorset come from "Pipiriki, 1936–39" (Mugar Memorial Library, box 4, folder 8), pp. 23–51.

[8] "Pipiriki, 1936–39" (Mugar Memorial Library, box 4, folder 8), p. 51 (emphasis in original). We have preserved Sylvia's occasional use of two dots for ellipses.

[9] "Pipiriki/February 23–November 26 [1941]" (Mugar Memorial Library, box 16, folder 2), p. 52.

[10] Regarding the identification of Joy Alley with the fictional Saul Mada, Sylvia wrote to her new daughter-in-law, Jacquemine Henderson, on September 29, 1967:

> I hasten to tell you that the man in the story called Saul is a fictionalisation of the District Nurse who lived across the road from us in Pipiriki—you need to know this. I turned her into a man in order to shield the nurse from embarrassment. Joy Alley. Elliot knows her. Also I had to point up the conversation & behaviour to make them more man-woman interchange. That's the only fiction in the book although Saul's behaviour is actually Joy's but pointed up. (Mugar Memorial Library, uncatalogued box)

Sylvia claimed to her editor and later to her biographer that Mada is a composite character based in part on a physician, Dr. Steele, who preceded Joy in Pipiriki. Our evidence demonstrates that Dr. Steele, a district health officer, did not reside in Pipiriki; furthermore, the early drafts of *Myself* show that Joy was Sylvia's companion on each of the occasions attributed to Dr. Mada.

[11] "Selah," a word derived from the Hebrew psalms that Sylvia understood to mean "a pause," was the term she appropriated to name her private space for thinking, writing, and her art. With each move to a new Maori school, Keith helped Sylvia fashion a Selah: sometimes a mud hut, a cave carved out of a bank, a room in the house. In her final home, Whenua in Tauranga, her Selah was a small apartment attached to the house at the end of a cloistered walkway.

[12] Joy Alley, personal interview with authors, Torbay, Auckland, New Zealand, July 29, 1998.

[13] Sylvia Ashton-Warner, "Pipiriki," 1941–1942, Sylvia Ashton-Warner papers, Alexander Turnbull Library, Wellington, New Zealand (4425–050), n.p.

[14] Sylvia Ashton-Warner, "Skylark," November 1965, draft 2, book 6 (Mugar Memorial Library, box 16, folder 4), p. 121. When Sylvia began to assemble her papers for deposit in the Mugar Memorial Library, she rediscovered and rewrote her Pipiriki diaries, believing they contained the raw material for several novels. Drafts of several manuscripts exist—"Pipiriki," "Skylark," "Thee," "Selah," and ultimately *Myself.* Each involves a character based on Joy. The "Skylark" manuscript referred to in this chapter should not be confused with the earlier "Skylark," 1948–1949 (Mugar Memorial Library, box 3, folder 3), which concerns a female teacher's love for a male Maori teacher.

[15] Sylvia Ashton-Warner, "Skylark," November 1965, draft 2, book 6 (Mugar Memorial Library, box 16, folder 4), pp. 11–12.

[16] Joy Alley, audiotape prepared for authors, July 29, 1998.

[17] Joy Alley, audiotape prepared for authors, July 29, 1998.

[18] Sylvia Ashton-Warner, letter to Bob Gottlieb, February 21, 1979 (Mugar Memorial Library, uncatalogued box) contains typescripts of several poems by Joy Alley, including this one. The typescripts also appear among rejected pages of *I Passed This Way* (Alexander Turnbull Library, MS Papers 4425–067).

[19] "Skylark," draft 2 (Mugar Memorial Library, box 16, folder 4), n.d., n.p.

[20] An example of this practice appears in Sylvia Ashton-Warner, letter to Joy Alley, September 19, 1943: "Really, I should count myself fortunate to have a friend who tells me who and what I am. My dear, I feel married and would like to talk to you in a married way." The letter remained in Joy's possession in 1998; she included a reading of it on the audiotape prepared for the authors on July 29, 1998.

21 Joy Alley, letter to Sylvia Ashton-Warner [August 1945] (Mugar Memorial Library, uncatalogued box). More than thirty letters and poems from Joy to Sylvia, along with a photograph of the bust Sylvia sculpted, are contained in a large envelope, across which Sylvia wrote "close to the bone."

22 Joy Alley, letter to Sylvia Ashton-Warner, October 26, 1945 (Mugar Memorial Library, "close to the bone" envelope).

23 Sylvia Ashton-Warner, "Thief," fourteen-page handwritten draft, October 22–29, 1945 (Mugar Memorial Library, box 9, folder 4).

24 Sylvia Ashton-Warner, "Tenth Heaven," miscellany, c. 1966–1967 (Alexander Turnbull Library, MS Papers 4425-079), p. 233.

25 Sylvia Ashton-Warner, "Skylark," draft 2, "Oct 27 '45 Saturday morning" (Mugar Memorial Library, box 16, folder 4), n.p.

26 Sylvia Ashton-Warner, "Selah," draft 2, March 23, 1966 (Mugar Memorial Library, uncatalogued box).

27 Personal diary, July 16, 1965 (Alexander Turnbull Library, MSX 3441). She had begun work on "Thee" (Mugar Memorial Library, box 16, folder 4) on July 8, 1965.

28 The idealized intimacy she called "fusion" appears more explicitly in *Teacher*, where Sylvia says, "When I teach people I marry them" (p. 209), later elaborating, "There is quietly occurring in my infant room a grand espousal. To bring them to do what I want them to do they come near me, I draw them near me, in body and in spirit. They don't know it but I do. They become part of me, like a lover" (pp. 210–11).

29 Sylvia Ashton-Warner, "Skylark," November 1965, draft 2, book 6 (Mugar Memorial Library, box 16, folder 4), pp. 11–12.

30 This verse (32) comes from the first edition of the poem (1859). See Louis Untermeyer (1947); Untermeyer reprints the first edition and the combined third through fifth editions.

31 Even Sylvia's New York editor, Bob Gottlieb, equated Saul Mada and Paul Vercoe, and wrote Sylvia appreciatively on September 17, 1996, when she changed the Joy character in *Myself* to Dr. Mada: "I see that the Saul story—of which we saw something, didn't we, in Spinster—is demanding to be released out of you. It seems to me to be something you have to do now, in one way or another. I'm so glad you've given him his proper sex in this version, and liberated the truth" (Mugar Memorial Library, uncatalogued box). Perhaps Dent and Gottlieb made the mistake of thinking that Saul was a version of Paul because of the almost irresistible biblical parallel. Neither understood the logic of Sylvia's imagination: Joy=Eugene; Joy=Saul.

32 Sylvia Ashton-Warner, "Pipiriki Diary," draft 1, December 29, 1942 (Alexander Turnbull Library, MS Papers 4425–050).

33 The Old Man of the Sea becomes a parasitical artist figure dependent on the services of a Sinbad "complement" in an unpublished novel written during the final eighteen months of Keith Henderson's life. We are currently editing "Artist," called "Five Women" in the several versions held by the Mugar Memorial Library (box 13, folders 1–7).

34 "Tenth Heaven," miscellany (Alexander Turnbull Library, MS Papers 4425-079), p. 47. Sylvia later crossed out the word "love" and replaced it with "learn."

35 "Tenth Heaven," miscellany (Alexander Turnbull Library, MS Papers 4425-079) p. 201.

36 "Tenth Heaven," miscellany, loose leaf (Alexander Turnbull Library, MS Papers 4425-079).

37 Sylvia Ashton-Warner, letter to Bob Gottlieb, March 22, 1967 (Mugar Memorial Library, uncatalogued box).

[38] Sylvia Ashton-Warner, "Skylark," draft 2, "Oct. 15. Monday, 10 a.m. [1945]" (Mugar Memorial Library, box 16, folder 4) n.p.

[39] Elliot Henderson, interview with authors, Napier, New Zealand, July 20, 1998.

[40] Sylvia Ashton-Warner's private papers have since been transferred from the Mugar Memorial Library to the Howard Gotlieb Archival Research Center at Boston University. All the box and folder numbers remain the same.

References

Ashton-Warner, S. 1958. *Spinster.* London: Secker and Warburg.

———. 1963. *Teacher.* New York: Simon and Schuster.

———. 1967. *Myself.* New York: Simon and Schuster.

———. 1979. *I passed this way.* New York: Knopf.

Benjamin, J. 1988. *The bonds of love: Psychoanalysis, feminism, and the problem of domination.* New York: Pantheon.

Hood, L. 1988. *Sylvia! A biography of Sylvia Ashton-Warner.* Auckland, New Zealand: Penguin.

———. 1990. *Who is Sylvia? A diary of a biography.* Dunedin, New Zealand: John McIndoe.

Read, H. 1943. *Education through art.* London: Faber and Faber.

Sylvia Ashton-Warner archives. Alexander Turnbull Library, Wellington, New Zealand.

Sylvia Ashton-Warner archives. Howard Gotlieb Archival Research Center, Boston University (formerly housed at the Mugar Memorial Library, Boston University).

Untermeyer, L., ed. 1947. *Rubáiyát of Omar Khayyám, Translated into English quatrains by Edward FitzGerald.* New York: Random House.

CHAPTER SEVEN

Who Is Sylvia?: (Re)reading, Con/structing, & (Re)constructing Textual Truth & Violence

Anne-Louise Brookes

In the course of writing her biography I learnt that I had more in common with Sylvia than I ever thought was possible. (Hood 1990, 302)

Sylvia Ashton-Warner's work changed the way I see the world and the way I understand teaching. She taught me to see art as dramatic, artists as dramatic, and to see teaching as an art form. I was thrilled when Lynley Hood's biography *Sylvia!* (1988) appeared, followed shortly by a second book, *Who Is Sylvia?* (1990). Finally, I thought, Ashton-Warner's work will be embraced by scholars. But after I read Hood's work, something terrible happened. I was stunned into silence by the shock of what I felt. While I continued to develop my own adaptation of Ashton-Warner's teaching scheme,[1] I found it impossible to reconcile my reading of Ashton-Warner with Hood's construction of her. The more I brooded over Hood's portrayal, the less I was able to write about Ashton-Warner herself. It took me some months to realize why I was affected by Hood's depiction of Ashton-Warner and how her picture contributed to my silencing. I could only write comfortably again when I understood how Hood's theoretical perspective shaped her analysis and when I realized that Hood's displacing of Joy Alley was a key to understanding Hood's biographical (re)construction of Ashton-Warner. My aim here is to examine how Hood's (1988) assumptions that her "story is true" and that she has "made up nothing" (9) do violence to the life and work of Ashton-Warner.

Lynley Hood's writing in *Sylvia!* is skillful and persuasive. Her sources are impeccable and authoritative—no one else who writes about Ashton-Warner will be able to interview so many key figures from Ashton-Warner's life. It is evident that Hood was fascinated by Ashton-Warner's appeal for others and became fascinated by the complex woman herself. Hood wrote her biography of Ashton-Warner to capture "the truth" about one of New Zealand's most famous characters; her promise to readers is that she knows the inside story and will deliver it without distorting anything. She claims she will present Sylvia's fantasies and her reality so that the intelligent reader can judge for herself what to make of the woman who achieved international fame. So persuasive is Hood, so confidently and determinedly "scientific" in her telling of the story of Ashton-Warner's life, that it took me many puzzled months to figure out why I found Hood's portrait so disturbing. By questioning Hood's (apparent) assumptions about what lay at the center of Ashton-Warner's story, I was finally able to see what has made *Sylvia!* and *Who Is Sylvia?* damaging studies.

From the very outset, Hood (despite her acknowledgment of Ashton-Warner's fame and achievements) places herself at odds with Ashton-Warner and fashions herself as the protector of an unsuspecting public duped into seeing Ashton-Warner through rose-colored glasses as some kind of supermodel teacher, mother, and writer. Hood seems determined to shatter this illusion—an illusion she suggests indirectly that Ashton-Warner may have tried to promote in her autobiographical writing. Perhaps Hood's determination to smash this false image was a necessary impulse in the New Zealand of the late 1980s. Nevertheless, her choice of perspective seems regrettable when there were, and are, so many (unacknowledged) alternative ways of reading the same material.

What makes Hood's biography damaging is that she writes throughout as though she is an objective recorder of the "truth"; since her sources include Ashton-Warner and Ashton-Warner's own writing, it is difficult at first to see Hood's shaping and apparently unexamined biases and assumptions. Hood's Sylvia is an oversimplified Freudian nightmare: a woman who is forever a child, forever looking for a mother, and forever messing up the lives of her husband and children through her own selfishness and inability to know her place. Supposedly describing the famous educator and author with detached truth, Hood scolds and scorns an infantile Sylvia. It is as though Hood does not recognize Ashton-Warner's attempts to break through what Sidonie Smith (1987) has called the "androcentric" (62) voice of the dominant culture. Notice how *Sylvia!* begins with a declaration of truth:

> This story is true. All the characters are real, even Sylvia Ashton-Warner. Her life is as strange a mix of truth and fantasy as you will find anywhere, but the important point is that it is her fantasy, not mine.... I have made up nothing. (Hood 1988, 9)

Right from the opening, Hood establishes herself as superior to and inviolable by the fantasy-loving Sylvia, who is clearly not to be trusted. Hood suggests that she herself will offer the trusted voice since Sylvia's story is so "strange a mix of truth and fantasy." If the reader accepts Hood's perspective at the outset, Sylvia does not have a chance to be perceived as adult or credible. Further, Hood's reconstruction perpetuates textual violence by establishing a tone for subsequent readings of Ashton-Warner's theory of education and by constructing and reinforcing the view that Ashton-Warner was a creative writer, a charismatic classroom teacher, but not a theoretician. Hood makes the reader ask: how could Ashton-Warner be credible on any level if she was deluded by her own fantasies? Never mind that it is Hood who has planted the suggestion that Ashton-Warner's views are fantasies.

How does Hood's view violate Ashton-Warner? Three key assumptions shape Hood's (1990) portrayal (I am tempted to call it betrayal) of Ashton-Warner: the assumptions that Ashton-Warner remained a child, that she hated her mother, and that her muse was the devil. Hood ties these three assumptions together and in so doing distorts the ways in which Ashton-Warner was supported by, and relied on, women for inspiration. Specifically, I shall argue that Hood minimizes the power held by the single most important woman in Ashton-Warner's life: Joy Alley. In my reading of Ashton-Warner's work, Joy Alley lies at the heart of much of what Ashton-Warner wrote. Joy Alley is the muse for the adult Sylvia, who dared to become a successful artist, teacher, writer, mother; who dared even to surpass her mother, whom she admired and respected[2] (see James and Thompson, this volume for an exploration of Joy Alley's and Sylvia's relationship). I will also examine how Hood writes Joy Alley into and out of the picture.

Hood (1988, 1990) suggests that Sylvia and Joy seem to love each other, but she also describes each woman's fear of the word "lesbian." By tacitly supporting the stigmatizing of the word "lesbian" and by recording but not contextualizing Joy and Sylvia's energetic rejection of the label, Hood neatly accomplishes two things: she taints the concept of lesbianism, and she deflects attention away from Sylvia's relationship with Joy Alley, under any label. Yet Hood's manner of raising the issue of lesbianism does not clear Sylvia of taint. Hood in fact leaves the reader with the impression that Sylvia is, as her opening lines suggest, "strange" and deluded. And so Hood's perspective encourages the reader's censure of Sylvia while apparently shifting the ground away from whether she was involved in a lesbian relationship. Hood's is a tough job. She writes as though Ashton-Warner needs defending from the label "lesbian" but at the same time wants to blame her for being difficult and different. Eventually she blames Sylvia for her relationship with Joy Alley and, in a curious way, dismisses the power of Sylvia's own description of this relationship.

Joy Alley's spirit is woven into the very fabric of Ashton-Warner's work. On one hand, Hood (1988) acknowledges the importance of the place where Joy and Sylvia met in the 1940s: "Pipiriki was a Maori village fifty miles upriver from the coastal town of Wanganui. The setting was beautiful … exhilarating … threatening … and Sylvia, struggling to recover from a shattering nervous breakdown, was vulnerable to all it had to offer" (89). On the other hand, Hood directs our attention to Ashton-Warner's vulnerability, implying that her time there with Joy was marred by Sylvia's excessive openness. From Hood's perspective, the setting itself is both exhilarating and threatening, suggesting that the very meeting ground—the physical context for their meeting—is somehow suspect.

In *I Passed This Way*, Ashton-Warner describes her life as an infant-room teacher in the two-room school in Pipiriki where her husband Keith was the headmaster. Only thirty-two years old, she writes about how she longed to "escape from teaching" (294), to become an artist, to write. But the conditions of war and the need for another salary to support their family made escape impossible. Opal (Sylvia's fictive name for Joy Alley), the "spinster" district nurse, lived across the road from Sylvia, Keith, and their three children. Sylvia's goal at Pipiriki, Hood (1988) reports, was to become a "better teacher" and a "worthwhile person" (90). I suggest Ashton-Warner was always driven by a desire to create, a passion ignited further when she met her muse, Joy Alley. Hood goes on to describe how Sylvia admired

> Joy's wide knowledge of philosophy, politics and the arts, and [how] Joy in turn was fascinated by Sylvia's creativity, passion, introspection and reckless unconformity. Sylvia's impressions of the relationship were recorded in a diary she kept at the time. When she revised it for publication in 1967 as *Myself*, she changed Joy to the fictional "Dr. Saul Mada" and she presented the same relationship in her autobiography as a stormy friendship with a nurse named Opal Owen. (1988, 96)

Drawing from her diary, Ashton-Warner rewrites Joy as an attractive male doctor with whom the protagonist is in love. Why is this love story not pursued in Lynley Hood's biography? Notice how Hood constructs Sylvia's relationship with Joy:

> In her love affairs with women Sylvia had a powerful need to be mothered.... Falling in love with a woman meant for Sylvia the explosive recognition of both the painfully unacceptable and the impossibly idealised parts of herself in the other, and a desperate craving to possess the other in order to make herself whole. (1988, 94)

Moreover, Hood assumes:

> From all the men and women she loved, Sylvia sought attention and admiration, but she was particularly anxious to be admired by men; they controlled the status heap. If she could make men worship at her feet, then everyone would see that she belonged at the top. So partly for this reason, and partly because she just couldn't help it, Sylvia flirted compulsively with men all her life. (1988, 94)

Surely the gap between flirtation and a love affair should be acknowledged, as should the commonly felt experience of wanting maternal nurture and wanting to feel whole.

Hood also points out that Keith, and not the women she loved, consistently mothered Sylvia: "Keith's mothering role ... had become a way of life at Pipiriki, for in Sylvia's self-defined reality the children occupied a very peripheral place, and in her inner world they barely existed at all" (1988, 93).[3] From Hood's perspective, Sylvia's "need to be loved was matched only by her need to love. Again, it was a matter of emotional survival. The euphoria of falling in love pushed back the depression that licked around the edges of her consciousness" (1988, 94). The assumption that Sylvia used love to forestall depression surely minimizes the power of the love itself. It was, in fact, within the boundaries of her relationship with Joy, as well as within the boundaries of Sylvia's private Selah—Sylvia's room of her own, away from the family home and Keith—that her creative work flourished. Hood does concede that "Joy was the inspiration" (1988, 104): "Sylvia shared with Joy her programme of study, and her search for an underlying design for her life" (1988, 102). Notice how Hood shifts the focus away from their love (and Sylvia's work) and into Sylvia's apparently impossible expectations when she says:

> Joy was not, and could not be, Sylvia's ideal woman but Sylvia cast her into the role regardless. At first Joy was thrilled by the attention and admiration, and by the gifts—books, sheet music for the piano, a ring, paintings—that Sylvia bestowed on her, and she tried very hard to play the part. For both of them life became a euphoric dream. All that mattered was that they loved and needed each other. They spent their waking hours either being together or wishing they were, and on some Saturday nights they slept together. Both women were convinced of their own heterosexuality and they regarded sharing a bed as an innocent giving and receiving of comfort and reassurance.... Gradually the dream turned sour. Joy could not be Sylvia's ideal-woman/ideal-mother/ideal-self. (1988, 104)

In a letter to Joy that Hood wrote following Ashton-Warner's death, she discusses Sylvia's love for Joy. Note her lucid, shrewd line of questioning and reasoning. Hood begins by asking Joy to correct her if she has it wrong:

> It concerns a summer during the Pipiriki years, when for a couple of weeks you and Sylvia slept together in a tent, and were totally absorbed with each other. I gather that at the time some people thought this shocking, presumably assuming a sexual component to the relationship. This is in sharp contrast to the pre-Freudian notion that women falling in love and engaging in displays of affection was of no consequence because women were not thought to be sexual beings. From the 1943 notes you lent me it is clear that you and Sylvia were aware of your sexuality and had discussed it—but did you relate this awareness to the relationship between you, or just to your relationship with men? (1990, 153–54)

Hood then records Joy's response but comments neither on the obvious sidestepping Joy does, nor on the implications of her own biases and assumptions about Joy and Sylvia. Here is Hood's record of the answer from Joy:

> She (Joy) seemed glad that I had brought the lesbian question out into the open. Yes, it was a passion. Yes, they sometimes slept in the same bed—she said it was not a sexual thing but something that nurses did for comfort and reassurance, or because there was a shortage of beds. She rejected the lesbian label mainly because of her negative image of lesbians. She saw them as strident, predatory man-haters.... She argued that the Health Department would never have appointed a lesbian to the high position she had held, and pointed out that she and Sylvia enjoyed good relationships with men. (1990, 164)

What can I, as reader, make of "Yes, it was a passion"? Volumes—whether of Hood's or Joy's or both—may be deliberately suppressed in Hood's careful words: "She rejected the lesbian label." Certainly Hood's biography, read in conjunction with *Who Is Sylvia?*, continues the suppression by blurring, muting, and subsuming Sylvia's and Joy's passion. Rather, it is the "good relationships" with men that get Hood's attention and approval. Perhaps Hood even encourages the reader to see between her lines—but if so, she makes it clear that whatever (distasteful) things we perceive there are our own fault or Sylvia's—certainly not Hood's.

While it may be the case that both Joy and Sylvia enjoyed good relationships with men, Sylvia says little about these relationships. Instead, she writes about her relationship with Joy. She writes about Joy in the same sexually charged language she uses to describe the very place she and Joy met. In *I Passed This Way*, Ashton-Warner describes the place where Joy Alley entered her life:

> Pipiriki is a hollow in the ranges shaped like a heart.... The valley is a cauldron of steaming passions irregularly stirred by Fate; a place where quiet orderly, usually routine people, tourists included, drop their guards like clothes on a riverbank before entering turbulent waters; to act themselves out for once in a lifetime with no accounting to God, man, past, or future, babbling in tongues of the red ranta worn in the hair of the forest.... There are so many dells and grassy nooks calling for people to fling themselves down in to kiss and kiss, that love-affairs flame with forbidden lovers and hate-affairs deepened unto death and guests are never the same again. (296)

Ashton-Warner's autobiographical reconstruction of Pipiriki is laden with references to Opal, a thinly disguised Joy. Only on occasion does she speak about another lover, Pan, whom she also names Hilton Morris, a mystery man who receives perhaps more attention from Hood than from Ashton-Warner. Hood concludes that Pan is Walter Harris, a school inspector who spent time with Sylvia and Keith at Pipiriki. Sylvia writes that "three major formative loves of my life, Keith, Hilton and Opal, were under way simultaneously in Pipiriki" (*I Passed This Way*, 316): "Three loves: my husband, a woman, a lover. Plenty of room. By my reckoning there was a place for two men in a woman's life simultaneously and most certainly for a woman too. Each love different from the other two; rather than overlapping complemented one another" (326).

Ashton-Warner's references to love-complements are not always clear, but Hood neither points to ambiguity nor questions Sylvia's use of the term (see James and Thompson, this volume; see Robertson, this volume). According to Hood (1988), Ashton-Warner believed that what "made the artist really unique was his need for a complement. A complement was a boring, untalented individual who drew joy, purpose and inspiration from caring for an artist … nothing sexual at all in the artist-complement bond; it was a simple matter of parasite and host" (182). Hood suggests that Ashton-Warner used the artist-complement bond to define her relationship with Joy Alley. How could Joy Alley, an active and productive person with her own work and writing—an inspiration for Ashton-Warner—have fit into the "parasite" side of the neat arrangement Hood defines? Elsewhere Hood argues that Ashton-Warner saw herself as two separate people: "She saw herself as a charming, compliant, sexy woman, and a rampaging male artist who lived life on his own unique terms.… That he required 'attention, praise, service, sacrifice and unflawed devotion' was a normal and proper consequence of his temperament" (1988, 181). In fact, it was a devoted Keith and not the women in Sylvia's life who consistently attended to and serviced the "boring" needs of the artist Sylvia. In a society that expected women to service the needs of men, Sylvia paid heavily for this attention, though less so to Keith, who did support her work.

Even in her autobiography, which was written close to the end of her life, Sylvia writes about Opal, and not about Keith or Pan. Only Joy is immortalized in Ashton-Warner's books. When asked by Hood (1990) about her favorite book, Sylvia indicates *Spinster* (17). Hood asks Sylvia:

> What were you sad about when you wrote it? She said she was lonely for her dearest friend from Pipiriki, Joy Alley—and then, protesting that the name had slipped out by accident, she began calling her "Opal".… She said she dealt with the pain of separation by stepping into the character of Anna Vorontosov, and that knowing Opal enabled her to understand spinsters. She said she based Anna Vorontosov on Opal. (But surely, I thought, Anna Vorontosov was based on Sylvia herself?) (Hood 1990, 17)

Since Hood did not see Joy as central to Sylvia, she could not, of course, understand why Sylvia would see herself as the frustrated, unsuccessful male lover of Anna rather than as Anna herself. Even the word "joy" is woven into the fabric of *Spinster*: "Look, they say, at all this juice and all this joy. Look where the sap runs. The sap has to run for joy" (230). In countless ways, Joy is written into Ashton-Warner's books.[4] Ashton-Warner's interest in women's relationships is also apparent in three unpublished manuscripts: "Barren Radiance," "Five Women," and another of Sylvia's favorites, "Tenth Heaven." These were bought by her publisher, Bob Gottlieb, during the late 1960s but were never published: it is as though Gottlieb, like Hood, was determined to silence the possibility or assumption that Ashton-Warner might have had a lesbian relationship with Joy Alley.

While in the archives of the Mugar Memorial Library[5] at Boston University, I examined early drafts of "Five Women."[6] In the second draft, Sylvia harkens back to Pipiriki (her meeting place with Joy), using the concept of complement in a positive way that makes Hood's "parasite and host" definition seem much too simple:

> I'm thinking of a time twenty years ago when the artist in me found its complement in a woman of my own age. Both of us staggering through youth. "Where have you been all this time?" I asked. "I couldn't find you," she said. And, we swore fidelity forever. But it was only a matter of four or five years before she fell in love and withdrew from me. At that time I held the ace in my hand which was that the art in me would survive, but I didn't know it.

Hood claims that Ashton-Warner stopped working on this manuscript because of her publisher's reaction to the explicit homosexuality and because "she couldn't cope with the idea of lesbianism. She abandoned the novel, and whenever necessary thereafter used the artist complement concept to explain her relationship with the woman she loved" (1988, 183).

Notice that Hood says it is the "idea" of lesbianism that distresses Ashton-Warner. Why doesn't Hood point out that Ashton-Warner seems caught in an apparent contradiction between the artist-complement as one who services her needs and the artist-complement as one with whom she shares her art and passion? Sylvia and Joy shared three passionate years in Pipiriki. Joy's decision to leave Pipiriki was followed by a two-month illness during which time she was cared for by Sylvia. Their separation caused unbearable grief for Sylvia, who wrote:

> The loss of Opal I couldn't stand.... I was no longer wonderful to her, or first with her since she'd fallen in love with a romantic young man. All she wanted from me was ordinary dry friendship, not inspiration or love or anything vital.... In the evenings ... I'd go to the big kitchen table ... with my dear paper and paints to make a book of pictures for Opal, to somehow tell her, explain to her by imagery, to communicate with her, to try to share with her again what we'd shared on the River

with barely a word spoken; to try to recapture peace I'd known. So that she'd love me again. (*I Passed This Way*, 324–25)

Quoting from an unposted diary entry/letter from Sylvia to Joy dated 1946, Hood acknowledges Sylvia's loss:

In her diary Sylvia reproached Joy with the story of Naomi and Ruth (whither thou goest, I will go), and wrote of her black night of the soul: "My love. Now the tear dogs are up again. I didn't go to school today. I told Keith I wanted to be excused for another week. I haven't been to school at all since that letter I burnt—I haven't sorted myself out." (1988, 108)

Throughout the year of her departure and for years afterward, Joy continued to write letters and poems to Sylvia. Some of them I discovered in an uncatalogued box in the Boston archives.

Sylvia's stormy post-Pipiriki relationship with Joy lived on through letters and occasional visits for another decade. In *Sylvia* (1988) Hood acknowledges that Ashton-Warner's goal of winning back Joy's devotion was never realized. Joy told Hood in an interview that "Sylvia made impossible demands on me that I couldn't fulfill" (Hood 1990, 90). Post-Joy, Sylvia developed several significant relationships with women, many through letter-writing, though none would compare with Joy, whom "she never forgot" (Hood 1988, 112).

Based on my readings of Ashton-Warner and Hood, I am surprised by Hood's compulsion to (mis)identify the mysterious Walter Harris as a significant character. Harris, a shadowy figure with whom Sylvia shared secret kisses, pales by comparison with Joy. But strangely, Hood highlights Sylvia's love for Harris and says confidently, "Although she (Sylvia) fell deeply in love with women, it was in the company of men that Sylvia really came alive" (1988, 126). What in Ashton-Warner's work supports this view?

From my perspective, Hood's assumptions about the focus of Sylvia's love exist in violent contradiction to Sylvia's descriptions of herself, her mother, and her muses. Living as we still do in a homophobic world divided by gender, race, and class, I can imagine why Hood is tempted to believe that Ashton-Warner's muse was the devil. As a successful and talented woman, she was bedeviled by frustrations, frustrations Sylvia herself describes in great detail in her autobiography. Because she is so explicit and writes so well about her childhood memories and experiences, she gives readers all they need to (mis)construct reasons for her choices. I can understand why Hood portrays her as a mother-searching child who confuses sexual love and mother-substitute love, but ultimately, I refuse the power of that suggestion. Hood conspires with those readers who want Ashton-Warner to be quiet, to somehow conform to the respectability Sylvia courted but herself scorned and moved beyond. In a stretch, perhaps I can also understand how Hood's repeated reassurances to her readers that she has "made up nothing" and is "telling the truth" could be meant to mollify those who would rather see Ashton-Warner as eccentric and immature rather than creative, radical, and frustrated.

To understand Sylvia Ashton-Warner's life, perhaps it does not matter how Ashton-Warner defined her relationship with Joy Alley. But from my perspective, it does matter that Hood's way of writing acts to demonize Ashton-Warner's character. As well, her writing works to demonize lesbianism and raises it as one of the specters that must beleaguer any conscientious, scientific, perfectly truth-abiding biographer of Ashton-Warner—such as herself. Symbolically, Hood's struggle with lesbianism parallels her struggle to make sense of the (social) context in which Ashton-Warner lived and wrote, a context once described by Carolyn Heilbrun (1988) thus: "These women had no models on which to form their lives, nor could they themselves become mentors since they did not tell the truth about their lives" (25). Hood fails to analyze the world in which Ashton-Warner struggled successfully to write and teach.

More damaging still is the ambiguous way Hood (1990) examines the impact of Ashton-Warner's work. She repeatedly praises Sylvia with one hand and strips her of worth with the other. Look at what she has to say to a young man "who had made a special study of Sylvia Ashton-Warner" (Hood 1990, 114) (it is noteworthy that Hood seems to assume she is defending Ashton-Warner to him):

> I talked about her spiritual impact—he was unimpressed. I mentioned her use of powerful emotions in her teaching—he claimed that all good teachers did that. I told him that she enabled each child to make a profound personal statement about themselves—he said that encouraging individuality was dangerous and anarchistic. By then it was clear that he hated her guts and nothing I said was going to make a difference. He went on to insist that her impact came from the power of her writing and her personal teaching style, and when you stripped those away there was nothing underneath. (Hood 1990, 114)

Hood's ambiguous response to his assessment neither supports nor examines his view: "Perhaps he's right, perhaps he's wrong, as far as I'm concerned the jury is out. I've got no particular ideological axe to grind.... I just want to make sense of all the contradictions in her life and work" (Hood 1990, 114). Hood, I suggest, ultimately fails to make sense of Ashton-Warner's contradictions precisely because of her "particular ideological axe"—her unwillingness to see and articulate how her perspective unfavorably positions Ashton-Warner. This position, I also suggest, is in keeping with Hood's assumption that her story is "true" and that she has "made up nothing" (1988, 9).

In a strange and complex way, Lynley Hood becomes the heroine of her own story about Sylvia—after all, she writes as if she has had to labor mightily to protect her readers from many things, among them a relationship with Joy that only Sylvia's immaturity has forced Hood into discussing at all. From Hood's perspective, Sylvia is certainly not the heroine of her own story since she is so clearly the willful child who deserves constant public scolding. Readers who accept Hood's "truth" inevitably disapprove of Sylvia, as did I in my first reading of Hood's biography—a reading that for a time rendered me silent and stopped me from writing about the woman whose work has changed my life.

I now wonder whose violence, or self-violence, is greatest in all of this interpreting: Hood's, in declaring and believing that she speaks the "truth"; Ashton-Warner's, in accepting her culture's and her editor's condemnation of homosexuality; or Hood's and Ashton-Warner's readers', in accepting that silencing, sublimation, and textual violence are inevitable and therefore unremarkable parts of all women's lives. Hood's basic assumptions—that she is telling the truth and that Ashton-Warner is a spoiled and damaged child who needs to be publicly scolded—invite challenge.

When I read Ashton-Warner first in the 1980s, I was struggling to find my own voice in an academy that still seemed to regard women as alien and secondary. Reading Ashton-Warner's stories and life gave me hope that the infantilizing voice of patriarchy was one I could write my way through. Ashton-Warner showed me how she wrote her way into adulthood, defying the voices that would have limited and silenced her. For me, Ashton-Warner is appealing not because she was any form of paragon, but because she made mistakes and struggled through anyway. For me, Ashton-Warner's stories of herself and others contain all the messiness of life—what Sidonie Smith (1987) characterizes as "the confusions, the crampedness, the compromises, the ambivalence—that is, the damages to woman of seeking to appropriate the story of man in a culture that would condemn her to its sentence" (62). Reading Ashton-Warner for the first time, I was thrilled to discover an educator who could teach me deeply about the art of reading and writing; a woman who talked about her loves, her strengths, her confusions, and her questions; a woman who had broken through the patriarchal constraints of her time, with full and acknowledged help from those who, if she had been sweetly compliant, would not have helped her at all. In other words, Ashton-Warner served as my muse in the classroom and in my writing because she was so clearly fallible. Another way of seeing the "truth" about her life is that Ashton-Warner struggled throughout her life to resist her culture's determination to infantilize and silence her. That she could conceive of the brilliant key-word scheme is noteworthy—that she could write about it and find an audience for it worldwide is miraculous. Rather than seeing Ashton-Warner as a permanent child grasping for attention and glory, I see her as a woman struggling against enormous odds to become a woman with a voice.

So much has developed in the understanding of life writing and of women's lives in the years since 1988. If Lynley Hood were writing her biography today, would she make the same claims to "truth" as she did in 1988? Ashton-Warner's way of writing—her admitted confusions and personal searching—now seems even more significant than it did in her lifetime. The way she positions herself, the way she takes up subjectivity and objectivity in her work as an educator, gives readers such as myself the courage to examine our own contexts and our conscious constructions of selves as well as the unconscious scripts, as Jill Ker Conway (1999) calls them, that we inherit and enact. I wonder when will there be another biography of Ashton-Warner, a biography that addresses some of the alternate readings Hood chose not to see as "true."

Notes

[1] I have adapted Ashton-Warner's Teaching Scheme and for several years I have used it to teach critical thinking skills in university classrooms (for example see Brookes, 1992, 2000). Most recently, I have been teaching pre-service teachers to use Ashton-Warner's Key Word theory in their own teaching.

[2] I spent a month in the Mugar Memorial Library at Boston University reading the entire Ashton-Warner collection. Copies of the letters Ashton-Warner wrote to her mother suggest a rich and deep connection between them (see, for example, Box 2 and Box 22).

[3] Ashton-Warner wrote copious letters to her children during the years she lived and taught in North America. Reading copies of this correspondence suggests that all of Ashton-Warner's children were very important to her. In *Who Is Sylvia?* Hood mentions Ashton-Warner's "20-year correspondence" (p. 132) with her son Elliott. Surely a 20-year correspondence with Elliott does not support Hood's assumption that Ashton-Warner was inattentive to her children (see, for example, Box 19, Mugar Memorial Library).

[4] See *Myself* and *Greenstone*.

[5] Sylvia Ashton-Warner's private papers have since been moved from the Mugar Memorial Library to the Howard Gotlieb Archival Research Center at Boston University. All the box and folder numbers remained the same.

[6] Box 13, folder 2, and Box 15, Mugar Memorial Library.

References

Ashton-Warner, S. 1958. *Spinster.* Repr., London: Virago, 1980.

———. 1966. *Greenstone.* New York: Simon and Schuster.

———. 1968. *Myself.* London: Secker and Warburg.

———. 1979. *I passed this way.* New York: Alfred A. Knopf.

Brookes, A-L. 1992. *Feminist pedagogy: An autobiographical approach.* Halifax, Canada: Fernwood Publishing.

———. 2000. *Teaching and learning liberation: Feminist pedagogies.* Regina, Canada: women's studies research unit, University of Saskatchewan.

Conway, J. K. 1999. *When memory speaks: Exploring the art of autobiography.* New York: Vintage.

Heilbrun, C. 1988. *Writing a woman's life.* New York: Ballantine Books.

Hood, L. 1988. *Sylvia! The biography of Sylvia Ashton-Warner.* New York: Viking.

———. 1990. *Who is Sylvia? The diary of a biography.* Dunedin, New Zealand: John McIndoe.

Smith, S. 1987. *A poetics of women's autobiography: Marginality and the fictions of self-representation.* Bloomington: Indiana University Press.

CHAPTER EIGHT

Reading in(to) Sylvia:
Interviews on Ashton-Warner's Influence

Kathleen Connor and Linda Radford
with Judith P. Robertson

Our interest in Sylvia Ashton-Warner as provocateur was initially provoked by *Cinema and the Politics of Desire in Teacher Education* (Robertson 1994). Robertson's study examines how white primary school teachers "read" teacher films in relation to their own identity work and how the collective phenomenon of the dream of love in teaching, a fantasy formation, emerges from viewer responses to alluring screen teachers/heroes. One of the films featured in the study is Michael Firth's film *Sylvia* (Reynolds and Firth 1984), which dramatizes the life and influence of Ashton-Warner as a radical and singular teacher. She defied the conventions of her time, rebelling against New Zealand's educational norms, marking herself as a defender of Maori interests through her innovative and culturally sensitive approaches to teaching and developing classroom readers. After viewing the film, we decided to revisit the life and legacy of Ashton-Warner to find out whether and how Ashton-Warner's works continue to have an impact larger than the sum of their parts. This chapter recounts where this excitation took us as we set out to engage with individuals who not only knew Ashton-Warner but were influenced by her and could comment on the impact of her work.

We settled on three prominent scholars.[1] C. K. Stead is a distinguished novelist, poet, and critic. He taught at the University of Auckland and remains a prominent voice and outspoken critic in New Zealand's literary landscape. Carole Durix is a French literary critic, professor, and managing editor at the Université de Bourgogne. She studied Ashton-Warner's work extensively for her graduate and postgraduate work and is an international leading literary theorist of

Ashton-Warner's brand of literary genius (Durix 1977, 1979, 1980, 1987, 1989). Both Stead and Durix met personally with Ashton-Warner in New Zealand. Herbert Kohl is a widely published radical thinker in the field of education in the United States, best known for his passionate endorsements of student-centered pedagogy in the open-classroom debates of the 1970s. Kohl established the Center for Teacher Excellence and Social Justice at the University of San Francisco's school of education and is currently the Lang visiting professor at Swarthmore College's educational studies. From the participants' interviews we were able to "read into" distinct yet overlapping experiences with the ideas, innovations, and life of Ashton-Warner. Each narrative sounded out the tensions winding around their thoughts of how Ashton-Warner influenced a commitment to education or a literary calling. Through our questions, designed to get at the history of each participant's engagement with the life and work of Ashton-Warner, we found that she endures as a provoking, productive, enigmatic, extraordinary, and controversial figure in pedagogy and in literature.

Carole Durix, January 22, 2003

INTERVIEWERS: What were the specific circumstances of your introduction to Ashton-Warner's work?

DURIX: In 1974 I attended the EACLALS [European Association for Commonwealth Literature and Language Studies] conference held at Stirling University in Scotland. At the time I was reading to decide on the subject of my M.A. thesis. For personal reasons my choice of zone was New Zealand. Well-known academics from all over the world were present at the conference, and so I asked Professor R.T. Robertson, a New Zealander who taught at the University of Saskatoon, and Professor Ian Gordon from the University of Victoria, Wellington for their advice. Both were pioneers in Commonwealth studies and both spontaneously suggested a study of Sylvia Ashton-Warner for, in their opinion, she was an important New Zealand writer and little had been written on her work. The conference bookstall supplied me with a copy of *Spinster* that I immediately read. The book initially fascinated me on two counts: the vivacity and immediacy of her prose intrigued me and Ashton-Warner's capacity to bring the Maori pupils to life through light touches of the paintbrush of words both delighted and consoled me. Her ability to express the fears and frustrations of her character Anna Vorontosov, her capacity for deflating the importance of the hierarchy by looking on tragic situations with humor, comforted me. My first teaching experience had been with a class of forty-eight seven-year-olds from a difficult area in Britain. Had I had the opportunity of reading *Spinster* at the time I am sure the experience would have been less traumatic.

INTERVIEWERS: What impact did her work and life have on yours?

DURIX: In 1976, having completed my master's dissertation, a close study of Sylvia Ashton-Warner's novel *Greenstone*, I decided to continue my research as a doctoral student. This was not possible without a visit to New Zealand to have access to library facilities. Consequently, in 1978 the whole family spent three months in Auckland so that I could gather the necessary documents for my study. At that time the Internet was unheard of. When I announced my research project to many *pakeha* academics on the campus in Auckland I was greeted with incredulity or a polite "Oh!" and the conversation turned to more serious subjects of consideration (British or American literature). New Zealand bookshops had only limited stocks of New Zealand literature that was often housed in the dark corners at the back of the shop! I persisted and, between secondhand bookshops and the 'Glass Case,' which contained the University of Auckland's collection of New Zealand literature together with the vast collection of journals, I managed to assemble the necessary documents for my studies. This consisted mainly of background reading to New Zealand literature in general, Ashton-Warner's short stories published in various journals, reviews of her novels, and just one critical article by Dennis McEldowney published in 1969. I also visited many of the communities where Ashton-Warner had taught and was able to appreciate the extent of the isolation that she suffered in places such as Pipiriki or the outposts of the East Cape.

She invited us all to her home in Tauranga for the weekend on condition that we cooked for ourselves. In fact we had the free run of her beautiful house for she lived in her granny-flat, Selah 7, at the end of the patio. Spending time with her enabled me to gauge her personality—her generosity with our children, the magic of her relationship with them—and at the same time to observe the barriers that she raised in order to protect her own independence. The rest of the family was firmly sent down to the beach while she showed me many of her private archives and personal paintings and I was the only one admitted into Selah. I realized even at that early date that her avowed credo of 'liberty' was ultimately framed and governed by her own desires. Her friends and acquaintances were gently but firmly fitted into the framework of her design. On the Saturday evening she organized a party for us with her extended family. I perceived that she felt once again that her work was being recognized by people from outside New Zealand, and she resented the fact that recognition 'at home' was still not forthcoming.

I returned to France with my research 'tools' and for the next few years 'lived' a monastic life with Ashton-Warner while I wrote my thesis. I think what perturbed me most came from the fact that, being the first to study her work in depth, I could not exchange ideas with other researchers. The danger was that my research, which consisted mainly of literary criticism, might become completely enveloped by Sylvia Ashton-Warner's writing and consequently lack the necessary distance for criticism. It was difficult to stand back and appreciate her techniques, which themselves were based on fusional strategies.

C. K. Stead's (1981b) seminal article appeared in his collection of essays *In the Glass Case* in 1981 just before I completed my thesis. This, I felt, indicated that the importance of the writings of Sylvia Ashton-Warner was beginning to be recognized within New Zealand and this, for me, was a source of great satisfaction.

INTERVIEWERS: What will be Ashton-Warner's legacy and effect? Was there resistance to her ideas?

DURIX: People's reactions to Sylvia Ashton-Warner are never indifferent. The woman charmed and exasperated; her curiosity was permanent, her ambitions great, and her thirst for recognition was never quenched. Her teaching methods have been espoused and rejected with equal passion. Her delight that she be the subject of discussion by intellectuals around the world via that international means of communication, the Internet, in the year 2003 would be immense. Perhaps her greatest legacy is precisely that over twenty years after her death her ideas and her writing continue to provoke discussion. Her capacity to shake the establishment out of complacency with controversial ideas, her ability to seize upon minute details of everyday life to enrich her storytelling either in the classroom or in her fiction, was unconventional but is still pertinent today.

Her importance for educational practices has to be examined within the history of education in New Zealand. In the fifties her ideas were revolutionary. At a time when the curriculum was binding and the individuality of the pupils was largely ignored, her theories disturbed the establishment. Even in the late seventies pupils in New Zealand were still being taught to read with books imported from Great Britain with stories of snow at Christmas and blue tits singing in the garden in springtime. The contents of these readers in no way corresponded to the experience of *pakeha* children, let alone the Maori living in the country.

Faced with the problem of reading materials, Sylvia Ashton-Warner was able to put her own artistic gift to good use and produce individual readers for her pupils. Each book was adapted to the particular interests of the child at a given time. Ideally these books were one-off creations not meant to be re-used. Their elaboration depended on the time and the talent of the teacher. This was possible because she was posted in isolated country schools with a limited number of pupils and because of the untiring support of her husband and headmaster, Keith Henderson. As an ideal, this is perfect but in practice.... The fact that these innovatory methods were instigated by a woman who radically questioned the authority of those who formulated the syllabus shook the foundations of the educational board.

Nevertheless her educational theories on the respect of the individual child and the need to adapt material to the requirements of the classroom were sound. Some of her contemporaries probably used similar methods but Sylvia Ashton-Warner was the first to formulate and publish them. This was no easy task as the history of her publications shows. Her educational treatise, *Teacher*, was repeatedly rejected by various New Zealand publishers. Undeterred, Ashton-Warner reformulated her text to produce the novel *Spinster*, published in London by Secker and Warburg in 1958. It was an immediate success. The education world became acquainted with her theories via this fictional text. In many ways I find that fiction served her purpose better than her 'treatise,' *Teacher*, which sits uneasily astride autobiography and educational theory.

The relative success of *Spearpoint: Teacher in America* proved that a single method cannot be systematically applied to very different situations and that education is a question of interaction, understanding, and exchange. Whereas Ashton-Warner was 'at home' and at ease with her Maori pupils, she failed to 'connect' with many of her students in North America. In my opinion this does not necessarily indicate a weakness in the theory but rather shows that a primary school teacher needs to have an intimate knowledge of the cultural attitudes of his or her pupils and this obviously takes time.

Sylvia Ashton-Warner considered herself an artist in the broadest sense of the term; her writing reflects this all-enveloping notion and adopts strategies from painting and music in an effort to integrate harmoniously various mediums of expression that have different appeal for the readers' senses. Her storytelling uses a number of narrative techniques—the elements of time and space—and an apparently naïve sense of humor to draw her audience into her stories. For Sylvia, the imagination was defined in terms of fluidity—a natural exchange is established between the narrator and the narratee who becomes so intimately involved in the process of story-making that the plot takes on a life of its own. In spite of this, the author controls the development of her text with an iron hand.

Perhaps the most original novels in terms of narrative technique are those in which Ashton-Warner uses a first-person narrator who can be a character, an omniscient outside narrator, and at times the author herself. The different narrators all have their own point of view and have access to the limited amount of information that the author is prepared to divulge. At times this leads to a fusional interchange between the first- and second-person narration. As a result, the various characters and narrators, instead of exchanging ideas, become undifferentiated and are susceptible to being manipulated by the author.

INTERVIEWERS: What factors or developments in autobiography and feminism have affected social memory or amnesia about this woman who has been called New Zealand's most distinctive writer, and who in 1959 was hailed as one of the ten best writers in the English language?

DURIX: I think it was *Time* [magazine] who hailed Ashton-Warner as one of the ten best writers in the English language in 1959. These hit-parades are to be taken with more than just a pinch of salt. I wonder who the other nine writers were. As far as New Zealand literature is concerned, Sylvia Ashton-Warner definitely stood out when, in 1958, she published *Spinster* with its touching evocations of Maori children; until then Maori characters in New Zealand fiction tended to be reduced to the stereotype of the 'noble savage.' The Maori themselves had produced little fictional writing.[2] Witi Ihimaera was the first to publish a book of short stories, *Pounamu, pounamu*, in 1972.

I feel ill equipped to comment on the sociological impact of Ashton-Warner for her educational theories and her feminism were peripheral to my enterprise of literary criticism. In the sphere of autobiography Sylvia Ashton-Warner left no fewer than four different works concerning her own life and writing. Such a rich corpus of autobiographical material over such a long period of time (1958–1979) is a significant indication of the importance she attached to the subject of her self. For the literary critic, this material is particularly interesting to study because of the varied choice of genre: the novel, the journal, the diary, and the 'official' autobiography. Here again I was more interested in studying the author's strategies for writing about her own life. Rather than examine the events themselves, I preferred to concentrate on the significance of memory, of ellipses, and on the author's reordering of events in order to fit a particular artistic agenda.

C. K. Stead, November 25, 2002

CONNOR: What were the specific circumstances of your introduction to Sylvia Ashton-Warner's work?

STEAD: You mean, when I first read her? Only as an interested New Zealand reader, I was pretty young at the time. Actually, I don't remember when or where I read which of her books.

CONNOR: Is it something that the young people were discussing at the time?

STEAD: Not very much, no. But I think things happened in reverse for her. Usually writers get a local reputation, and then maybe it extends outward to become an international reputation. In her case, I think she was a pretty obscure figure in New Zealand, and then there was the success of *Spinster* and the movie made from it [*Two Loves* (Blaustein and Walters 1961), starring Shirley MacLaine]. That meant that there were articles about her in the popular press and so on, and at the time that gave her quite a public profile. There were mixed reactions to that. In those days there was still a certain snobbery about the idea of Hollywood. It gave her much more publicity, but among some academics and literary people it also produced a feeling that well, after all, she was just a popular item not to be taken seriously. So it wasn't all a plus for her, but it did give her a New Zealand literary identity that she hadn't had significantly until that time.

CONNOR: That gives me a picture of how it comes about that someone would have been introduced to her. Were you a student at that time?

STEAD: Yes. I would have read [*Spinster*] then, and admired it. And so after that, with most of her work, I would have read it in sequence as it came out. But as I developed some sort of literary identity myself as a young poet and critic, of course I heard her work discussed.

CONNOR: Would you have had a meeting with her at that time, as a literary person?

STEAD: No, I never met her until years later, 'til the late '70s. I only met her twice. I remember I was present in Wellington when she was awarded the New Zealand Book Award for her autobiography; I think that would have been 1979 or 1980. Then, within a year of her death, my wife and I visited her in Tauranga. I had written about her and we exchanged letters, I can't remember why, maybe I wrote and asked her a point of fact or perhaps I might even have sent her a copy of the original article in the *London Review of Books* (Stead 1981a). She just said, "If you're passing, do call," so I made a time and we called on her. I imagine that would probably have been in 1983, [before] she died in 1984.

CONNOR: Could you describe the key impact of her words and her life on yours? What ideas has she provoked in you?

STEAD: She's not one of those writers I would feel has had a direct effect on my own work, except in the generalized way that I admired it. She is one of those writers that added to my feeling about New Zealand society and the problems of being an artist of any kind in New Zealand. She did dramatize [that]. No doubt many people felt, not without reason, that she overstated it. But if it was overstated, it was nevertheless the truth, particularly at that time—the repressive, conformist pressure of New Zealand society on people who want to deviate in any way, be extravagant, or colorful. She just felt that repression all the time. She felt that original ideas, new ideas, that she was clearly bringing into teaching, were not welcomed. That was something I just accepted then, true of New Zealand society, but she was the person who dramatized it in her own life and in her own writing. I think that was, for me, the importance of her work. She was a figure who lived out this drama and, as I say, exaggerated it, but in exaggerating it she revealed the truth—that it was very difficult to be liberated, original, and flamboyant in New Zealand; you got punished for it, and she got punished quite severely. [As example,] I met a woman who was with [Sylvia] when she was a training college student, and this woman spoke so slightingly of her because they regarded her as egotistical and a show-off. But you know, those colorful qualities she had as a person are probably what made her so successful as a teacher.

CONNOR: So there was a fairly profound theme in her life, in that she was always breaking out. And yet, she had what would be considered the conventional life of mother, teacher?

STEAD: The life was more conventional, except that the way they lived it, with the husband as the sole charge headmaster, in small schools, and in very isolated places, meant she had a certain freedom to do in the classroom what she wanted to do. Then when the inspectors came, and they found this unorthodox, rather flamboyant woman, they didn't give a very good report. In one sense she had this conventional life; she was a wife and mother—I'm sure she wanted to be a wife and mother. Also, in a way, she was an old-fashioned wife in the sense that she lived to some extent under the protection of a husband who, I suppose, in practical ways was dominant. But then under that conventional surface, she was so totally unconventional. She found a way to be free without throwing everything overboard.

CONNOR: In "Living on the Grand" (Stead 1981b), you state that she had recognized the alienation of the Maori child in the colonial classroom. Is that part of her genius?

STEAD: Maori children were not necessarily alienated from their own situations, but they were cut off from the educational system to some extent. Her ways of getting over that gap, as she describes them in her books about teaching, I find completely convincing. I believe that it worked and that it deserved much greater attention and recognition than it got. There's no doubt there's another side to this story and other people would say, "Look, we *were* interested and she was determined to be a victim." They say all these things, and there would be some truth in all of them, but I think there's much more truth, and a much more important truth, in what she said about it: that she had original ideas, and that they weren't given proper attention and respect, and their potential wasn't utilized. The educational problems with Maori children existed and to some extent still exist. It almost does seem too bad that there wasn't more of a network at the time, of educators, possibly other people, who saw that. But certainly in her work she seemed to show that she had the will and the way, the initiative to do something about it right in her classroom.

I think the fact that she wrote that book *Teacher* and couldn't get it published, that's a terrible indictment of New Zealand attitudes at that time. I remember that she only went on to write *Spinster* because it was a way of getting across in fiction some of the ideas that she tried to put forward in *Teacher*. But it was years before that book was published, and it had such important things to say and such important suggestions to make. It's appalling that she couldn't find a publisher for it. Mind you, in those years, there was not very much of a New Zealand publishing industry—there wouldn't be the same problem now. In fact, publishers would compete for a book like that.

CONNOR: Speaking as a New Zealander, what does Ashton-Warner's work, her legacy and effect, currently provoke in New Zealand?

STEAD: She's somewhat neglected at the moment. I've said in the introduction to *Kin of Place*[3] (Stead 2002) that one of the great puzzles to me is why, in the period from the mid-'80s to the mid-'90s, when universities were full of people desperately searching around for neglected women writers—and were often discovering not very significant writers and making an awful lot of them *because* they were women—here was a relatively neglected and certainly brilliant woman writer, and somehow, she wasn't taken up. Right at this moment I think that the [fictional] work is out of print. As far as I know, the fiction books and *I Passed This Way*, which I think is a superb book, are not in print in New Zealand. She's the sort of writer that you would expect to be reissued from time to time in New Zealand, even if her work went out of print overseas. That's what would happen with other writers from the recent past.

CONNOR: It is hard to put one's finger on what would lead to reprinting.

STEAD: It would only need somebody enterprising and one of the publishers to say, "Good heavens, why is this work out of print?" Today I'm having lunch with a person from Auckland University Press. I'm going to say to her, "Look, why is everything of Sylvia Ashton-Warner's out of print? Why don't you bring the autobiography back in print?"

I've just picked up the *New Zealand Herald Review* of *Kin of Place* (Hewitson 2002) and it says: "In the introduction to *Kin of Place*, Stead notes that his advocacy of Sylvia Ashton-Warner had the effect of producing no sign of a revival of serious interest in her work, a fact, all the more puzzling when considered against the background of 1987 and the determined search in the universities for prospective women writers." Then the review goes on in parenthesis, "It's not that difficult to work out why. Ashton-Warner was bound to be too hysterical, too needy to be embraced." And that's by a woman who said earlier on in the review that she was in the women's studies department at the University of Auckland in the 1980s. To say Ashton-Warner was always going to be too hysterical, too needy to be embraced, it's a very surprising statement from someone who came through that training.

CONNOR: Could you discuss her writing style? You wrote on page 99 of "Living on the Grand" that she had a "straight expository prose which has a clear, sharp efficiency of a first rate mind." What would you say most appeals to you about her literary style and her fictional works? You've mentioned *Incense to Idols* [in the article "Living on the Grand"] and *Greenstone*. What of *Bell Call* and *Spinster*?

STEAD: It's something I'd call "immediacy." A lot of prose you read seems to come through cotton-wool to you, through layers that are intermediate between you and the writer. It's very hard to pin down, or to define, or to demonstrate how a writer brings that about. It's a rare talent, so few writers have it. Another New Zealand writer who has [this immediacy] is Katherine Mansfield, particularly in her letters and journals. It comes partly from a sense of urgency and a very good, a high intelligence. What happens with other people in the process of copyediting, happens instantly in the mind of the writer. Everything is shaved right down to the essentials. The other thing is that she can also project her own personality. So as well as conveying information, she can convey along with it the varying emotions that for her are attached to that information. Thus, you feel in the presence of the writer. It's also partly a dramatic quality in the sense of acting.

CONNOR: Would some of these books translate well onto the screen? Do you think films could have been made of *Greenstone* or *Bell Call*?

STEAD: That's another line of possibility because there is quite a New Zealand film industry now. Somebody only needs stumble on this. Usually the way it happens is somebody finds the book. I think that'll happen in New Zealand sooner or later, and more likely sooner than later.

Herbert Kohl, November 22, 2002

RADFORD: What were the specific circumstances of your introduction to Sylvia Ashton-Warner's work?

KOHL: I read *Teacher* when it came out in the United States and found it illuminating, especially since at the time I was teaching kindergarten and first grade. I really liked the whole notion (that is not unique to her) of the idea of eliciting primary vocabulary from the students themselves and building literacy in some substantial way out of their own worlds and their own experiences and their own needs and concerns. Paulo Freire (1968) did the same thing with adults. His core vocabularies were elicited somewhat differently than the way in which she did it, but that had to do with an age difference and a difference in politics and motivation. The approach resonated with me primarily because it was a way to reach through past the barriers, to enable literacy for poor people that the [economic/power] system often gives rise to.

RADFORD: Could you describe the key impact of her words and life on yours? What ideas has she provoked in you?

KOHL: I would call myself a translator. I don't care where any educator works or with whom, an interesting idea is an interesting idea. It is my role to transform it and modify it rather than imitate it in the context of the situation that I work.

RADFORD: In an interview you did in March 2001, you assert the notion that every student can learn and every teacher must find creative ways to facilitate learning. Ashton-Warner also seemed to ascribe to this belief.

KOHL: It wasn't just the primary vocabulary, but the way that it was so brilliantly crafted, so that you get elaboration on ideas, the use of the visual, the capacity to develop a literate memory by a constant reuse of the language, that was just so elegant. It was also so appropriate that I actually—in some cases, not for all kids—just used what she was doing with a couple of little twists to great effect.

What was really so beautiful about Ashton-Warner's work, and continues to be, is that she has the skill of a novelist, the grace of a real writer. You have access to stories in ways that are very powerful in [*Teacher*] and so what happens is that it is alive and it is real. The kids were Maori, but they are kids. She created a density of life for kids that otherwise would have been stereotyped. I really love that, because that is one of the things that I have been struggling against for years—the whole attempt to stereotype kids who come from certain backgrounds and say they all act alike and all have the same mentalities—if in fact you acknowledge that they have any. So what I found there was a deep respect for the kids. There was also a way of drawing out of them the kind of depth that requires feeling the world and then using that as a way to help them learn and grow. It really affected me in a very positive way, in the sense of providing me with both a concrete image of how certain things might be done, but also with a very humane image of the calling.

RADFORD: Was there any resistance to Ashton-Warner's ideas or dissonance with your own experience in education or the arts? Could you see Ashton-Warner's ideas informing pedagogical practices in terms of feminism, anticolonialism, psychology, or antiracism?

KOHL: *Teacher* is the book that affected me. After that, I was not obsessed with her work. She said a lot of stuff about those of us in the '60s who were trying to create social transformation in the United States [ref. here to *Spearpoint*], and I became uninterested. I would say that *Teacher* influenced me, but her opus did not. I come from an old socialist background. I have been struggling with antiracist stuff since I was about fourteen years old. I have learned a lot more about colonialism from a lot of other people. [For example], about economics from Marx. [Ashton-Warner] was not at all an influence in forming my moral values or [political] understandings. Remember, I started out at age twenty teaching in an all-black school in New York before her book was published. I was involved in antiracist issues. Ashton-Warner seemed to me to have no politics. I can't imagine her influencing my politics when she didn't have any. I mean, she may have had some, but I don't know what they were. What I do know from some of the other books she wrote when she spent a year in America, in Colorado, is that she didn't like a lot of the stuff we were doing on the left.

RADFORD: Do you know others who are reading and exploring Ashton-Warner's work? How are new teachers or artists working with the implications of what Ashton-Warner's work established? For example, how has the notion of the dynamic vitality of inner life and experience influenced contemporary teaching?

KOHL: At this stage in the history of education and at this stage of educational thinking in the United States, there is no influence except on old-timers like myself. I am going to be using her text in a class on integrated language arts that I am teaching next semester.[4] None of my students have ever heard of her, but they haven't heard of John Dewey, either. There is a kind of historical amnesia in education, especially with the obsession with high-stakes testing and technology. This is a climate in which we stand in the face of danger of losing the best pedagogy to right-wing obsessions. There are a number of people struggling to keep her ideas alive. I have said in my book *Discipline of Hope* (Kohl 2000), *Teacher* is one of the three or four most powerful and long-lasting things that I have read on education.

RADFORD: What do you believe will be Ashton-Warner's legacy and effect?

KOHL: Her work was really very well thought of, and used, in America. For example, it is referred to and reflected upon in the whole-language movement with Ken and Yetta Goodman. Even so, whole-language movements have been totally destroyed in some parts of the States, partly arising from the dogmatism of the whole-language movement itself. [Ashton-Warner] fell down the hole with the whole-language movement. In effect, she fell out of all but some of the most progressive teacher-education schools, all of which are under siege right now from the far right. So it is not that the ideas aren't appropriate or shouldn't be current, it is that the current politics make it very hard for students to be exposed to them.

I still use *Teacher*. I had one teacher who was having an awful time last year. I teach in the teacher education program. My students all teach with emergency credentials. They are on the frontlines at the same time as they are getting some education about how to teach. My student was in a panic and couldn't reach the kids she was teaching. It was a first- or second-grade class. It was multilingual, multiracial, multi-everything except white kids. So I actually bought a copy [of *Teacher*] for her, and it really worked. It really transformed her practice. I decided I am going to have to share it with all my students, and she began to share it with others. It still works because it is right! What Ashton-Warner is doing—the way she went about respecting kids and provoking something they could give her back to learn quickly but deeply—this is a very profound educational strategy.

Readings of Ashton-Warner's Influence

If we are to believe Carole Durix, C. K. Stead, and Herbert Kohl, Sylvia Ashton-Warner still merits attention in the world of letters and pedagogy. She is a crucible of contradictions and misunderstandings even as she keeps alive an infinity of meanings and chances at life through her writing and life-work. Our interviewees spoke of three spheres of influence: Ashton-Warner's literary prowess in navigating between fictional and autobiographical representations of the life of the teacher and work in the classroom; Ashton-Warner's nonconformist bent and ordeal of being a life-long outsider, even at the height of her acclaim; and the alluring impact, whether acknowledged or somehow resisted, of Ashton-Warner on the life of the mind.

Firstly, we draw from the interviews evidence of Ashton-Warner's literary talents, which spanned various genres and made an international impression. We appreciated Durix's ease of transition between the educational and literary impacts of Ashton-Warner as we searched through the three interviews for explanations to bridge the autobiographical books of Sylvia's canon and the "fictional" representations of her "life" or the life she imagined for other teachers. Durix considered Ashton-Warner's fictional writing from the perspective of the artist at work—and a multitalented artist at that—for her writing drew dimensionality from her painting and musical skills and interests. The fluidity of imaginative re(construction) Ashton-Warner was capable of invoking established the relationship of intimacy, trust, and fascination so crucial between storyteller and audience.

Durix characterizes the compelling artistry of the books as partially due to Ashton-Warner's narrative techniques: omniscient narration and first-person narration of the author. All techniques of first- and second-person narration were subject to the author's control as the final referent and authority. Durix sees this fusional interchange in narrative technique as masterful and integral to Ashton-Warner's style of writing. This "we," resulting from the alchemy of identifications, continues to draw readers and teachers into the stakes of Sylvia's world.

Discussing Ashton-Warner's writing style, Stead notes that she has a "straight expository prose which has a clear, sharp efficiency of a first rate mind." Asked what about her style most appeals to him, Stead responded without reservation, "immediacy," praising Ashton-Warner's style for its clarity and precision of meaning. There is an intensity, an unsettling powerfulness that is linguistically profound in her work. He also touched upon the dramatic quality of the writing, which prompted a question of whether or not some of her other books would translate well onto the screen. Stead was enthusiastic, feeling that the time was right for an Ashton-Warner revival, including the possibility of interest from that most perfect venue of shock and dream, the screen, given the burgeoning New Zealand film industry.

With the words "brilliantly crafted," Kohl describes Ashton-Warner's *Teacher* as having the stature of a literary classic. He argues that with "the skill of a novelist, the grace of a real writer," Ashton-Warner brings alive an educational testament of what can be done in the name of literacy. In *The Discipline of Hope*, Kohl (2000) sketches out his own refusal to accept limits on what students can learn or on what teachers can do to facilitate learning. His statement that *Teacher* is one of the most powerful books he has read on education is a significant revelation, considering his intensive and long-lasting work in the field. For Kohl, Ashton-Warner's talent as a writer works in the service of critical education as she provides a "humane image of the calling." Teaching for Herbert Kohl—via Sylvia—assumes the right to be expansive, revolutionary, extraordinary—a summoning (Buber 1964) not to be equated with the shameful breach of the standards/accountability discourses.

Durix sensitizes us to how richly Ashton-Warner produced herself in four different works concerning her life and writing. Durix notes that the nature of production in varied genres—"the novel, the journal, the diary, and the 'official' autobiography"—comprise, for her as literary analyst, a fascinating view of Ashton-Warner's lucid, courageous strategies for self-exploration. An important point Durix makes is that the educational world had the opportunity to become acquainted with Ashton-Warner's theories via a fictional text (*Spinster*) *or* via an informational text (*Teacher*). Ashton-Warner's ideas were conveyed through the personae of Anna Vorontosov in *Spinster* and Sylvia Ashton-Warner Henderson in *Teacher*, offering explicit options to ensure the widest audience appeal. This versatile, accommodating, expansive symbolization of self leaves an iconic impact on Ashton-Warner's readers. She is able not only to imprint and impress through her leading-lady role in all genres but also to model ways in which the feminine self can distinguish, sustain, and expand itself in multiple, polyvocal ways.

However, as Stead signaled, those at home in New Zealand still shunned the dramatic-rebellious aspect of Ashton-Warner's representations of her life as a woman and a teacher. Stead was puzzled by the paradox of feminist researchers and women's studies departments who overlooked Ashton-Warner's work while "desperately searching" for women to spotlight. Stead notes that his advocacy of Sylvia Ashton-Warner in *Kin of Place* did not produce any sign of a revival of serious interest in her work, a fact he found all the more puzzling when considered against the backdrop of a determined search in the universities, from 1987 onward, for women writers for prospective study.

Kohl similarly points out how Ashton-Warner remained outside the inner circle of American progressives in the critical education movement taking place around the time she worked in Colorado. His statement that "she had no politics" contributes to our reading of Ashton-Warner as iconoclastic: she refused to be co-opted into the tight knot of any particular movement. The radical milieu to which Kohl refers could have drawn on Ashton-Warner's pedagogical example for support, and she could have actively joined that milieu, but she remained a difficult critic and an outsider through her refusal to attach herself to any sort of status quo. Hers was first and foremost the realm of an artist, a domain without national or theoretical ties, and she had an overarching need to meet educational ideas on her own terms.

Each of the three interview participants demonstrated the impact Ashton-Warner had on their work and life of the mind. Durix, through more than thirty years of sustained work on Ashton-Warner, has achieved an apparently vigilant and respectful understanding of her life and work. Durix closely observed the intertwined reality of who and how Sylvia was, and in her communication with us related how she performs her own study of Ashton-Warner: Durix displaces her focus from the *events* that Sylvia's narratives represent to better understand what Ashton-Warner works to produce on the subject of *self*. This approach evokes the strategy of cultural receptionist theorists (Staiger 1992) as well as that of a committed lover and reader of Sylvia's oeuvre.

Stead recounts how Ashton-Warner's public reception in New Zealand had an impact on his own emerging consciousness as a writer and literary critic when he first read her work. Stead notes that one of the major tendencies in Ashton-Warner's work was her ability to "dramatize" her existence in the sober New Zealand society of the 1960s, a society that frowned on flamboyance and insisted upon conformity. Stead also mentions the contrary motion of Ashton-Warner's fame: whereas writers normally go from local reputation to international recognition, Ashton-Warner went from the dizzying international success of the book *Spinster* to film and was only later featured in articles in the New Zealand press. She became a popular icon upon whom some looked down, because of the Hollywood connection of film, but simultaneously she came to occupy a recognized New Zealand literary identity. Thus Stead allows us to revision Ashton-Warner's dynamic trajectory as international figure who must be reconciled to her New Zealand. Within the upheavals of this space, Stead underscores her commitment to educational reform, particularly as a Maori educational advocate. Yet it is her literary achievements and style that continue to beckon him and cause him to write about her and remember her as an inspiring figure.

Kohl's memory work suggests that Ashton-Warner was original in her presentation and passionate influence for the educational ideas she promoted through her lifework, especially in *Teacher.* He draws an interesting distinction between how Ashton-Warner's ideas "resonated" with him as a young teacher but did not influence his politics. The image of Kohl passing on *Teacher* years later to his own teachers-in-training, who work in the most challenging classroom situations, illustrates the lasting effect of such resonations and affirms the transformative value of Ashton-Warner's inspiration, presentation, and practice of humane educational strategies.

Closing Thoughts on Sylvia Ashton-Warner

The interviews with Durix, Kohl, and Stead put Sylvia Ashton-Warner in perspective as an educational beacon for her time. Readings of the Ashton-Warner canon, along with the interviews we collected, portray the struggles of a female artist straining to give voice to a rebellious genius and inner vision. In getting educators and readers to think of language and the life of the teacher, and of what matters most in the life of the classroom, Ashton-Warner's life and writings dramatically opposed the conformity of her place and time.

Through our research, we read Ashton-Warner as an (icon)oclastic figure in the twentieth-century educational scene, defying educational and literary conventions of her time, marking her teaching tenure with innovative approaches and materials for "her" Maori pupils. She did not shrink away, even when her presentation of self (think of the titles *Myself* and *I Passed This Way*, along with her autobiographical penchants in her fictional works) led to reactions of extreme enchantment or severe aversion. She was a female teacher whose enthusiasms were dismissed by male school administrators in New Zealand. She was subject to self-doubt and emotional breakdowns. At times, her personal life seemed at odds with her self-vision as artist/teacher/author. She knew that she needed a room of her own (it was called Selah). She persevered in the face of obstacles.

It seems somehow important to picture Ashton-Warner's classroom pedagogy as a means for an unconventional female teacher to rebel against the same system that repressed her Maori pupils. Even in her Auckland Teachers' Training College days, Ashton-Warner was not a conformist (Hood 1988). In her classroom and in her personal life, she worked through her own rebellions, power, and genius, and did not waver in her insistence on the inner life of the woman-teacher-artist. For those in education, literature, and other callings, Ashton-Warner reads as a distinctive, persistent provocateur across time and space.

Acknowledgments

We would like to thank Dr. Stead, Dr. Durix and Dr. Kohl for their invaluable contribution and generosity of response to this chapter imparting their knowledge of Sylvia Ashton-Warner's work and insights into her legacy.

Notes

[1] In contacting potential participants, we approached individuals who knew Ashton-Warner or had a close professional or scholarly relationship to her work. We sent letters and emails contextualizing our project in relation to the collection of essays to appear in this book. With a firm commitment from Stead, Durix, and Kohl, we followed through with the interviewing process. Carole Durix answered our interview questions via email. Kathleen Connor and Linda Radford carried out telephone interviews with Karl Stead and Herbert Kohl respectively, taping and later transcribing them.

[2] In fact, there exists a rich classical tradition of Maori literature, as surveyed in the *Oxford History of New Zealand Literature in English*, edited by Terry Sturm (1998). Sturm explains the apparent discrepancy as follows:

> Literature in Maori is a large, vital, and compact literature including texts of an ancient oral tradition, translated works, and a well-defined body of historical and contemporary documents. Yet, in its physical form, it appears to be a small, antiquated, and fragmented literature, a scattered mass of published and unpublished texts, some of which are inaccessible to readers. Because of conventions about dissemination of the oral tradition on the unsympathetic climate into which a published form of the tradition might have emerged, a public literature in Maori (except for the material translated and collated by Pakeha) has grown slowly and tentatively while a private literature has prospered. (1998, 26)

[3] *Kin of Place* is a collection of essays on leading New Zealand literary figures of the last decades of the twentieth century.

[4] At the time of the interview, Herbert Kohl was teaching at the Center for Teacher Excellence and Social Justice at the University of San Francisco.

References

Ashton-Warner, S. 1958. *Teacher.* Repr., London: Virago, 1980.

———. 1958. *Spinster.* Repr., London: Virago, 1980.

———. 1960. *Incense to idols.* London: Secker and Warburg.

———. 1964. *Bell Call.* New York: Simon and Schuster.

———. 1966. *Greenstone.* Repr., New York: Bantam Books, 1967.

———. 1967. *Myself.* New York: Simon and Schuster.

———. 1972. *Spearpoint: "Teacher" in America.* New York: Alfred A. Knopf.

———. 1980. *I passed this way.* Wellington, New Zealand: Reed.

Blaustein, J., prod., and Walters, C., dir. 1961. *Two loves.* USA: MGM.

Buber, M. 1964. *Between man and man.* London: Collins.

Durix, C. 1977. Natural patterns and rhythms in *Greenstone* by Sylvia Ashton-Warner. *Commonwealth Essays and Studies* 3: 29–37.

———. 1979. The Maori in Sylvia Ashton-Warner's fiction. *Literary Half-Yearly* 20, no. 1: 13–26.

————. 1980. Sylvia Ashton-Warner: Portrait of an artist as a woman. *World Literature Written in English* 9, no. 1: 104–10.

————. 1987. Literary autobiography or autobiographical literature? The work of Sylvia Ashton-Warner. *Ariel* 18, no. 2: 3–12.

————. 1989. Orality as literary finality in the prose of Sylvia Ashton-Warner. In *Subjects worthy of fame: Essays on Commonwealth literature in honour of H. H. Anniah Gowda*, ed. A. L. McLeod, 27–34. New Delhi: Sterling.

Freire, P. 1968. *Pedagogy of the oppressed*. Trans. by Myra Ramos. New York: Continuum / Seabury Press.

Hewitson, M. 2002. C. K. Stead: *Kin of place*. *New Zealand Herald*, August 10.

Hood, L. 1988. *Sylvia! The biography of Sylvia Ashton-Warner*. Auckland, New Zealand: Viking.

Ihimaera, W. 1972. *Pounamu, pounamu*. Auckland, New Zealand: Reed.

Kohl, H. 2000. *The discipline of hope: Learning from a lifetime of teaching*. New York: The New Press.

McEldowney, D. 1969. Sylvia Ashton-Warner: A problem of grounding. *Landfall* 23, no. 3: 230–45.

Reynolds, D., prod., and M. Firth, prod./dir. 1984. *Sylvia*. New Zealand: MGM/UA Classics Release.

Robertson, J. 1994. Cinema and the politics of desire in teacher education. PhD diss., University of Toronto, Ontario, Canada.

Staiger, J. 1992. *Interpreting films: Studies in the historical reception of American cinema*. Princeton, NJ: Princeton University Press.

Stead, C. K. 1981a. Rebellion: Review of *Spinster, Teacher*, and *I passed this way*. *London Review of Books* 3, no. 8 (May 7): 16–17.

————. 1981b. Sylvia Ashton-Warner: Living on the grand. In *In the glass case*, C. K. Stead, 51–66. Auckland, New Zealand: Auckland University Press.

————. 2002. *Kin of place: Essays on Twenty New Zealand writers*. Auckland, New Zealand: Auckland University Press.

Sturm, T., ed. 1998. *The Oxford history of New Zealand literature in English*. 2nd ed. Auckland, New Zealand: Oxford University Press.

CHAPTER NINE

Recovering Education as Provocation:
Keeping Countenance with Sylvia Ashton-Warner

Judith P. Robertson

On everything I have written, and have yet to write, I should like the epigraph: "Do not understand me too easily." Who made that plea? Gide? And possibly every writer. (Shadbolt 1999, 15)

How is provocation useful to understanding, and what would happen in the absence of provocation? If provocation is what Sylvia Ashton-Warner made for metaphor, what would it have been for this artist, teacher, writer, musician, and woman *not* to provoke? Fellow New Zealand author Maurice Shadbolt (1999) identifies her as "the most distinctive writer in New Zealand history" (70); we have wondered in this book what else Ashton-Warner might have done in the absence of her thumping capacity for provocation. We have asked readers to consider what losses would have accrued, for women, for poets, and for pedagogues. Shadbolt notes that "she thrived on imagined enmity. She needed to be seen leading the charge against the philistines. Otherwise her persona would fall apart. In that respect she had more in common with other New Zealand writers than she was likely to admit" (1999, 71). Shadbolt leads us to consider (as have contributors to this volume) the ways in which Ashton-Warner's provocation emanated from her psychological needs as artist. What hungers did provocation satisfy in her, and what impulses has it awakened in others? "Angela Carter's proposition that writers write to be loved might be true," Shadbolt suggests; "It was certainly true that they needed to be stroked now and then" (1999, 72). The critics of provocation tend to assume too much when they trail (or ignore) the huge history and drama of a teacher who could write and a writer who could teach. And so we have asked: what are the persistent provocations (excitements and uncertainties) at play in the life and legacy of Sylvia Ashton-Warner? How do her insights impress with consequence, even twenty years after her death, the arts and humanities of education? Why is a reassessment of her ideas and effects, including her disturbances, so important at this time?

In exploring the question of why Sylvia is so seductive, most would agree that at least for teachers, her magnetism resides in her writer's capacity to convey the living tissue of classroom experience: "She couldn't have become so influential had she not been such a very good writer" (Shallcrass 1984, 343). Far back into the nineteenth century, New Zealand women of letters had filled books with deft records of women's oppression, but none burned the page with shiny scenes of schooling. Most of Sylvia's dozen novels and more than a score of stories took shape under the blue swell of New Zealand sky, often in schoolrooms. Heather Roberts (1989) tells of a tradition within the New Zealand feminine novel in which "women can find strength in access to the inner world of the imagination and emotions, a world which may also be the source of artistic creation" (5). And so Sylvia belongs to a select sorority of New Zealand women, including Robin Hyde and Janet Frame, who have a penchant for unraveling "the invisible, the intangible, the real" (Frame 1967, 72). Her scenes of classroom life are lapped by tides of light in which commonplace people have uncommon roles in crashing dramas. Her ironic perspective on teaching is impolite and funny: "At last our lord the bell rings, freeing all the other little prisoners" (*Spinster*, 52). It is worth noticing how Ashton-Warner's refusal of the assigned script wins out through humor and comic perspective. Her mocking voice is particularly noteworthy considering that the tradition she inherited from her feminist foremothers contained anger and nostalgia rather than comic satire (Heilbrun 1988, 15). The subversive power and disruptive energy of Ashton-Warner's satire, mimicry, and wordplay (i.e., the "non-livingroom" in *Three*) possess a moral purpose. They function as a form of intelligent encouragement, provoking readers to reassess and question those values long taken for granted. With righteousness, you risk becoming a joke to your detractors; with irony, you *get* the joke.

Moreover, as Cathryn McConaghy elaborates in chapter 4 of this volume, Ashton-Warner is a phenomenologist of the eros of classroom life, giving flesh to intimacy and excitement in learning. Intruding into its times of disruption, she hears the song beneath the text. For example:

> The infant room rocks along like a dinghy in a storm … dozens of infants talking and working and playing and laughing and crying and embracing and quarrelling and singing and making … Lovely movement. Lovely grouping. Talks on the way; fights on the way. And pushing. And caressing … All sorts of involved caressing. (*Spinster*, 51)

The poet-teacher takes command of language, here using potent, single-syllable words ("rocks," "storm," "talks," "fights") to communicate something elemental about times of learning. She shapes her two-foot verbal adjectives into dynamic couplets ("singing," "making," "talking," "working," "playing," "laughing," "crying"), thus provoking in her reader a sense of urgency about something that feels like a continuous present ("on the way"). She piles up "and" (ten times over the course of a few lines) to convey not only unbounded association (inviting all and sundry to jump into the fray) but also the notion of "in addition to," thus drawing attention to the interminability of learning. In associating Ashton-Warner's command of narrative imagery to the phenomenology of being a teacher, fellow teacher Walizer (1995), commenting on *Spinster*, elaborates:

> The passage captures the multiplicity of experiences as one teaches. First there is the layering of time, memories of past people and experience and of recent work, all coloring the present moment, supporting and conflicting with present concerns.... She shifts between the sadness produced by memories from the past and the forgetfulness induced by the demands of the present. She is insightful about the need to lose oneself in teaching and resentful of being constantly consumed by others. She lowers herself constantly to the physical level of the children, unsure whether this constitutes a rise or a fall. (48)

If these are the incitements that produced Ashton-Warner's reputation fifty years ago, it is worth wondering if and how Sylvia continues to provoke response today, especially in women. What kind of object is *provocation* for today's teachers, and what does education have to do with it?

A trip to the library reveals that "provocation" and "education" are etymological siblings, each containing a root memory related to the act of drawing out. According to the *Oxford Dictionary of English Etymology* (Onions 1966), "provocation" means "to incite," especially "to anger, to call forth or evoke." The word comes from the fifteenth-century Old French *provoquer* or Latin *provocare,* from *pro* + *vocare* (meaning "call," same root as "vocation"). *Provo* is the effect of action upon something through the stimulus of irritation or inspiration. Similarly, "educate" comes from *educe*, meaning "to lead or draw forth, to bring out or to develop" from a latent condition; this is based on the Latin *e* + *ducere*, "to lead somewhere," as a duct. "Provocation" and "education" thus share a common house. They are sibling rivals, each intended to stimulate dynamic response in the other, punctuated by movement, reaction, and change.

Recovering education as provocation invites us to view it as something dynamic and unfrozen, or as Phillips (1994) would say, "as a resource to be thought about rather than a persecution to be endlessly re-enacted" (69). It is worth noticing that "the erotic character of a pedagogy of possibility" is founded on such ideas, "a fascination with the dignity and worth of those whom we teach" (Simon 1992, 72). Pedagogy is erotic in the sense of sponsoring life instincts and forces and locating these "within personal and political investments" (Kelly 1997, 6). In more temperate moments Ashton-Warner also saw education this way, as falling in love: "When I teach people I marry them" (*Teacher,* 178); "I'm glad I know this at last, that to teach I need first to espouse" (*Teacher,* 180); and [quoting Gide] "I never feel myself living so intensely as when I escape from myself to become no matter who" (*Teacher,* 181).

When thinking serves as transformative action (as in Sylvia's associations of teaching with love and education with war), it constitutes a fantastic and even a dangerous form of provocation, as Alison Jones (this volume) observes. When thought experiments arise from conditions of risk (as in Ashton-Warner's trading of the syllabus for Schubert), they may survive only when exercised in opposition to public opinion. Alan Mulgan, writing for *Author's Week* in 1936, gives some sense of the difficult commonplaces of literary existence upon which the young Sylvia was forced to sharpen her lead: "Until a few years ago there was very little New Zealand fiction worthy of the name" (as cited in Roberts 1989, 10). "New Zealand was a land of literary kamikazes," echoes Shadbolt (1999, 65). And novelist Janet Frame (1967) lengthens the view through her representation of the New Zealand of the 1950s as "provincial, prejudiced, puritanical" (50). These conditions have no place in a writer's vocabulary, and in the case of Ashton-Warner, they provoked her to delay easy conclusions about the work of education, encouraging her to reopen and to rework the plot. That feat was not so much a "magical transmutation of unbearable reality into bearable fiction ... a technique for coping ... throughout her life" (Hood 1988, 27) as evidence of a sharp mind forging its metal on the fires of talent and time. "If teaching is to be a work of dignity, wit, and grace, then teachers must be neither tyrants nor doormats, but real people with genuine interest, skills, and feelings," Ashton-Warner said (as cited in Shallcrass 1999, 9). Shoring up the long arm of desire with words like these, Sylvia was the herald of the new woman teacher.

She smoked in public when it was illicit for female teachers to do so. She built a room of her own—before *A Room of One's Own* was written. She drank at a time when alcohol abuse was considered a male prerogative. She lived a bohemian existence at the edge of the sky when most of the pure white sisterhood stuck to towns and cities, and she slept with men (and possibly women) and wrote about it in novels that blazed with daring. The effects of such discourtesies were likely consummately exciting to both writer and readers. It is not stretching the point to apply to Sylvia Ashton-Warner what has been said of Katherine Mansfield: that she possessed an "'intuition' that 'New Zealand's obstinate social hedonism, marching with the littleness and the isolation and already taking shape in its laws, stood between her and the knowledge of life (and death) she needed'" (Curnow 1960, as cited in Brown 1993, 50). To expose the limitations of the contemporary prescribed view, in Ashton-Warner's time the artist required hope and a transcendent imagination, the ability to occupy faithfully a space of fantasy. And if it is true that the sky had to cave in on her before she could dig herself out, it is also true that she eventually learned how to test her fantasy life against the starchy functions of reality. She performed this task ably, partly by action and partly in the imagination, as she played through different imagined actions and their consequences.

Psychoanalyst Hanna Segal (1997) writes about the writer's want of a plumb line to the likes of Sylvia's unconscious: "This leads to the consideration of 'What would happen if …' which enables even wildly surrealistic scenarios to be imagined in a non-delusional manner" (7). Sylvia Ashton-Warner did not waste her life wondering what it would feel like to live it. Undoubtedly, this is why her memory has spawned so many outrageous stories: of dinners gone cold and guests departed hungry against the triumphal strains of Chopin; of fickle trajectories abroad to procure … *gloves*; of wading into the sea fully gowned to experience the long wash of Oceania. As one countryman reflects, "We regarded [*Teacher's*] author, rather patronizingly, as an off-beat novelist, an eccentric, to be tolerated, but not to be taken seriously" (Mitchell 2001, 56). But of those who still may question Ashton-Warner's capacities to think clearly and with courage, C. K. Stead (see Connor and Radford with Robertson, this volume) has this to say: "those who have thought of Ashton-Warner as a woman all heart and of small intellect (she sometimes writes of herself as if this were true) should look in particular at her straight expository prose, which has the clear sharp efficiency of a first-rate mind" (1981, 17).

Ashton-Warner used provocation as a way of thinking for herself. Arguably her capacity for boldness served, as did Edna St. Vincent Millay's expression of defiance in "First Fig"," as "an anthem of her generation" (Milford 2002b, xiii):

My candle burns at both ends;
It will not last the night;
But ah, my foes, an oh, my friends—
It gives a lovely light!

Ashton-Warner, like St. Vincent Millay, "was quite clear about what form her insulation from the world of domesticity should take" (Milford 2002a, 336). Another way of thinking about the uses of provocation in education, then, is to ask what private catastrophe provocation seeks to avert. Writing in her diary in 1944, Ashton-Warner draws an analogy between land and woman: both, she argues, are "cultivated" to make them "produce" (*Myself*, 171). And both are objects of male ownership. What exactly are these regulatory practices in society that govern women as "cultivated" producers, and in what sense are men the "owners" of these practices? Ashton-Warner's work represents a submerged heretical voice within the overall bureaucratic discourse of education, then and even now. Long before the emergence of a critical pedagogy with its theorization of schooling as "a mode of social control" (McLaren 1994, 173), Ashton-Warner made words out of wounds that would not heal.

In straining against the expectation of organizational loyalty, she fights to locate herself as a subject. "How in heaven can I free myself from the tyranny of traditional thinking?" she cries (*Spinster*, 41); "A good teacher does not break out from the curriculum, even when it is deficient. A worthy teacher does not defy an order of a Director" (*Spinster*, 207). Weighty with satire, her words are those of an insurgent. The writer, like the teacher, wants something, and registers the exemplary force of the drive to create in the face of deadly composure. It is of interest that the motto of the Crown of Scotland and of all Scottish regiments, *Nemo me impune lacessit*, recounts the dangers of such provocation: "No one provokes me with impunity." That phrase draws attention to the high stakes at play in games of provocation, in which no soul (teacher, escape artist, or adult child) is permitted freefall from provocation's effect.

And this brings us to one element of the most obvious effect of Sylvia's life of provocation. It is a way that endangers life (as in war and as in love, says Adam Phillips [1994]), giving proof of the serious consequences of being alive and having deep stakes in existence. "Working among my Little Ones and fingering continually the tender truths they show me, I come nearer to God. But peace still avoids me," Ashton-Warner writes in *Spinster* (156). Here again, she stings the mind through living registers of language that convey the agony and the ecstasy of provocative teaching. Her psalm-like lines, "How blessed to weep in the sun" give concrete iambic expression to education's hunger for experiences like these—elemental, alive, essential.

The psychoanalytic question at any given moment in the story of provocation and education might be: what is the unconscious nature of the demand and to whom is it addressed? This question carries in its wake material associated with emotional crisis in the life of the provocateur; crisis itself can serve as a life-sustaining form of provocation, reparative or cathartic in effect. "My arms have become itchy on the inside to hold children," Ashton-Warner writes in a moment of missing the classroom (*Spinster*, 169). Provocation can function as a cure for skepticism or despair, a way of taking chances with ideas, of claiming strange freedoms with language and high risks with life. "Can honour's voice provoke the silent dust, Or flatt'ry soothe the dull cold ear of death?" wrote Thomas Gray, thereby also associating provocation with character and configuring its use as a challenge to deathly stasis.

Hanna Segal invokes the notion of mid-life crisis to have us think about how time passing must feel within the life-world of a poet-teacher. Segal (1997) writes, "Mid-life puts the individual in touch with the passage of time and with the often painful facts of ageing and personal death. In all individuals, but perhaps most sharply in creative ones, this recognition takes the form of a crisis, and some fail to surmount it and cease to work creatively" (11). Ashton-Warner's most productive writing and thinking occurred at exactly mid-life. Her literary formulations (especially *Spinster* and *Teacher*) performed as profound psychic achievements. These were attempts to visualize, to symbolize, and to represent phenomena from her inner world previously inaccessible to her, phenomena to which she had consequently not felt accountable. Restlessness and severe depression had marked her early thirties, as though it was too difficult for her to take command of the state of her internal world and her feelings of futility. "My dreams are too heavy," she said (*I Passed This Way*, 276). In the final analysis, the only way to bear the weight of her dreams (and the weight of the voiceless child within) was to enable other children to give voice to the contents of their inner worlds. She had "to release the native imagery." In this version of provocation, there is immediacy. It "draws out" heated conflicts. It speaks to the passage of time and the imminence of death: one's own death and the death of parents (and the concomitant obligations of *being* a parent), losses full of reminders of unresolved infantile anxieties, failures, and angers. "I am a bird.... Rebuilding," Sylvia wrote (*Spinster*, 171).

Provocation then, adds to the available stock of good educational stories. Its effects may be radical and socially transformative, awakening consciousness in the form of insight, as in Ashton-Warner's inspired association of war with education. Ashton-Warner survived two world wars and, closer to home, war in Korea and war in Vietnam. Her catapult onto the world stage in the late 1950s with *Spinster* occurred at the height of American witch hunts and the Cold War. No stranger herself to combat, she situated the roots of violence in the seedbed of infant experiences of language, where cultural meanings of consequence get attached to first words. Her insight into the motives and consequences of the early collective symbolizing experiences of childhood is profound. It is no exaggeration to say that the library of education has been enriched by the multiple plots of Ashton-Warner's life that sought cure in her theory of organic teaching (see Anne-Louise Brookes, this volume). Take, for example, the following examples of her painful awakening to the sounds of education and violence:

> The clock and the strap did much of the teaching, successful teaching too, for [the children's] handwriting was copybook standard and no one talked. (*I Passed This Way*, 165)

> I've seen other schools in other countries since then with different education philosophies but I've not seen anything like that at all. In my work later in life I've

addressed myself to the violence in classrooms, in teachers as well as in children, to find out why. (*I Passed This Way*, 168)

> I have found there is violence in us all in the jungle of the undermind, in nations as
> well as in a person. If any of these children—excluding the fools—grow up wanting
> to kill, then that is my personal failure.... I think I might know now, with the World
> War over, what this work has to do with war. (*Myself*, 239)

Written at the same historical conjuncture as Virginia Woolf's *Three Guineas* (1938) the words of the two women—so otherwise severed by continent, class, and comfort—bear remarkable resemblance: "How ... are we to prevent war? Here we are only concerned with the obvious fact, when it comes to considering this important question—that education makes a difference" (Woolf, 8).

But—and this is important—not only does Ashton-Warner (as a New Zealand teacher) draw meticulous attention to the foundational cultural significance of learning to survive the infant room, but she hints at how interpellation into dominant forms of social representation may be linked to subjective behaviors and speaking positions that have barbarous collective consequences. A defiant cultural worker and critic (like Paulo Freire, but earlier and more accessible), Ashton-Warner struggles to find a new and more adequate way of easing children's entry into the sociosymbolic order. It is as though at some level she understands (as has been observed about Janet Frame's protagonists) that as the subject acquires identity and a speaking position, "this entry into language and the social order is seen to deprive the subject of its unique and individual voice, the voice of imagination and dream, the unrestrained expression associated with the primal drives" (Barringer 1993, 71).

The style of *Teacher* illustrates the artist approaching her epic vision of subjectivity in an exploratory way, as though she must first tell the story to herself. The narrative voice and structure ("heard as an explosion of inner pressures" [*Spinster*, 35]) are fragmentary, discontinuous, piecemeal, and stream of conscious. Like the associative method of the analysand (but without the comfort of the analytic dyad), Ashton-Warner's thinking about the uses of education registers a dreamlike curiosity, courage, and freshness: she can "see some shape breaking through the chalk ravage" (*Spinster*, 180). It is as though the semantic and narrative fragments of these early writings incorporate the chaos of Ashton-Warner's inner world with its shadowy, impalpable, and hazy contents. Small wonder that Bob Gottlieb had his work cut out as her American editor. "The fire within my body takes possession," she writes, as though fully and fiercely committed to its consequences (*Spinster*, 45).

The experiment of her new teaching methods stimulated Ashton-Warner's growth and discovery. She discovered the importance of providing an educational holding environment in which infants can elaborate, from symbol into story, the objects of greatest issue in their inner worlds: "There's no teaching at all," she remarks with wonderment (*Spinster*, 183). In forging this stunning discovery of the importance of containment in times of learning (and here we are reminded of Winnicott), she is assisting herself (assisted by the children) to take measure of the long-lost objects of her own unruly childhood. There reside closeted objects long hidden within the quiescent archives of dangerous memory, the key words that will catapult her to self-knowledge and fame: "ghost," "drunk," "cry," "hit," "kiss," "dead baby," "fight," "sing," "mommy," "daddy." The approach is essentially iconographic, in which the dramatis personae of (other) children's "dreamwork" serve as condensations and displacements of the artist's working-through of representations of her own persona non grata. "It's the easiest way I have ever begun reading," she writes, with an irony that may or may not have been intended (*Spinster*, 183). This is why the discovery is so amazing and grievous to her, a paralyzing, riveting, "exciting and frightening business" (*Spinster*, 40). "If only I could get it out and use it as working material," she wishes; "If I had a light enough touch it would just come out under its own volcanic power" (*Spinster*, 40).

Sylvia tells us here not only of her own life, but also of the ways in which lives—ours as well as hers—are always other lives, and always in the making. The words she chooses to hear and to record for the Maori children to remember are not only words drawn from life on the *pa*. These are also the dead babies, the hit children, the songs, the drunken adults, the corpses, the "skellingtons," and the vengeful ghosts closeted within her own beleaguered internal world: "it is I who am the Little One," she registers on the opening page of *Spinster* (3). Later, she writes:

> I make this little girl. I draw her in pencil first, a few lines-worth of long dress, bare feet, straggly hair and tears. I choose the finest of my pre-war brushes to turn the paint the colour I mean and, by the time the rain has settled down heavily on the low roof, here is this little girl wailing from the page. (*Spinster*, 39)

And later still: "I have a refuge after all, I realize: other people's children. There is stability in the boy body against mine which I have lost in my own, and communion in the up-gazing eyes. This borrowing from a body so small!" (*Spinster*, 101). In words that are weighted with feeling and foresight, she writes, "I consider Mere, who has no mother, slightly mine" (*Spinster*, 111).

"Mere" is, of course, the name that Ashton-Warner claimed as her own in her last years. The word claims a complex lexical ancestry. In the Maori language, *mere* refers to a short flat weapon of stone, sometimes restricted to greenstone, used for hand-to-hand fighting. Another Maori meaning associates the word with Venus, an evening star (Williams 1975). But also arising from many old European languages as a word meaning "sea," *mere* frequently denotes variations in gender as well as boundaries or landmarks. Its primary auditory associations (given the Maori inflections) are to (sacred) mother. Curiously, another buried meaning of the word from the sixteenth-century Old French is "done without another's help; unmixed, pure, absolute, entire, that is only what it is said to me" (Onions 1966). In a mythological context, Mere is a shortened form of Merope, one of the Pleides who married a mortal and, for this reason, became the faintest star in the constellation (Kaster 1964). Tellingly, Ashton-Warner's diminutive is a window that lets light into the many shades of her being. As the French psychoanalyst Pontalis once wrote, "One shouldn't write one autobiography but ten of them, or a hundred because, while we have only one life we have innumerable ways of recounting that life to ourselves" (as cited in Phillips 1994, 73). "Mere" contains all of these innumerable presences of a life recounting itself to itself: of southern surf bursting on reef, of fences that make good boundaries, of resolute determinations in combat with sacred stone, of quotidian longings that can turn desire into itself, and of a teacher-poet's search for a lasting home under starlit antipodean skies.

Ashton-Warner's earliest works are, above all, works of mourning; her mourning is itself an art "in renewing the possibilities of communication, in the commitment to language" (Phillips 1994, 81). Alternatively, we might say that her identity "is in a constant state of negotiation as the subject in process struggles to gain, and maintain, balance at the edge of the alphabet" (Barringer 1993, as cited in Prentice 1993, 4). A crucial feature of the teacher's pedagogical innovation comes from the incorporation of children's unconscious thoughts, which have a linguistic structure, into learning material—not only for them, *but also for herself*—material situated, to plunder from Janet Frame (1962), "at the edge of the alphabet." "They are my arduous teachers," Ashton-Warner writes of her characters (*Spinster*, 158). In a pedagogical restaging of the psychoanalytic method, not only does she elicit primary process thinking from the children, but in bringing it to collective consciousness, she uses it as creative material to decode the enigmatic mysteries of cultural iteration: reading and writing. Alongside this she seeks to liberate the children's key words from the social opprobrium that attaches to them. This revolution in pedagogy is comparable to assisting children in deciphering a rebus or hieroglyph insofar as once the key is found, it may be used and reused forever to decipher and translate the forces that dominate in both inner life and external reality. The children's sex and aggression words are not discrepancies to Sylvia. Even though they pose striking challenges to the respectable lingua franca of the dominant fare (basal readers), Ashton-Warner cuts across the manifest meanings of first words to reconstruct their latent and unconscious intentionality, which she then demonstrates as crucial to the process of learning. Paradoxically, she also utilizes the primary classic Eurocentric texts of literature and music (such as Ibsen, Chekhov,

Schubert, and the Grimm brothers) to stimulate the Maori children in other forms of cultural expression (such as performance and dance).

So it is in her refusal of the conventional satisfactions of pedagogical narrative that Ashton-Warner proves herself most provocative to teachers. She pays homage to the precarious journey through which human beings totter into language and reality. This delicate time, she believes, is "the vital thing so often cut off in a schoolroom" (*Spinster*, 181). In so doing, she hallows as sacred those inner objects of psychic life that circumspection denies and convention condemns in more orthodox tales of schooling. As Jeannette Veatch wrote in 1973, "Her books came to all of us as humane documents" (127). C. K. Stead (1981) eloquently elaborates: "Most of her life Sylvia Ashton-Warner has been in the classroom, which is, I think, *the furnace in which the new society is forged*. There, as in her writing, she has offered passion, style, extravagance, a lavish public expenditure of the self, as her form of rebellion against that uniformity which comes from fear and uncertainty" (17, italics added).

Granted, there are slippages in the Sylvia canon. Writing in the *New York Times* in 1976, one reviewer comments, "Ashton-Warner's passages of self-revelation are, as she acknowledges, distraught, and some will be put off by them, but overall, she is a comfortable writer to be with" (Meras). An embarrassing example of a moment when she is *not* comfortable to be with occurs in *Spearpoint*. *Spearpoint* reads at times like a comic opera of the classroom gone bad, as in her unfortunate characterization of Aspen's children as "Muperson," lacking in "the normal pattern of the outward flow" (*Spearpoint*, 79). When Denver's "wannadowanna" children refuse to take up Ashton-Warner's gracious invitation of the key vocabulary, "her slightly complacent progressive formulas shatter" (Maddock 1972, 80). "No comfort here for those who draw sustenance from the example of chosen lives," writes another reviewer (Harrison 1979). But such lapses tend to be small blips on the big screen of her writings about education.

If Sylvia's inner world is populated by marvelous and mysterious creatures, so also is the inner world of childhood, beset as it is by crises of separating, being alone, feeling bored, getting lost, and loving and hating: "all the young with grief in their being that I ever knew. I may even be weeping for my own lost youth" (*Spinster*, 48). We could do worse as teachers than to be reminded that education is pierced by such passions (being wounded, feeling hurt and neglected, out of favor, disappointed). Ashton-Warner's conjuring of the cruelties of childhood in *Stories from the River* inspired reviewer J. H. Bentley (1987) to put her alongside Katherine Mansfield as a sublime storyteller (see Moeke-Maxwell, this volume). Like Mansfield, "[a]fter exerting herself to escape home, family, and country, she seems to spend the rest of her life trying to return there" (Murray 1990, 18). Lynley Hood's (1990) research for *Sylvia*!

provoked many odd confessions from many people, but one of the most heartfelt came from a teacher who confessed, "She made me feel that if you're a teacher it's okay to be nuts" (184). Preserving intact these objects of uncertainty and understanding their significance is absolutely central to learning and teaching, to psychic survival and to a vision of education as a practice of humanity. In tracking the logic of desire in children's learning, Sylvia led an adventure that makes thinkable the rich and fractious contents of the inner life of all human beings, including those who teach.

Ashton-Warner's provocations arose against the backdrop of the 1960s and that decade's hope, idealism, dreams of peace, rebellion against authority, and fear of nuclear holocaust and annihilation. Through her own genres of self-telling, Ashton-Warner provided a collective self-image for an entire generation of teachers. As Hood (1990) puts it:

> [W]hat's coming through in her in possibly a quite unconscious way is what is prophetic in the culture. Whether it was part of her experience or whether it was part of her fantasy it came to the reading public at a time when the spirit of the age was saying the same thing in many different ways. And she was more readable and more poetic, and therefore more accessible. She will go down in history as one of the seminal thinkers of our time. (200)

Nearly half a century after Sylvia's earliest works appeared, Hood's words find new contexts in which to resonate. Amid the forces of hard-nosed, profit-driven, means-tested, corporate educational management and standardization, a teacher of the new millennium remembers another time in teaching. As Brookes (2000) put it, "In this shift, I feel a changed classroom tone and rhythm, and for a moment I imagine our souls know Ashton-Warner's espousal method of teaching" (35).

Yet it is also true that anyone who heard Sylvia Ashton-Warner expound her espousal theories at teacher workshops and educational department meetings during the mid-century would not have thought of her as the Mother Teresa of education (see Jones, this volume; see also Middleton, this volume). Her shenanigans created a problem for the educational establishment that most frequently exercised (and exorcised) itself as ambivalence. At one moment she could write, "The truth is I am enslaved. I'm enslaved in a vast love affair with seventy children" (*Spinster*, 169). But at other times a fierce hatred reigned: "But the last thing in God's heaven or earth I wanted to be was a teacher. If I had one hate it was the inside of a schoolroom" (*I Passed This Way*, 141). Writing from a rear base in the war against domination, she cries, "How does a teacher resist those practices of regulation and standardization" (the "numbing analgesic against the cross-currents of living") (*Myself*, 207), that cause five-year-olds to roll "off the other end of the assembly line reading, writing, adding up, subtracting and obeying, to supply in the future good little soldiers of the queen m'lads" (*I Passed This Way*, 152). If it is true that ambivalence is a form of provocation (it provokes a response), then it is also true that provocation may produce forms of ambivalence. When love and hate are directed to the same object, conflict inevitably occurs—as in Ashton-Warner's ambivalence about being a teacher, and in teachers' responses to Sylvia. Adam Phillips (1994) writes how ambivalence may be a kind of safety device for use against giving up our idealizations: "Since we generally prefer to believe in progress narratives, ambivalence is dangerous, challenging us to consider another way of believing in *the Real Thing*" (xvii, italics added).

"It must have been hell for Sylvia, to be loved or hated so violently by the people around her," Hood points out (1990, 98); "[h]alf of them loved [reading her autobiography] and half of them hated it—no one was indifferent" (69). On the one hand she ranks "as one of the major educational innovators of this century" (Hood 1990, 98), challenging readers (as Diane Caney observes about Janet Frame) "with the limitations of socially sanctioned conformist thinking" (as cited in Prentice 1993, 7). On the other hand, she is impossible to love easily. C. K. Stead (1981) writes: "At the centre of much of her work there is the figure of a teacher who is at once brilliant and erratic, reluctant and original; failing to satisfy the pedestrian requirements of a system which itself fails to foster the true individuality and needs of the growing child" (16). There are times when Sylvia attracts followers like a grim reaper: "Of course you know she was a hopeless teacher—and mad as a meat axe" (reportedly said by a New Zealand educationalist; in Hood 1990, 89).

C. K. Stead (1981) has compared Sylvia Ashton-Warner to Janet Frame and Katherine Mansfield: "raw, untrammelled" New Zealand women who wrote with "a sense of comedy which is also a form of revolt against all prevailing pieties" (16). All three women wrote in places of exile from whence their attachment to native soil was ambivalent. Provocation may have allowed them to take command, to experience crisis, and to respond by making a commentary, a surprise, a fantasy, or even a reparative gesture in the face of painful experience. When Ashton-Warner writes, "This word is the caption of a very big inner picture.... It's the caption of a huge emotional picture" (*Spinster*, 161), she crosses continents by air, taking command of rooms through language. Such provocation is generous in its impulse to sustain life, because it creates space in which psychological aims may work out—not only for the artist, but for others who identify with her. In Hood's (1990) interviews with individuals at Simon Fraser University, where Sylvia taught in the late 1970s, one colleague remembered Sylvia's transmission of "spiritual energy from one person to another" (135) and experienced this spiritual transmission as a powerful form of communication. Another memorialized Sylvia for teaching him that he could be the hero of his own adventures and that he could make his dreams come true.

But within the corpus of Sylvia love stories, she exerts special power over women. "Today I would regard her work as my introduction to feminist educational theory," writes Middleton (1992, 23; see Middleton, this volume). Hood (1990) argues that her gendered purchase springs from the tenacious pursuit of her dreams: "Everyone has achievement dreams, but most women are forced to abandon them in childhood. With the singleminded pursuit of her dreams Sylvia would be like a beacon in the dark" (70). Walizer (1995) similarly embodies Sylvia with a powerfully feminine, procreative force: "the teacher here is creator, an intellectual earth mother whose own ideas require fertilization through exchange with others in a kind of intellectual intercourse through which she is also reborn" (59). Thompson (1994, see also this volume) finds Ashton-Warner's focus on "the importance of children's imagery as the raw working material for education" (40) to be the basis of her special appeal. Durix (see Connor and Radford with Robertson, this volume), in her considerable scholarship on Ashton-Warner, traces the artist's feminine seductions to three wellsprings: first, the forcefulness of Ashton-Warner's aesthetic depictions of woman's multiple, beleaguered roles (1980); second, her masterful orality—"not only the author's mastery of dialogue but also the conciseness of her narration" (1989, 27); and third, her original crafting of a new feminine genre, "literary autobiography or autobiographical literature" (1987, 3). Jones (1985) also ascribes Sylvia's seductions to the forcefulness of a feminine voice honed through autobiographical form to criticize the New Zealand provincialism of her day. Stead (1981) observes quite simply that Ashton-Warner had the face "of the modern woman who wants both kinds of self-fulfillment," fulfillment at work and at home: "freedom, the life of the artist ..., a studio, intellectual friends ..., health, a stable marriage, children, a garden, and outdoor life" (16).

Ashton-Warner's ability to provoke extreme responses had much to do with her extraordinary talent for self-dramatization. According to Stead (1981), she possessed "a perfect ear for the speech of others, and the ability to cast [herself] into a role" (16). Hood (1990) concurs: "There's a powerful spiritual dimension in her work that seems to strike her fans with the impact of an electric shock" (66). Her thespian instinct for self-protection ran like fire in her blood. Her directness as well as her insolence was provocative. While one New Zealand inspector recalls her as a "pushy eccentric" (Hood 1990, 51) whose drive to have her reading material published was a nuisance to the education department, others applauded her efforts and were then "dumbfounded by her attack on them in *Spinster*" (Hood 1990, 205). Whether experienced as a "paranoid liar" or a "gifted visionary" (Hood 1990, 228), Sylvia got under the skin.

With one foot in Oceania and the other in the stars, Sylvia was sometimes stretched apart. She had an unlovable side. "To lift the lean of that black bluff," as Edna St. Vincent Millay put it ("God's World"), was not easy for her. Hood (1990) asks: "Are artists born selfish and therefore driven to create something in their own image that they can control, or are they born with an intense creative drive which makes them want to use people as well as things as raw material for their art?" (42); "[D]o they need to feel misunderstood in order to become really outstanding (112)?"

In her critique of the history of female powerlessness, Myra Jehlen (1984) poses the issue as a feminist one: "All women must destroy in order to create," she states flatly (583). But in response to Jehlen's "brutal truth" (Heilbrun 1988, 17), my own questions multiply. Does something always need to be destroyed in order to create? Is it other people's burning noise or is it our own? (Sylvia hated noise.) Is creation possible without destruction? Do love and aggression codetermine the capacity for aesthetic glory, and must aesthetic glory always incorporate aggression in the service of love?

There were times when Sylvia experienced no boundaries in her capacity to recruit love in the service of aggression. She could not get the world close enough. "She's a witch," concludes one of Ashton-Warner's acquaintances; "If she'd been born in the Middle Ages she would have been burnt at the stake" (Hood 1990, 29). Hood speculates (unconvincingly) about Ashton-Warner's muse: "she was possessed by, and worshipped, a demonic lover" (1990, 73). More to the point, Selma Wassermann recounts: "I re-read some of Sylvia's letters last night. The feeling that came pouring over me like a bucket of cold water was her enormous capacity to be cruel" (Hood 1990, 179; see Wassermann, this volume for another perspective). Ashton-Warner's immense openness to aesthetic experience seemed to demand that she conduct her life as if in a theater of war, complete with sniper artillery.

How are we to understand provocation as aggression? Ashton-Warner experienced a rugged, complicated childhood in conditions of material distress in a house teeming with children. In physical and emotional terms, she endured her early years out on the hinterlands. Hood (1988) speculates that Sylvia's lack of an early holding environment to answer her emotional needs interfered with her capacity to commit herself to later relationships. Out of the unforgiving landscape of her childhood, Ashton-Warner carried little but her labor and the capacity, forced upon her by the economic exigencies of the 1930s, to exchange one set of talents for another, to turn her hand to whatever came along, which in her case was teaching. The "specificity of place and politics has to be reckoned with in making an account of anybody's life, and their use of their own past," cautions Carolyn Steedman (1986, 6). Economic injury, exile, isolation, and the politics of class-consciousness ensure that poor children (especially working-class girls) will develop what Steedman calls "a structure of feeling ... learned in childhood, with one of its components a proper envy, the desire of people for the things of the earth" (7).

Ashton-Warner's mature relations were often marked by a defensive devaluation of those who loved her. This is a dynamic of envy. So are emotional distancing and revengeful neediness. Her novel *Three* brilliantly captures these difficult emotions, conveyed (in aching Pinter-esque fashion) within the fiery constellation of intergenerational family relations, "where the sparse commentary between the dialogues reads almost like the brief stage directions of a play" (Durix 1989, 27). Promiscuity—wildly alive in Ashton-Warner's fantasy life and certainly in her legendary flirting—is also a performance of envy. Arguably, these behaviors (played out upon others) allowed the artist to defend herself against the conflicts around aggression she experienced with loved ones in her earliest years. This kind of "crazy" interaction in her intimate relationships (recounted by so many of Sylvia's friends and family) may have even amounted to a kind of "private madness," to use André Green's (1986) term. Such a dynamic could be "both frustrating and exciting because it occurs in the context of a relationship that may well have been the most exciting and satisfactory and fulfilling one that both partners could have dreamt of" (Kernberg 1991, 50). Tellingly, Ashton-Warner confided to Lynley Hood (1990) that her finest writing was fueled by sadness. Sadness stems from buried anger, which draws attention to another consequence of provocation: it incites vengeance. It is possible that Sylvia unknowingly needed to provoke others to become the rejecting mother, thus justifying her devaluation of them and, retrospectively, of her own mother, while guaranteeing her search (through her muse) for a new, idealized woman (Kernberg 1991).

"For much of his life this scarred and tormented man had won music from black bouts of depression, from a lame body and an often befuddled brain" (Shadbolt 1999, 218): although written about another New Zealand writer, these lines remind us of one of Sylvia's many selves. In psychoanalytic terms, the longing for complete fusion and the overcoming of boundaries replays infant desires that can never be fulfilled. The love object may be treated as a mirror-image of the self in which there is a demand for complete and continuous intimacy; it first seems an intimacy of love but eventually becomes an intimacy of hatred (Kernberg 1991). This leads us to consider another aspect of provocation, the problem of the artist treating the partner as a slave. Hood (1990) writes of Sylvia's "enormous capacity" to inspire others in a "profoundly meaningful way" while simultaneously cutting them cold with her ability to "exploit, corrupt and degrade" (263). Judith James and Nancy Thompson (1993) explore this difficult dynamic in their essay, "Sylvia Ashton-Warner's Lost Novel of Female Friendship" (see also James and Thompson, this volume).

James and Thompson examine an abandoned (unpublished) manuscript consisting of multiple drafts written by Ashton-Warner between 1967 and 1968, during the time of impending loss of her husband, Keith Henderson. Holding together the various layers of narrative is a theme of eros among women, which Sylvia called "the concentric pattern of passion." But what is extraordinary in both the unpublished work and in James and Thompson's treatment of it (given our discussion of the aggressive components of provocation) are Ashton-Warner's speculations on "the artist's need for the special devotion of a complement" (as cited in James and Thompson 1993, 45), by which she appears to mean a counterpart or equivalent, a twin. But Ashton-Warner sees this counterpart as an extension of the artist's self, "a parasite," a sponger or freeloading guest, who feeds off the energy of the host and yet in so doing provides fuel for the host's aesthetic vitality. Ashton-Warner writes, "the complement is part of the body of the host.... So when this alter-ego is attracted away and attaches itself to another host the pain is beyond jealousy. Its [sic] a matter of the life or death of art" (as cited in James and Thompson 1993, 46). Elsewhere, Ashton-Warner imagines the artist as controlling "his complement as naturally as his own limbs and body, thoughtlessly, unconsciously, unwittingly arrogant, demanding and expecting from the other all he demands and expects for himself, or herself, until the parasite has to withdraw in self-preservation" (as cited in James and Thompson 1993, 51).

Sylvia reveals herself in these texts as "a woman reliant on the vitality of others for both energy and inspiration" (James and Thompson 1993, 51). But what if we also try to understand her narrative form and forming as a creative process, "an upshot of a process of externalization" in which "content is provided by them rather than packaged within them" (Rose 1993, xv)? Then, arguably, the subtext provides powerful material for the artist's working-through of fantasies of object choice, fears of loss (heightened in reality by the impending loss of her beloved partner), and desire for control (to stave off the pain of grief). Indeed, the artist of these texts is someone who cannot abandon—who laments the possible loss of—control. Arguably, that loss of control would itself preserve the integration of the (dead) object. There is little demonstrated desire for reciprocity in this painful limning of space. It is as though the artist's attempt at understanding the world aims to possess all the richness of the object, beyond the need of the self and possibly beyond the capacities of the object. In this work, I suggest, Ashton-Warner symbolically explores (beyond the limits of childhood) the primitive experience of introjection, in which the object serves the host as none other than an extension of her own body (cf. Segal 1997). In reality, when destructiveness is directed in this way toward objects (people or possessions), it serves as a defensive deflection of self-destructiveness to the outside. In creative life, when deeply incorporated into a sense of art, it makes for a very good story. When repeated throughout a person's life—in fractious relations with beloved others, in inconstancy in work and commitment, in heavy drinking ("Drink ... is a great provoker," says the porter to Macduff in *Macbeth*)—then we may see at work a melancholic superego whose teeth are ever positioned for attack. When tamed through art into words, such embodiment may be an account of nothing less than the *mana* of deeply lived trauma, surrender, struggle, and strength.

These speculations may help to shed light on Ashton-Warner's consistently edgy attacks on middle-class mothering. For example, we read in *Spinster*, "Mark is one of these 'can't' children whose mothers taste everything first" (35). It is as though Ashton-Warner directs a primitive form of hate toward love and food and care. Arguably, such envy masks a deeper desideratum: to have been one of those coddled children or to have had (or been?) "the perfect mother and all these children, brown, white and yellow, are my own" (*Spinster*, 42). Elsewhere too, it is as though Ashton-Warner targets for destruction any parent (mother) who exercises her love in ways that might curb the child's frustration: "I can't stand this phrase 'not allowed' from a parent ... all married women are unacceptable to me in any capacity" (*Spinster*, 72). Seeking to destroy the very attributes most absent in her early years of life, Ashton-Warner's destructive projective identifications with nurturing adults provide strong evidence for Hood's observation that she was frustrated by early neglect. Tellingly, Hood writes of Sylvia's defensive anxiety and lack of trust as Hood began her biographical research into Ashton-Warner's life in 1983. "I didn't think you would come back," Ashton-Warner childishly confided: "I thought you'd feel I wasn't worth the trouble" (Hood 1990, 18). When Hood remarks on Ashton-Warner's intense need to be admired, she draws attention to the ways in which provocation is a bid for attention, a plea for love and acknowledgment that might restore to the subject her (idealized) original state of integrity.

Throughout the writing of *Sylvia!* (Hood 1988), Ashton-Warner's provocations plagued the progress of her biographer: "Her behaviour outrages me so much at times that I have trouble even liking her" (Hood 1990, 23). At times Hood bares her fists with Dostoevskian fervour: "I want to pursue Sylvia with an axe for invading my privacy" (1990, 24). But then she discovers similar feelings in others: "What impressed me most was his anger. He was a striking example of the way Sylvia polarises people—in some she provokes a hatred that leaves me stunned, while others speak of her with religious reverence" (1990, 114). She was like "Mother Courage," concludes Jack Shallcrass (1984), who left her "peasant qualities" behind; she "used her high intelligence, a complex imagination and an endless capacity to play the world off against itself, sometimes with wicked pleasure" (343). Lehmann-Haupt, reviewing *Three* in the *New York Times* (1970), perhaps best captures the quandary of Sylvia Ashton-

Warner as provocateur, underscoring her capacious talent for getting to the heart (the disagreeable heart) of the truth of human relationships but also its difficult effects: "I confess that my underlying inclination was to shun the bleak landscape of her interior. All the same, one recognizes art when one sees it. And one respects one's elders."

Acknowledgments

In bringing my thoughts about Sylvia's difficult provocations to life, I wish to acknowledge the generous responses to earlier versions of this chapter provided by Cathryn McConaghy, Deborah Britzman, Emma Stodel, and Gretchen Knapp.

References

Ashton-Warner, S. 1958. *Spinster.* Repr., New York: Simon and Schuster (Touchstone), 1985.

———. 1958. *Teacher.* Repr., New York: Simon and Schuster (Bantam), 1961.

———. 1967. *Myself.* Repr., New York: Simon and Schuster (Bantam), 1968.

———. 1970. *Three.* New York: Alfred A. Knopf.

———. 1972. *Spearpoint: "Teacher" in America.* Repr., New York: Vintage, 1974.

———. 1979. *I passed this way.* New York: Alfred A. Knopf.

———. 1986. *Stories from the river.* Auckland, New Zealand: Hodder and Stoughton.

Barringer, T. 1993. Powers of speech and silence. *Journal of New Zealand Literature* 11: 71–88.

Bentley, J. H. 1987. Review of *Stories from the river. Landfall* 43, no. 3: 368.

Brookes, A-L, 2000. Teaching and learning liberation: Feminist pedagogies. Paper presented at the women's studies research unit, University of Saskatchewan, Canada.

Brown, R. 1993. A state of siege: The sociable frame. *Journal of New Zealand Literature* 11: 49–58.

Curnow, A., ed. 1960. *The Penguin book of New Zealand verse.* Auckland, New Zealand: Penguin.

Durix, C. 1980. Sylvia Ashton-Warner: Portrait of an artist as a woman. *World Literature Written in English* 9, no. 1: 104–10.

———. 1987. Literary autobiography or autobiographical literature? The work of Sylvia Ashton-Warner. *Ariel* 18, no. 2: 3–12.

———. 1989. Orality as literary finality in the prose of Sylvia Ashton-Warner. In *Subjects worthy of fame: Essays on Commonwealth literature in honour of H. H. Anniah Gowda,* ed. A. L. McLeod, 27–34. New Delhi: Sterling.

Frame, J. 1962. *The edge of the alphabet.* Christchurch, New Zealand: Pegasus.

———. 1967. *A state of siege.* London: W. H. Allen.

Green, A. 1986. *On private madness.* London: Hogarth.

Harrison, B. G. 1979. Teacher's story: Review of *I passed this way. New York Times,* December 23.

Heilbrun, C. 1988. *Writing a woman's life.* New York: Ballantine Books.

Hood, L. 1988. *Sylvia! The biography of Sylvia Ashton-Warner.* Auckland, New Zealand: Viking Penguin.

———. 1990. *Who is Sylvia? The diary of a biography.* Dunedin, New Zealand: John

McIndoe.

James, J. G. and N. S. Thompson. 1993. Sylvia Ashton-Warner's lost novel of female friendship. *Phoebe: Journal of Feminist Scholarship, Theory and Aesthetics* 5, no. 2: 43–53.

———. 1995. Flashpoints: Sexual/textual politics in editing "Five women." *Documentary Editing* 17, no. 2: 45–49.

Jehlen, M. 1984. Archimedes and the paradox of feminist criticism. *Signs* 6, no. 4: 575–601.

Jones, L. 1985. The one story, two ways of telling, three perspectives: Recent New Zealand literary autobiography. *Ariel* 16, no. 4: 127–50.

Kaster, J. 1964. *Putnam's concise mythological dictionary.* New York: Capricorn Books.

Kelly, U. A. 1997. *Schooling desire: Literacy, cultural politics, and pedagogy.* New York: Routledge.

Kernberg, O. F. 1991. Aggression and love in the relationship of the couple. *Journal of the American Psychoanalytic Association* 39: 45–70.

Kristeva, J. 1984. *Revolution in poetic language.* New York: Columbia University Press.

Lehmann-Haupt, C. 1970. Mother-in-law and order: Review of *Three. New York Times*, May 22.

Maddock, M. 1972. Now, children: Review of *Spearpoint. Time*, October 2.

McLaren, P. 1994. *Life in schools.* 2nd ed. New York: Longman.

Meras, P. 1976. End papers: Review of *Myself. New York Times*, October 16.

Middleton, S. 1992. Towards an indigenous university women's studies for Aotearoa: A Pakeha educationalist's perspective. In *Feminist voices: Women's studies for Aotearoa/New Zealand*, ed. R. du Plessis et al., 22–38. Auckland, New Zealand: Oxford University Press.

Milford, N. 2002a. *Savage beauty: The life of Edna St. Vincent Millay.* New York: Random House.

———, ed. 2002b. *Selected poetry of Edna St. Vincent Millay.* New York: Modern Library.

Mitchell, I. 2001. Sylvia Ashton-Warner in the secondary school: A reassessment of the work of New Zealand's most famous teacher. Special edition on Sylvia Ashton-Warner. *Auckland College of Education Papers* 10: 56–61.

Murray, H. 1990. *Double lives: Women in the stories of Katherine Mansfield.* Otago, New Zealand: University of Otago Press.

Onions, C. T., ed. 1966. *Oxford dictionary of English etymology.* Oxford: Clarendon.

Phillips, A. 1994. *On flirtation.* Cambridge, MA: Harvard University Press.

Prentice, C. 1993. Introduction. *Journal of New Zealand Literature* 11: 1–10.

Roberts, H. 1989. *Where did she come from? New Zealand women novelists 1862–1987.* Wellington, New Zealand: Allen and Unwin in association with Port Nicholson Press.

Rose, J. 1993. *Why war? Psychoanalysis, politics, and the return to Melanie Klein.* Oxford: Blackwell.

Segal, H. 1997. *Psychoanalysis, literature and war: Papers 1972–1995.* New York: Routledge.

Shadbolt, M. 1999. *From the edge of the sky: A memoir.* Auckland, New Zealand: David Ling.

Shallcrass, J. 1984. In memoriam: Sylvia Ashton-Warner. *Landfall* 38, no. 3: 342–44.

———. 1999. Voices from the past. *New Zealand Principal* 14, no. 2: 9.

Simon, R. I. 1992. *Teaching against the grain: Texts for a pedagogy of possibility.* South Hadley, MA: Bergin and Garvey.

St. Vincent Millay, E. 1922. *A Few Figs from Thistles: Poems and Sonnets.* New York: Harper and Brothers.

Stead, C. K. 1981. Rebellion: Review of *I passed this way*, *Spinster*, and *Teacher*. *London Review of Books* 3, no. 8 (May 7): 16–17.

Steedman, C. 1986. *Landscape for a good woman*. New Brunswick, NJ: Rutgers University Press.

Thompson, N. S. 1994. Imaging, literacy and Sylvia Ashton-Warner. In *Images in language, media, and mind*, ed. R. F. Fox, 29–41. Urbana, IL: National Council of Teachers of English.

Veatch, J. 1973. Teaching Americans: Review of *Spearpoint: "Teacher" in America*. *Teachers College Record* 1: 127–30.

Walizer, M. 1995. The volcanic mind: The story of Sylvia Ashton-Warner. In *Reasons for learning: Expanding the conversation on student-teacher collaboration*, ed. J. Nicholls and T. Thorkildsen, 36–61. New York: Teachers College Press.

Williams, H. W., ed. 1975. *A dictionary of the Maori language*. 7th ed. Wellington, New Zealand: Government Printer.

Woolf, V. 1938. *Three guineas*. Repr., Harmondsworth, England: Penguin, 1977.

Contributors

Anne-Louise Brookes, associate professor of education at the University of Prince Edward Island, Canada, is a practitioner-researcher who teaches critical literacy to university students using a teaching method she developed from Sylvia Ashton-Warner's work with key words. She won a teaching award for this method at St. Francis Xavier University in 1993. Dr. Brookes lived in New Zealand for a time in her childhood and has studied Ashton-Warner's teaching sites and archives in New Zealand as well as her papers in Boston in preparation for a new project, *Sylvia Ashton-Warner: A Critical Study*. Her publications include *Feminist Pedagogy: An Autobiographical Approach* (1992) and the internationally award-winning CD-ROM on L.M. Montgomery, *The Bend in the Road* (2000).

Kathleen Marie Connor is a doctoral candidate in the faculty of education at the University of Ottawa, Canada. Her dissertation, "Imagined Texts and Social Reality: The World and Works of Children's Author Thornton W. Burgess," investigates the cultural production of childhood literature through psychoanalytic readings of selected cases from the works of Thornton W. Burgess. She became interested in the educational and literary influence of Sylvia Ashton-Warner through her doctoral supervisor, Judith Robertson. Kathleen has published in *Home-Work: Postcolonialism, Pedagogy, and Canadian Literature*, edited by Cynthia Sugars (2004).

Judith Giblin James is an associate professor of English and associate dean of the graduate school at the University of South Carolina, United States. Recent publications include essays on Julia Peterkin, Lillian Smith, and Carson McCullers and a book chapter on the history and value of women's studies. In addition to her collaboration with Dr. Nancy S. Thompson on a biographical and textual study to be called *Intimate Fictions: The Life in the Work of Sylvia Ashton-Warner*, Dr. James is completing *Dramatizing Difference: Southern Novelists on Broadway*. Her most recent book is *Wunderkind: The Reputation of Carson McCullers 1940-1990* (1995).

Associate Professor *Alison Jones* has taught in the fields of feminist/poststructuralist theory, sociology of education, cross-cultural pedagogy, and education and the body at the University of Auckland, New Zealand. Her publications in journals such as *Discourse, British Journal of*

Sociology of Education, and *Journal of Curriculum Theorizing* explore the impact that social anxiety about touching children has on teachers. She is editor of the international collection *Touchy Subject: Teachers Touching Children* (2001).

Associate Professor *Cathryn McConaghy* researches in the sociology of education at the University of New England, Australia. She is the author of *Rethinking Indigenous Education: Culturalism, Colonialism, and the Politics of Knowing* (2000), has published widely, including in *The Journal of Curriculum Theorizing, Teaching Education,* and *The Australian Journal of Indigenous Education,* and was guest editor of a special edition of *Discourse: Studies in the Cultural Politics of Education* (1998) on feminist postcolonial studies in education. She is currently researching teachers' responses to children and trauma; is team leader of the Bush Tracks Research Collective to investigate transitions in rural teaching; and is completing two Australian Research Council projects, one on the challenges of Indigenous teachers within the racialized structures of Australian schooling, and the other in collaboration with the New South Wales department of education on identifying the new social and spatial dynamics of inequities in education.

Professor *Sue Middleton* is head of the department of policy, cultural, and social studies in education in the school of education at Waikato University, New Zealand. Her books include *Educating Feminists: Life Histories and Pedagogy* (1993), *Disciplining Sexuality: Foucault, Life-histories, and Education* (1998), and (edited with Kathleen Weiler), *Telling Women's Lives: Narrative Inquiries in the History of Women's Education* (1999).

Tess Moeke-Maxwell (*Ngati Pukeko* and *Ngai Tai*–Umupuia) had her PhD conferred in 2003 by the University of Waikato, New Zealand. Since the 1990s, Dr. Moeke-Maxwell has worked as a specialist (Maori) counselor in her capacity as an independent sexual-abuse clinician for the New Zealand Government's Accident Compensation Corporation. More recently Dr. Moeke-Maxwell has developed her business, Te MAIA Cultural Services: Education and Training Consultancy, which provides consultation on cultural competency issues related to Maori identity. She also supplies contract research for the mental health sector.

Linda Radford is a doctoral student in education at the University of Ottawa, Canada. She is currently working on her thesis, "Reading the Teacher's Apprentice: Juvenile Historical Fiction and Reading Practices in Teacher Education." She is interested in how the reading and teaching of literature has an impact on social and psychic histories that perpetuate social injustices. Her most recent publication, *The Teacher Reader: Canadian Historical Fiction, Children's Learning and Teacher Education*, is in print in *Home-Work: Postcolonialism, Pedagogy, and Canadian Literature*, edited by Cynthia Sugars (2004).

Judith P. Robertson holds a PhD in education from the University of Toronto, Canada and teaches in the faculty of education at the University of Ottawa, Canada. Her work compels readers to explore ways in which discourse, narrative, reading, and viewing experience are punctuated by the personal, including the vicissitudes of unconscious life. Her first book, *Teaching for a Tolerant World, Grades K–6: Essays and Resources* (1999) assisted elementary teachers in teaching about genocide and intolerance through literary works for children. Dr. Robertson's other work has appeared in *Journal of Curriculum Theorizing*, *Canadian Journal of Film Studies*, *Reading Teacher*, *English Quarterly*, *Children's Literature Association Quarterly*, *Changing English: Studies in Reading and Culture*, *SIGNS: Journal of Women in Culture and Society*, and *TABOO: A Journal of Culture and Education*. She is the recipient of the distinguished University of Ottawa Award for Excellence in Teaching (2004), as well as the Ontario Confederation of University Teachers' Teaching Award of Excellence (2004) and the University of Ottawa's Faculty of Education Teaching Award (2003).

Associate Professor Emerita *Nancy S. Thompson*, now retired from the English department at the University of South Carolina, United States, is director of the Research Communications Studio, a three-year research project funded by the National Science Foundation and housed in the USC College of Engineering and Information Technology. Widely published in journals such as *College Composition and Communication*, *Writing Program Administration*, and *English Journal* and in book chapters on literacy and pedagogy, she is currently completing a book-length manuscript (with Rhonda Grego) on *The Writing Studio Model: Teaching Writing in Third Spaces*. With Judith James, she is working on a biographical and textual study called *Intimate Fictions: The Life in the Work of Sylvia Ashton-Warner* as a tribute to Sylvia's influence on her pedagogical approaches for some thirty-five years.

Professor Emerita *Selma Wassermann* is retired from Simon Fraser University. She has published many books including *Getting down to Cases: Learning to Teach with Case Studies* (1993), *Introduction to Case Method Teaching: A Guide to the Galaxy* (1994) and the recently released, *This Teaching Life*: *How I Taught Myself to Teach* (2004). She taught with Sylvia Ashton-Warner at Simon

Fraser in the 1970s. She was one of the first researchers in North America to explore the theoretical underpinnings of Ashton-Warner's work. Her early articles about Sylvia's significance for educators appeared in the *Journal of the Association for Childhood Education International* and *Phi Delta Kappan*.

Bibliography

Anderson, Benedict. *Imagined Communities: Reflections on the Origin and Spread of Nationalism.* London: Verso, 1983.

Anthias, Floya, and Nira Yuval-Davis. "Woman-Nation-State." In *Woman-Nation-State,* edited by Nira Yuval-Davis and Floya Anthias, 1–17. Basingstoke, England: Macmillan, 1989.

Appadurai, Arjun. Putting Hierarchy in its Place. *Cultural Anthropology* 3, no. 1 (1988): 36–49.

Appel, Stephen, ed. *Positioning Subjects: Psychoanalysis and Critical Educational Studies.* Westport, CT: Bergin and Garvey, 1996.

Ashton-Warner, Sylvia. 1958. *Spinster.* London: Secker and Warburg. (New York: Simon and Schuster, 1958; London: Virago, 1980).

———. 1960. *Incense to idols.* London: Secker and Warburg.

———. 1963. *Teacher.* New York: Simon and Schuster. (Harmondsworth, England: Penguin, 1966; London: Virago, 1980; New York: Simon and Schuster, 1986).

———. 1964. *Bell Call.* New York: Simon and Schuster. (Christchurch, New Zealand: Whitcombe and Tombs, 1969).

———. 1966. *Greenstone.* New York: Simon and Schuster. (Christchurch, New Zealand: Whitcombe and Tombs, 1966).

———. 1967. *Myself.* New York: Simon and Schuster. (Christchurch, New Zealand: Whitcombe and Tombs, 1967; London: Secker and Warburg, 1968).

———. 1970. *Three.* New York: Alfred Knopf.

———. 1972. *Spearpoint: "Teacher" in America.* New York: Alfred A. Knopf.

———. 1979. *I Passed This Way.* New York: Knopf. (Wellington, New Zealand: Reed, 1980).

———. 1986. *Stories from the River.* Auckland, New Zealand: Hodder and Stoughton.

Ausubel, David. *Ego Development and the Personality Disorders.* New York: Grune and Stratton, 1952.

———. *The Fern and the Tiki.* Sydney, Australia: Halstead, 1960.

———. Review of *Teacher. Education* 12, no. 9 (1963): 27–28.

Awatere, Donna. *Maori Sovereignty.* Auckland, New Zealand: Broadsheet Collective, 1984.

Ball, Douglas G. "What Does Integration Mean?" *Education* 1, no. 3 (1948): 114–115.

Barringer, Tessa. "Powers of Speech and Silence." *Journal of New Zealand Literature* 11 (1993): 71–88.

Barrington, John, and Tim Beaglehole. *Maori Schools in a Changing Society.* Wellington, New Zealand: New Zealand Council for Educational Research, 1974.

Beeby, Clarence E. *Biography of an Idea: Beeby on Education.* Wellington, New Zealand: New Zealand Council for Educational Research, 1992.

Benjamin, Jessica. *The Bonds of Love: Psychoanalysis, Feminism, and the Problem of Domination.* New York: Pantheon, 1988.

Ben-Peretz, Miriam. *Learning from Experience: Memory and the Teacher's Account of Teaching.* Albany, NY: State University of New York Press, 1995.

Bentley, John H. Review of *Stories from the River. Landfall* 41 (1987), no. 3: 368.

Bernstein, Basil. "On the Classification and Framing of Educational Knowledge." In *Knowledge and Control*, edited by M. F. D. Young, 47–69. London: Collier Macmillan, 1971.

Bhabha, Homi. *The Location of Culture*. New York: Routledge, 1994.

———. "The Third Space." Interview with Homi Bhabha. In *Identity: Community, Culture, Difference*, edited by J. Rutherford, 207–22. London: Lawrence and Wishart, 1990.

Blaustein, Julian, producer, and Charles Walters, director. *Two Loves*. USA: MGM, 1961.

Boire, G. "Thieves of Language." Review of *Dreams of speech and violence: The art of the short story in Canada and New Zealand*. *Landfall* 43, no. 1 (1989): 199–224.

Bond, Russell. Review of *I Passed This Way*. *National Education* (July 1, 1980): 115.

Brickman, Celia. *Aboriginal Populations in the Mind: Race and Primitivity in Psychoanalysis*. New York: Columbia University Press, 2003.

Britzman, Deborah. *After-Education: Anna Freud, Melanie Klein and Psychoanalytic Histories of Learning*. Albany, NY: State University of New York Press, 2003.

———. "If the Story Cannot End: Deferred Action, Ambivalence and Difficult Knowledge." In *Between Hope and Despair: Pedagogy and Remembrance of Historical Trauma*, edited by Roger Simon et al., 27–58. Lanham, MD: Rowman and Littlefield, 2000.

———. *Lost Subjects, Contested Objects: Toward a Psychoanalytic Inquiry of Learning*. Albany, NY: State University of New York Press, 1998.

———. "The Tangles of Implication." *QSE: International Journal of Qualitative Studies in Education* 10, no. 1 (1997): 31–37.

Brookes, Anne-Louise. *Feminist Pedagogy: An Autobiographical Approach*. Halifax, Canada: Fernwood Publishing, 1992.

———. "Teaching and Learning Liberation: Feminist Pedagogies." Paper presented at the women's studies research unit, University of Saskatchewan, Canada, 2000.

Brown, Ruth. "A State of Siege: The Sociable Frame." *Journal of New Zealand Literature* 11 (1993): 49–58.

Buber, Martin. *Between Man and Man*. London: Collins, 1964.

Butler, Judith. *Bodies that Matter: On the Discursive Limits of "Sex."* New York: Routledge, 1993.

———. *Gender Trouble: Feminism and the Subversion of Identity*. New York: Routledge, 1990.

———. *The Psychic Life of Power: Theories in Subjection*. Palo Alto, CA: Stanford University Press, 1997.

Campbell, A. E., ed. *Modern Trends in Education: Proceedings of the New Zealand New Education Fellowship Conference*. Wellington, New Zealand: Whitcombe and Tombs, 1938.

Caruth, Cathy. Introduction to *Trauma: Explorations in Memory*, edited by Cathy Caruth, 3–12. London: Johns Hopkins University Press, 1995.

———. *Unclaimed Experience: Trauma, Narrative and History*. Baltimore, MD: Johns Hopkins University Press, 1996.

Chatterjee, Partha. *The Nation and Its Fragments: Colonial and Postcolonial Histories*. Princeton, NJ: Princeton University Press, 1993.

———. "The Nationalist Resolution of the Women's Question." In *Recasting Women: Essays in Indian Colonial History*, edited by Kumkum Sangari and Sudesh Vaid, 233–54. New Delhi: Kali for Women, 1990.

Chernaik, Judith. "A True Visionary." *New Society* 54 (1980): 244.

Christianos, Bronwyn, Eliza Tepania-Carter, and Te Whanau O Waipareira. *Te Whanau: A Celebration of Te Whanau O Waipareira*. Waitakere City, New Zealand: Authors, 2001.

Clemens, Sydney Gurewitz. *Pay Attention to the Children: Lessons for Teachers and Parents from Sylvia Ashton-Warner*. Napa, CA: Rattle O.K., 1996.

Collins, Heeni. "*Nga Tangata Awarua*: The Joys and Pain of Being both Maori and Pakeha." In *Oral History in New Zealand*, vol. 11, edited by Megan Hutching, Linda Evans, and Judith Byrne, 1–5. Wellington, New Zealand: National Oral History Association of New Zealand, 1999.

Connor, Kathleen Marie. "Cornering the Triangle: Understanding the 'Dominion-itive' Role of the Realistic Animal Tale in Early Twentieth-Century Canadian Children's Literature." In *Home-Work: Postcolonialism, Pedagogy, and Canadian Literature*, edited by Cynthia Sugars, 487-501. Ottawa, Canada: University of Ottawa, 2004.

Conway, Jill Ker. *When Memory Speaks: Exploring the Art of Autobiography*. New York: Vintage, 1999.

Culley, Margo, and Catherine Portuges, eds. *Gendered Subjects: The Dynamics of Feminist Teaching*. New York: Routledge, 1985.

Curnow, Allen, ed. *The Penguin Book of New Zealand Verse*. Auckland, New Zealand: Penguin, 1960.

"Difficult Woman." *New Zealand Women's Weekly*, August 20, 1962.

Durix, Carole. "Literary Autobiography or Autobiographical Literature? The Work of Sylvia Ashton-Warner." *Ariel* 18, no. 2 (1987): 3–12.

———. "The Maori in Sylvia Ashton-Warner's Fiction." *Literary Half-Yearly* 20, no. 1 (1979): 13–26.

———. "Natural Patterns and Rhythms in *Greenstone* by Sylvia Ashton-Warner." *Commonwealth Essays and Studies* 3 (1977): 29–37.

———. "Orality as Literary Finality in the Prose of Sylvia Ashton-Warner." In *Subjects Worthy of Fame: Essays on Commonwealth Literature in Honour of H. H. Anniah Gowda*, edited by A. L. McLeod, 27–34. New Delhi: Sterling, 1989.

———. "Sylvia Ashton-Warner: Portrait of an Artist as a Woman." *World Literature Written in English* 9, no. 1 (1980): 104–10.

Endeavour Television. *Sylvia Ashton-Warner* [Television broadcast]. Wellington, New Zealand: National Film Library, 1977.

Epperly, Elizabeth, Deirdre Kessler, and Anne-Louise Brookes. *The Bend in the Road: An Invitation to the World and Work of L.M. Montgomery*. CD-ROM, L.M. Montgomery Institute, 2000.

Ewing, John L. *The Development of the New Zealand Primary School Curriculum 1877–1970*. Wellington, New Zealand: New Zealand Council for Educational Research, 1970.

Fabian, Johannes. *Time and the Other: How Anthropology Makes Its Object*. New York: Columbia University Press, 1983.

Felman, Shoshana, ed. *Literature and Psychoanalysis: The Question of Reading: Otherwise*. Baltimore, MD: Johns Hopkins University Press, 1997/1980.

———. *The Juridicial Conscious: Trails and Traumas in the Twentieth Century*. Cambridge, MA: Harvard University Press, 2002.

———. *What Does a Woman Want? Reading and Sexual Difference*. Baltimore, MD: Johns Hopkins University Press, 1993.

Felman, Shoshana, and Dori Laub. *Testimony: Crises of Witnessing in Literature, Psychoanalysis and History*. New York: Routledge, 1992.

Foster, Rose. "The Bilingual Self: Duet in Two Voices." *Psychoanalytic Dialogues* 6, no. 1 (1996): 97–98.

Foucault, Michel. *The Care of the Self: A History of Sexuality*. Vol. 3. Translated by R. Hurley. London: Penguin, 1986.

———. *Discipline and Punish.* Translated by A. Sheridan. Harmondsworth, England: Penguin, 1977.

———. *Power/Knowledge: Selected Interviews and Other Writings 1972–1977.* Edited by C. Gordon and translated by C. Gordon. New York: Pantheon, 1980.

———. *The Use of Pleasure: A History of Sexuality.* Vol. 2. Translated by R. Hurley. London: Penguin, 1985.

Frame, Janet. *The Edge of the Alphabet.* Christchurch, New Zealand: Pegasus, 1962.

———. *A State of Siege.* London: W. H. Allen, 1967.

Freire, Paulo. *Education, the Practice of Freedom.* London: Writers and Readers Co-operative, 1976.

———. *Pedagogy of the Oppressed.* Translated by Myra Ramos. New York: Continuum / Seabury Press, 1968.

———. *Pedagogy of the Oppressed.* Translated by Myra Ramos. Harmondsworth, England: Penguin, 1972.

Freud, Sigmund. *Civilisation and Its Discontents.* 1930. Translated by James Strachey. Reprinted in The Penguin Freud Library, 243–340, 1991.

———. "Family Romances." 1908. Translated by James Strachey. Reprinted in *Standard Edition of the Complete Psychological Works of Sigmund Freud*, vol. 9, 17th edition, edited by James Strachey, 217–52, London: Hogarth Press, 1959.

———. *Moses and Monotheism.* 1939. Translated by James Strachey. Reprinted in The Penguin Freud Library, 237-386, 1991.

———. "Screen Memories." 1899. Translated by James Strachey. Reprinted in *Standard Edition of the Complete Psychological Works of Sigmund Freud*, vol. 3, edited by James Strachey, 301–22. London: Hogarth Press, 1962.

———. "Totem and Taboo: Some Points of Agreement between the Mental Life of Savages and Neurotics." 1913. Translated by James Strachey. Reprinted in *Standard Edition of the Complete Psychological Works of Sigmund Freud*, vol. 13, edited by James Strachey, London: Hogarth Press, 1964.

———. "The Uncanny." 1919. Reprinted in *Complete Psychological Works of Sigmund Freud*, vol. 17, edited by James Strachey, 217–56. London: Hogarth Press, 1962.

Friedman, Susan. *Mappings: Feminism and the Cultural Geographies of Encounter.* Princeton, NJ: Princeton University Press, 1998.

Furedi, Frank. *Culture of Fear: Risk-Taking and the Morality of Low Expectation.* Revised edition. London: Continuum, 2002.

———. *Paranoid Parenting: Why Ignoring the Experts May Be Best for Your Child.* Chicago: Chicago Review Press, 2002.

Gallop, Jane. *Feminist Accused of Sexual Harassment.* Durham, NC: Duke University Press, 1997.

———. "Knot a Love Story." *Yale Journal of Criticism* 5, no. 3 (1992): 209–18.

———, ed. *Pedagogy: A Question of Impersonation.* Bloomington: Indiana University Press, 1995.

Gordon, Colin. Afterword to Foucault, *Power/Knowledge*, 229–59.

Green, André. *On Private Madness.* London: Hogarth, 1986.

Griffith, Penelope, Douglas Ross Harvey and Keith Maslen, eds. 1997. *Book and Print in New Zealand: A Guide to Print Culture in Aotearoa.* Wellington, New Zealand: Victoria University Press, 1997.

Grumet, Madeleine. *Bitter Milk: Women and Teaching.* Amherst: University of Massachusetts Press, 1988.

Hall, Stuart, ed. *Representation: Cultural Representations and Signifying Practices.* London: Sage, 1997.

Harrison, Barbara Grizzuti. "Teacher's Story." Review of *I Passed This Way. New York Times,* December 23, 1979.

Harrison, Bernard T. "Organic Teaching: Sylvia Ashton-Warner." *Literary Review* (January 1981): 1–14.

Heilbrun, Carolyn. *Writing a Woman's Life.* New York: Ballantine Books, 1988.

Hewitson, Michele. "C. K. Stead." Review of *Kin of Place. New Zealand Herald,* August 10, 2002.

Higgin, G. "Contribution to Symposium on Modern Teaching." *Education* 1, no. 3 (1948): 125.

"Historical Survey of Maori Schools." *Education* 1, no. 2 (1948): 75.

Hood, Lynley. *Sylvia! The Biography of Sylvia Ashton-Warner.* Auckland, New Zealand: Viking Penguin, 1988.

———. *Who Is Sylvia? A Diary of a Biography.* Dunedin, New Zealand: John McIndoe, 1990.

hooks, bell. *Teaching to Transgress: Education as the Practice of Freedom.* New York: Routledge, 1994.

Ihimaera, Witi. *Pounamu, Pounamu.* Auckland, New Zealand: Reed, 1972.

Irwin, Kathie. "Towards Theories of Maori Feminism." In *Feminist Voices: Women's Studies Texts for Aotearoa/New Zealand,* edited by Rebecca du Plessis et al., 1–22. Auckland, New Zealand: Oxford University Press, 1992.

Jacobus, Mary. *Psychoanalysis and the Scene of Reading.* Oxford: Oxford University Press, 1999.

Jagodzinski, Jan, ed. *Pedagogical Desire: Authority, Seduction, Transference and the Question of Ethics.* Westport, CT: Bergin and Garvey, 2002.

James, Judith Giblin. *Wunderkind: The Reputation of Carson McCullers 1940-1990.* Columbia, SC: Camden House, 1995.

James, Judith Giblin, and Nancy S. Thompson. "Flashpoints: Sexual/Textual Politics in Editing 'Five Women'." *Documentary Editing* 17, no. 2 (1995): 45–49.

———. "Sylvia Ashton-Warner's Lost Novel of Female Friendship." *Phoebe: Journal of Feminist Scholarship, Theory and Aesthetics* 5, no. 2 (1993): 43–53.

Jehlen, Myra "Archimedes and the Paradox of Feminist Criticism." *Signs* 6, no. 4 (1984): 575–601.

Jones, Alison, ed. *Touchy Subject: Teachers Touching Children.* Dunedin, New Zealand: University of Otago Press, 2001.

———. *"At School I've Got a Chance." Culture/Privilege: Pacific Islands and Pakeha Girls at School.* Palmerston North, New Zealand: Dunmore Press, 1991.

———. "Risk Anxiety, Policy and the Spectre of Sexual Abuse in Early Childhood Education." *Discourse* 25, no. 3 (2004): 321–34.

———. "Touching Children: Policy, Social Anxiety and the 'Safe' Teacher." Special issue: Childhood and cultural studies. *Journal of Curriculum Theorizing* 19, no. 2 (2003): 103–16.

Jones, Lawrence. "The One Story, Two Ways of Telling, Three Perspectives: Recent New Zealand Literary Autobiography." *Ariel* 16, no. 4 (1985): 127–50.

Kaster, Joseph, ed. *Putnam's Concise Mythological Dictionary.* New York: Capricorn Books, 1964.

Kelly, Ursula A. *Schooling Desire: Literacy, Cultural Politics, and Pedagogy.* New York: Routledge, 1997.

Kelsey, Jane. "Legal Imperialism and the Colonization of Aotearoa." In *Tauiwi: Racism and Ethnicity in New Zealand*, edited by Paul Spoonley et al., 15–44. Palmerston North, New Zealand: Dunmore Press, 1984.

Kernberg, Otto F. "Aggression and Love in the Relationship of the Couple." *Journal of the American Psychoanalytic Association* 39 (1991): 45–70.

Khanna, Ranjana. *Dark Continents: Psychoanalysis and Colonialism.* Durham, NC: Duke University Press, 2003.

Kohl, Herbert. *The Discipline of Hope: Learning from a Lifetime of Teaching.* New York: New York Press, 2000.

Kohu, Hinewirangi. "Hinewirangi Kohu." In *Faces of the Goddess: New Zealand Women Talk about Their Spirituality*, edited by C. Kearney, 38–61. North Shore City, New Zealand: Tandem Press, 1997.

Kristeva, Julia. *Revolution in Poetic Language.* New York: Columbia University Press, 1984.

Lacan, Jacques. Translated by Dennis Porter. *The Seminar of Jacques Lacan, Book VII. The Ethics of Psychoanalysis, 1959-1960,* edited by Jacques-Alain Miller. New York: W.W. Norton and Co., 1997.

Lehmann-Haupt, Christopher. "Mother-in-Law and Order." Review of *Three. New York Times*, May 22, 1970.

Levine, Judith. *Harmful to Minors: The Perils of Protecting Children from Sex.* Minneapolis: University of Minnesota Press, 2002.

Maddock, Melvin. "Now, Children." Review of *Spearpoint. Time*, October 2, 1972.

McConaghy, Cathryn. "Curriculum and Accountability in an Age of Trauma." Paper presented at the annual meeting of the American Educational Research Association, Chicago, IL, 2003.

———, ed. *Discourse: Studies in the Cultural Politics of Education* 19, no 3 (1998).

———. *Rethinking Indigenous Education: Culturalism, Colonialism, and the Politics of Knowing.* Flaxton, Australia: Post Pressed, 2000.

McDowell, Linda. *Gender, Identity and Place: Understanding Feminist Geographies.* Oxford: Blackwell, 1999.

McEldowney, Dennis. "Sylvia Ashton-Warner: A Problem of Grounding." *Landfall* 23, no. 3 (1969): 230–45.

McLaren, Peter. *Life in Schools.* 2nd edition. New York: Longman, 1994.

McWilliam, Erica. *Pedagogical Pleasures.* New York: Peter Lang, 1999.

McWilliam, Erica, and Alison Jones. "Eros and Pedagogical Bodies: The State of (non)Affairs." In *Pedagogy, Technology and the Body*, edited by Erica McWilliam and Peter Taylor, 127–36. New York: Peter Lang, 1996.

Meras, Phyllis. "End Papers." Review of *Myself. New York Times*, October 16, 1976.

Meridith, Paul. "Being 'Half-Caste': Cultural Schizo or Cultural Lubricant?" *Tu Mai* 4 (July 1999): 24.

———. "Don't you like kina bey? Et, you're not a real Maori!" *Tu Mai* 3 (June 1999): 4–6.

———. "Hybridity in the Third Space: Rethinking Bi-Cultural Politics in Aotearoa/New Zealand." *He Pukenga Korero* 4, no. 2 (1999): 12–16.

Middleton, Stuart. "Releasing the Native Imagery: Sylvia Ashton-Warner and the Learner of English." *English Teacher* 10, no. 2 (1982): 16–31.

Middleton, Sue. "American Influences in the Sociology of New Zealand Education 1944–1988." In *The Impact of American Ideas on New Zealand's Educational Policy, Practice and Thinking*, edited by D. Philips, G. Lealand and G. McDonald, 50–69. Wellington, New Zealand: N.Z.–U.S. Educational Foundation/New Zealand Council for Educational Research, 1989.

———. *Disciplining Sexuality: Foucault, Life-histories and Education.* New York: Teachers College Press, Columbia, 1998.

———. *Educating Feminists: Life-Histories and Pedagogy.* New York: Teachers College Press, Columbia, 1993.

———. "Educating Researchers: New Zealand Education PhDs 1948–1998." *New Zealand Association for Research in Education State of the Art Monograph.* No. 7. Palmerston North, New Zealand: Massey University/New Zealand Association for Research in Education, 2001.

———. "Feminism and Education in Post-War New Zealand: A Sociological Analysis." PhD diss., University of Waikato, Hamilton, New Zealand, 1985.

———. "Schools at War: Learning and Teaching in New Zealand 1939–1945." *Discourse* 19, no. 1 (1998): 53–74.

———. "Towards an Indigenous University Women's Studies for Aotearoa: A Pakeha Educationalist's Perspective." In *Feminist Voices: Women's Studies for Aotearoa/New Zealand,* edited by Rebecca du Plessis et al., 22–38. Auckland, New Zealand: Oxford University Press, 1992.

Middleton, Sue, and Helen May. *Teachers Talk Teaching 1915–1995: Early Childhood, Schools, and Teachers' Colleges.* Palmerston North, New Zealand: Dunmore Press, 1997.

Milford, Nancy. *Savage Beauty: The Life of Edna St. Vincent Millay.* New York: Random House, 2002.

———, ed. *Selected poetry of Edna St. Vincent Millay.* New York: Modern Library, 2002.

Mitchell, Ian. "Sylvia Ashton-Warner in the Secondary School: A Reassessment of the Work of New Zealand's Most Famous Teacher." Special edition of Sylvia Ashton-Warner, *Auckland College of Education Papers* 10 (2001): 56–61.

Moeke-Maxwell, Tess. 2003. "Bringing Home the Body: Bi/multi Racial Maori Women's Hybridity in Aotearoa/New Zealand." PhD diss., University of Waikato, New Zealand, 2003.

Mohanram, Radhika. *Black Body: Women, Colonialism and Space.* New South Wales, Australia: Allen and Unwin, 1999.

Moscoso-Gongora, P. *An Educator's Escape into Art.* Chicago Tribune Book World, 1981.

Murray, Heather. *Double Lives: Women in the Stories of Katherine Mansfield.* Otago, New Zealand: University of Otago Press, 1990.

New Zealand Department of Education. *Reading in the Infant Room: A Manual for Teachers.* Wellington, New Zealand: Government Printer, 1956.

———. *Syllabus of Instruction for Public Schools.* Wellington, New Zealand: Government Printer, 1929.

Newmann, Fred, et al. *Authentic Achievement: Restructuring Schools for Intellectual Quality.* San Francisco, CA: Jossey-Bass, 1996.

Onions, Charles Talbut, ed. *Oxford Dictionary of English Etymology.* Oxford: Clarendon, 1966.

Orange, Claudia. *The Treaty of Waitangi.* Wellington, New Zealand: Allen and Unwin, 1987.

Pearson, David. "Biculturalism and Multiculturalism in Comparative Perspective." In *Nga Take: Ethnic Relations and Racism in Aotearoa/New Zealand,* edited by Paul Spoonley et al., 194–215. Wellington, New Zealand: Dunmore Press, 1991.

———. *A Dream Deferred: The Origins of Ethnic Conflict in New Zealand.* Wellington, New Zealand: Allen and Unwin, 1990.

Pearson, Leigh. "Challenging the Orthodox: Sylvia Ashton-Warner, Educational Innovator and Didactic Novelist." Masters thesis, University of Waikato, Hamilton, New Zealand, 1984.

Pere, Rangimarie Rose. *Te Wheke: A Celebration of Infinite Wisdom.* Gisborne, New Zealand: Ao Ako Global Learning, 1991.

Phillips, Adam. *Darwin's Worms.* London: Faber and Faber, 1999.

———. *Houdini's Box: The Art of Escape.* New York: Pantheon Books, 2001.

———. "Keeping It Moving." In Butler, *The Psychic Life of Power,* 151–59.

———. *On Flirtation.* Cambridge, MA: Harvard University Press, 1994.

Pitt, Alice. 2003. *The Play of the Personal: Psychoanalytic Narratives of Feminist Education.* New York: Peter Lang, 2003.

Pitt, Alice, and Deborah Britzman. "Speculations on Qualities of Difficult Knowledge in Teaching and Learning: An Experiment in Psychoanalytic Research." Paper presented at the American Educational Studies Association Conference, Vancouver, Canada, 2000.

Prentice, Chris. "Introduction." *Journal of New Zealand Literature* 11 (1993): 1–10.

Price, Hugh. "Educational Publishing." In *Book and Print in New Zealand,* edited by Penny Griffith, Ross Harvey and Keith Maslen, 144–46. Wellington, New Zealand: Victoria University Press, 1997.

Radford, Linda. "The Teacher Reader: Canadian Historical Fiction, Children's Learning and Teacher Education." In *Home-Work: Postcolonialism, Pedagogy, and Canadian Literature,* edited by Cynthia Sugars, 502-516. Ottawa, Canada: University of Ottawa, 2004.

Read, Herbert. *Education through Art.* London: Faber and Faber, 1943.

Review of *Myself. Christchurch Star,* December 7, 1968.

Reynolds, Don, producer, and Michael Firth, producer/director. *Sylvia.* New Zealand: MGM/UA Classics Release, 1984.

Rich, Adrienne. *On Lies, Secrets and Silence.* New York: Norton, 1979.

Roberts, Heather. *Where Did She Come From? New Zealand Women Novelists 1862–1987.* Wellington, New Zealand: Allen and Unwin in association with Port Nicholson Press, 1989.

Robertson, Judith. "Art Made Tongue-Tied by Authority: A Literary Psychoanalysis of Obstacles in Teacher Learning." *Journal of Curriculum Theorizing* 17, no. 1 (2001): 27–44.

———. "Cinema and the Politics of Desire in Teacher Education." PhD diss., University of Toronto, Toronto, Ontario, Canada, 1994.

———, ed. *Teaching for a Tolerant World, Grades K–6: Essays and Resources.* Urbana, IL: National Council of Teachers of English, 1999.

Rose, Jacqueline. *On Not Being Able to Sleep: Psychoanalysis and the Modern World.* London: Chatto and Windus, 2003.

———. *Why War? Psychoanalysis, Politics, and the Return to Melanie Klein.* Oxford: Blackwell, 1993.

Rutherford, Jennifer. *The Gauche Intruder: Freud, Lacan and the White Australia Fantasy.* Melbourne, Australia: Melbourne University Press, 2000.

Scott, Sue, Stevi Jackson, and Kate Backett-Milburn. "Swings and Roundabouts: Risk, Anxiety and the Everyday Worlds of Children." In Alison Jones, *Touchy Subject,* 15–26. Dunedin, New Zealand: University of Otago Press, 2001.

Segal, Hanna. *Psychoanalysis, Literature and War: Papers 1972–1995.* New York: Routledge, 1997.

Shadbolt, Maurice. *From the Edge of the Sky: A Memoir.* Auckland, New Zealand: David Ling, 1999.

Shallcrass, Jack. "In Memoriam: Sylvia Ashton-Warner." *Landfall* 38, no. 3 (1984): 342–44.

————. Review of *Myself. New Zealand Listener* 1527 (1969): 16.

————. "Voices from the Past." *New Zealand Principal* 14, no. 2 (1999): 9.

Sharp, Andrew. *Justice and the Maori: Maori Claims in New Zealand Political Argument in the 1980s.* Auckland, New Zealand: Oxford University Press, 1990.

————. *Why Be Bicultural? Justice and Identity.* Wellington, New Zealand: Bridget Williams Books, 1995.

Simmons, Monty. Review of *I Passed This Way. Roanake Times and World News*, February 3, 1980.

Simon, Judith. *Nga Kura Maori: The New Zealand Native Schools System 1867–1969.* Auckland, New Zealand: Auckland University Press, 1998.

Simon, Judith, and Linda Tuhiwai Smith, eds. *A Civilising Mission? Perceptions and Representations of the New Zealand Native School System.* Auckland, New Zealand: Auckland University Press, 2001.

Simon, Roger I. *Teaching against the Grain: Texts for a Pedagogy of Possibility.* South Hadley, MA: Bergin and Garvey, 1992.

Sinclair, Keith. *A Destiny Apart: New Zealander's Search for National Identity.* Wellington, New Zealand: Allen and Unwin, 1986.

Smith, Linda Tuhiwai. *Decolonizing Methodologies: Research and Indigenous Peoples.* New York: Zed, 1998.

Smith, Sidonie. *A Poetics of Women's Autobiography: Marginality and the Fictions of Self-Representation.* Bloomington: Indiana University Press, 1987.

Somerset, Hugh D. C. *Littledene: Patterns of Change.* Wellington, New Zealand: New Zealand Council for Educational Research, 1938.

————. "What Makes a Good School?" *Education* 1, no. 4 (1948): 170–76.

Staiger, Janet. *Interpreting Films: Studies in the Historical Reception of American Cinema.* Princeton, NJ: Princeton University Press, 1992.

Stead, C. Karl. *Kin of Place: Essays on 20 New Zealand Writers.* Auckland, New Zealand: Auckland University Press, 2002.

————. "Rebellion." Review of *Spinster, Teacher,* and *I Passed This Way. London Review of Books* 3, no. 8 (May 7, 1981): 16–17.

————. "Sylvia Ashton-Warner: Living on the Grand." In *In the glass case,* C. K. Stead, 51–66. Auckland, New Zealand: Auckland University Press, 1981.

Steedman, Carolyn. *Landscape for a Good Woman.* New Brunswick, NJ: Rutgers University Press, 1986.

Stevens, Joan. *The New Zealand Novel 1860–1960.* Wellington, New Zealand: Reed, 1961.

Stoler, Ann. *Race and the Education of Desire.* Durham, NC: Duke University Press, 1995.

Sturm, Terry, ed. *Oxford History of New Zealand Literature in English.* 2nd edition. Auckland, New Zealand: Oxford University Press, 1998.

Sylvia Ashton-Warner archives. Alexander Turnbull Library, Wellington, New Zealand.

Sylvia Ashton-Warner archives. Howard Gotlieb Archival Research Center, Boston University [formerly housed at Mugar Memorial Library, Boston University].

Sylvia [Ashton-Warner]. "The Maori Infant Room: 4. Organic Reading." *National Education* 8, no. 409 (1956): 97–98.

————. "The Maori Infant Room: 6. Nature Study and Number: The Golden Section." *National Education* 8, no. 413 (1956): 248–49.

————. "The Maori Infant Room: 7. Organic Teaching: The Unlived Life." *National Education* 8, no. 414 (1956): 294–95.

————. "The Maori Infant Room: 8. Tone." *National Education* 8, no. 415 (1956): 342–43.

———. "Organic Reading and the Key Vocabulary." *National Education* 7, no. 406 (1955): 392–93.

———. "Organic Reading Is Not New." *National Education* 8, no. 410 (1956): 141.

———. "Organic Writing." *National Education* 8, no. 408 (1956): 54–55.

———. "Private Key Vocabularies." *National Education* 8, no. 407 (1956): 10–12.

Tai, Ruth. "Ruth Tai." In *Faces of the Goddess: New Zealand Women Talk about Their Spirituality*, edited by C. Kearney, 77–96. North Shore City, New Zealand: Tandem Press, 1997.

Thompson, Nancy S. "Imaging, Literacy and Sylvia Ashton-Warner." In *Images in Language, Media, and Mind*, edited by Roy F. Fox, 29–41. Urbana, IL: National Council of Teachers of English, 1994.

Tobin, Joseph, ed. *Making a Place for Pleasure in Early Childhood Education.* New Haven, CT: Yale University Press, 1997.

———. "The Missing Discourse of Sexuality in Contemporary American Early Childhood Education." In *The Annual of Psychoanalysis, Volume 23: Sigmund Freud and His Impact on the Modern World*, edited by J. Winner and J. Anderson, 179–200. Hillsdale, NJ: Analytic Press, 2001.

Untermeyer, Louis, ed. *Rubáiyát of Omar Khayyám: Translated into English Quatrains by Edward FitzGerald.* New York: Random House, 1947.

Veatch, Jeannette. "Teaching Americans." Review of *Spearpoint: "Teacher" in America. Teachers' College Record* 1 (1973): 127–30.

Walizer, Marue. "The Volcanic Mind: The Story of Sylvia Ashton-Warner." In *Reasons for Learning: Expanding the Conversation on Student-Teacher Collaboration*, edited by John G. Nicholls and Terri A. Thorkildsen, 36–61. New York: Teachers College Press, 1995.

Walker, Ranginui. *Ka Whawhai Tonu Matou: Struggle without End.* Auckland, New Zealand: Penguin, 1990.

———. *Nga Tau Tohetohe: Years of Anger.* Auckland, New Zealand: Penguin Books, 1987.

Walkerdine, Valerie. "Developmental Psychology and the Child-Centred Pedagogy." In *Changing the Subject*, edited by J. Henriques et al., 153–202. London: Methuen, 1984.

———. "Sex, Power and Pedagogy." *Screen Education* 38 (1981): 14–23.

Wassermann, Selma. *Getting Down to Cases: Learning to Teach with Case Studies.* New York: Teachers College Press, 1993.

———. *Introduction to Case Method Teaching: A Guide to the Galaxy.* New York: Teachers College Press, 1994.

———. *This Teaching Life: How I Taught Myself to Teach.* New York: Teachers College Press, 2004.

Watson, John. "The Widening Research Scene in New Zealand." Supplement: The Ministerial Conference on Educational Research, *New Zealand Journal of Educational Studies* 14 (1978): 1–18.

Weiler, Kathleen, and Sue Middleton, eds. *Telling Women's Lives: Narrative Inquiries in the History of Women's Education.* Philadelphia, PA: Open University Press, 1999.

Wevers, Lydia. "Reading and Literacy." In *Book and Print in New Zealand,* edited by Penny Griffith, Ross Harvey and Keith Maslen, 212–20. Wellington, New Zealand: Victoria University Press, 1997.

Williams, Herbert William, ed. *A Dictionary of the Maori Language.* 7th edition. Wellington, New Zealand: Government Printer, 1975.

Winnicott, Donald. *Playing and Reality.* London: Tavistock, 1972.

Woolf, Virginia. *Three Guineas.* 1938. Reprint, Harmondsworth, England: Penguin, 1977.

Yeatman, Anna. "Interlocking Oppressions." In *Transitions: New Australian Feminisms*, edited by Barbara Caine and Rosemary Pringle, 42–56. New South Wales, Australia: Allen and Unwin, 1995.

Young-Bruehl, Elizabeth. *From Subject to Biography: Psychoanalysis, Feminism, and Writing Women's Lives*. Cambridge, MA: Harvard University Press, 1998.

Žižek, Slavoj. "Love Thy Neighbor? No Thanks." In *The Psychoanalysis of Race*, edited by Christopher Lane, 176–92. New York: Columbia University Press, 1998.

Index

OMPLICATED

CONVERSATION

A BOOK SERIES OF CURRICULUM STUDIES

This series employs research completed in various
disciplines to construct textbooks that will enable
public school teachers to reoccupy a vacated public
domain—not simply as "consumers" of knowledge,
but as active participants in a "complicated
conversation" that they themselves will lead. In
drawing promiscuously but critically from various
academic disciplines and from popular culture, this
series will attempt to create a conceptual montage for
the teacher who understands that positionality as
aspiring to reconstruct a "public" space. *Complicated
Conversation* works to resuscitate the progressive
project—an educational project in which self-
realization and democratization are inevitably
intertwined; its task as the new century begins is
nothing less than the intellectual formation of a public
sphere in education.

The series editor is:

Dr. William F. Pinar
Department of Curriculum and Instruction
223 Peabody Hall
Louisiana State University
Baton Rouge, LA 70803-4728

To order other books in this series, please contact our Customer
Service Department:

(800) 770-LANG (within the U.S.)
(212) 647-7706 (outside the U.S.)
(212) 647-7707 FAX

Or browse online by series:

www.peterlangusa.com